This Is My Flesh

This Is My Flesh

John's Eucharist and the Dionysus Cult

JAE HYUNG CHO

PICKWICK Publications · Eugene, Oregon

THIS IS MY FLESH
John's Eucharist and the Dionysus Cult

Copyright © 2022 Jae Hyung Cho. All rights reserved. Except for brief quotations in critical publications or reviews, no part of this book may be reproduced in any manner without prior written permission from the publisher. Write: Permissions, Wipf and Stock Publishers, 199 W. 8th Ave., Suite 3, Eugene, OR 97401.

Pickwick Publications
An Imprint of Wipf and Stock Publishers
199 W. 8th Ave., Suite 3
Eugene, OR 97401

www.wipfandstock.com

PAPERBACK ISBN: 978-1-7252-9852-1
HARDCOVER ISBN: 978-1-7252-9853-8
EBOOK ISBN: 978-1-7252-9854-5

Cataloguing-in-Publication data:

Names: Cho, Jae Hyung, author.

Title: This is my flesh : John's eucharist and the Dionysus cult / Jae Hyung Cho.

Description: Eugene, OR: Pickwick Publications, 2022 | Includes bibliographical references and indexes.

Identifiers: ISBN 978-1-7252-9852-1 (paperback). | ISBN 978-1-7252-9853-8 (hardcover). | ISBN 978-1-7252-9854-5 (ebook).

Subjects: LCSH: Bible.—John—Criticism, interpretation, etc. | Lord's Supper—History—Early church, ca. 30–600. | Dionysia. | Cults—Greece.

Classification: BS2615.6 C46 2022 (print). | BS2615.6 (ebook).

01/13/22

Unless otherwise noted, Scripture quotations contained herein are from Revised Standard Version of the Bible, copyright © 1946, 1952, and 1971 National Council of the Churches of Christ in the United States of America. Used by permission. All rights reserved worldwide.

Dedicated to My Parents,
Byungseong Cho and Kyungja Choi,
and in Memory of John and Mary Solberg

Contents

Preface ix
Acknowledgments xi
Abbreviations xiii
1 | Introduction 1
2 | Greco-Roman Background for the Johannine Eucharist 22
3 | Greco-Roman Sacred Meals in the Johannine Eucharist 52
4 | The Dionysus Cult and John's Eucharist 78
5 | Conclusion 130
Bibliography 135
Subject Index 145
Ancient Document Index 149

Preface

THE CONTENT OF THIS book was originally written in 2010 for my doctoral dissertation. The dissertation title was "The Johannine Eucharist in the Light of Greco-Roman Religion." I studied the New Testament in the School of Religion at Claremont Graduate University in California, USA from fall 2002 to the end of 2010. I investigated the New Testament from a Jewish background before meeting with Professors Dennis McDonald and Gregory Riley there. I haven't thought of the "heroic Christology" that interprets Jesus from the perspective of the Greco-Roman heroes, nor the literary connection between the Homeric epic and the New Testament. It took me a total of eight years to get my doctorate, but I was able to study the origins of Christianity from a new perspective by comparing the New Testament with the Greco-Roman religion and literature. After returning to Korea in 2012, I started to publish my articles in theologically specialized journals in Korea. The limitation of academic papers was that they could not easily reach the general public except for professional researchers. I have tried to publish my dissertation as a book through various channels, however, my situation has not allowed me to concentrate on its publication until 2020.

I believe that the Johannine Eucharist is influenced by the sacred meal tradition and the Dionysus cult in Greco-Roman religion, which is different from the Synoptics and Paul's writings that focus on Jewish Passover meal traditions. Using literary criticism and the history of ideas as its main methodologies, this book traces why John replaces "body" with "flesh" and "cup" with "blood" in cannibalistic language. Thus, this study investigates Greco-Roman meal customs, sacrificial meals, the hero cult, the image of Dionysus and the Dionysus cult to show that sacred meals profoundly shaped the Dionysiac sacrificial ritual. Among various Dionysiac features, wine and cannibalistic rituals significantly impact the Johannine Eucharist. This study also argues that John describes Jesus as the sacrificial animal in order to emphasize the suffering and death of Jesus in the idea of sacrifice. Although Jewish sacrifice shares commonalities with Greek sacrifice, because of its universal blood taboo, it does not use blood. The historical fact that Jewish sacrifice officially ceased in 70 CE. supports the influence of the Greek *thysia* sacrifice, which continued in the Roman Empire until the fourth century, on the Johannine Eucharist with its emphasis on the union between the god and the worshippers. Eating the animal's body and blood represents ingesting divine power, which does not appear in the Jewish sacrifice.

I discuss how John describes Jesus and his ministry by modeling Dionysus, especially in Jesus' wine miracle (2:1–11), walking on the sea (6:16–20), Eucharistic words (6:51–59), and the vine discourse (15:1–11). The Dionysiac ritual of eating and tearing raw flesh shows cannibalistic elements. Unlike other negative descriptions of cannibalism in ancient literature, Dionysus is described as both an eater and a giver of raw flesh. By reevaluating the negative term of cannibalism, John positively applies this Dionysiac cannibalism to the Eucharistic words in 6:51–59. Thus, Jesus' hard saying (6:60) is a consequence of this cannibalistic language and the ambiguous features of Dionysus. While in Greco-Roman religion the Dionysus cult shows the cannibalistic and manic ritual of sacred meals, in the New Testament the Johannine Eucharist presents the best model of the Dionysus cult.

Acknowledgments

I THANK GOD WHO gave me the patience and wisdom to publish this work through Pickwick Publications. Only with the great support of my dissertation committee members at Claremont Graduate University, my family, and friends, have I been able to produce this work. My greatest debt is to my dissertation advisor, Dr. Dennis MacDonald, who guided me to finish this project. He carefully read my manuscript chapter by chapter and thoughtfully provided advice throughout my writing process. My work owes a great deal to his criticism and perspective. I thank Dr. Karen Jo Torjesen who provided emotional support and kindness during my years in Claremont. I also thank Dr. Michael Robbins who was my teaching mentor at Claremont Graduate University (CGU), and Dr. Gregory Riley who inspired me through his class, "Greco-Roman Religion and the New Testament," in 2002.

My many thanks go to Dr. Geunhee Yu, the former Executive Pastor of North American Pacific Asian Disciples, and the former president, Mrs. Mary Ann Parrot of the Disciple Seminary Foundation. I also thank Mr. Vance Martin, Rev. Young Sook Kim, Rev. Jinseok Chun, and Mrs. Patsy Wander. I am always counting my blessings through my many friends in South Korea and the United States. My gratitude to them cannot be understated. My delight at completing my dissertation was mirrored by late Mrs. Pat Trent, late Mrs. Mary Solberg and the late Mr. John Solberg. I wish they were here to celebrate this publication.

I deeply thank Dr. Janet Wright, Mrs. Misoon Hur, Dr. Sejeong Oh, Evangelist Moon Kyo Park and my friend Hwa Joon Lee. They have always encouraged my studies and continued to share valuable friendship since I met them. I cannot express my thanks in words to my family members. In particular, my brothe-in-law, Seung Kie Choi, my two sons, and my wife Young Lim Choi. Particularly, Young Lim has made many sacrifices. My family's very existence makes me smile, laugh, and wonder at God's blessings, and they have allowed me to remain optimistic and enjoy the beauty of life in even the most difficult times.

Abbreviations

AB	Anchor Bible
ABD	*Anchor Bible Dictionary*. Edited by David Noel Freedman. 6 vols. New York: Doubleday, 1992
AJA	*American Journal of Archaelogy*
ATR	*Anglican Theological Review*
BTB	*Biblical Theology Bulletin*
CBQ	*Catholic Biblical Quarterly*
ET	*Expository Times*
HTR	*Harvard Theological Review*
IAC	Institute for Antiquity and Christianity
IB	*The Interpreter's Bible*. Edited by George Arthur Buttrick. 12 vols. New York: Abingdon, 1951–1957
IDB	*The Interpreter's Dictionary of the Bible*. Edited by George Arthur Buttrick. 4 vols. New York: Abingdon, 1962
Il.	*Iliad*
Int	*Interpretation*
JBL	*Journal of Biblical Literature*
JHI	*Journal of History of Ideas*
JHS	*Journal of Hellenic Studies*
JRS	*Journal of Ritual Studies*
JSNT	*Journal for the Study of the New Testament*

JSNTSup	Journal for the Study of the New Testament: Supplement Series
LCL	Loeb Classical Library
NTS	*New Testament Studies*
NovT	*Novum Testamentum*
Od.	*Odyssey*
SNTSMS	Society for New Testament Studies Monograph Series
TS	*Theological Studies*
ZNW	*Zeitschrift für die neutestamentliche Wissenschaft und die Kunde der älteren Kirche*

1

Introduction

THIS BOOK DISCUSSES THE Johannine Eucharist from the perspectives of the sacred meal tradition and the Dionysus cult in Greco-Roman religion. Arguing that the discourses of the Johannine Eucharist reflect the influence of Greco-Roman religion, it is particularly concerned with the history of eucharistic ideas, especially as it appears in John 6 and its related literature. It is also argued that the discourse can be understood, within this influence, as part of the development of early Christian eucharistic theology.[1]

From the perspective of the Gospels and Christian tradition, Jesus established the institution of the Christian Eucharist, but he did not create it from a vacuum. He drew ideas from the ancient Mediterranean world and synthesized them in the Eucharist. The Jewish background of the Eucharist is one part, and many parts of the Eucharist come from a Greco-Roman background. In this regard, the Johannine eucharistic discourses show a religious and cultural synthesis of the Greco-Roman world to reflect various

1. Whenever the World Council of Churches and other important Christian assemblies are held, Christians participate in the Eucharist because it ensures the wholeness of Christian communities "in fragments" Ruggieri and Tomka, ed. *Church in Fragments*, 43. Participating in the one body of Christ, all Christians are able to experience a true fellowship and Christian unity as God has united us at the table of the Eucharist. Participation is always associated with a deepening commitment to Christian spirituality because in the New Testament Jesus imperatively says that one must "eat his flesh and drink his blood" to obtain life (John 6:53–54) and "Do this in remembrance of me" (1 Cor 11:24; Luke 22:19).

traditions in Johannine literature.[2] In so doing, the Johannine Eucharist makes Christians one in Christ's body. Before developing my arguments, I will briefly sketch a historical overview of the Johannine Eucharist accomplished by other scholars.

HISTORICAL OVERVIEW OF THE JOHANNINE EUCHARIST

In the modern study of the Eucharist, the three most important works are Hans Lietzmann's *Mass and Lord's Supper*,[3] Gregory Dix's *The Shape of the Liturgy*,[4] and Joachim Jeremias' *The Eucharistic Words of Jesus*.[5] Lietzmann's work was originally published in 1926 under the title of *Messe und Herrenmahl*. Lietzmann proposes that two types of Eucharist originally existed in the primitive churches: one was a joyful commemoration of Jesus' resurrection with bread only, another was a commemoration of Jesus' passion with bread and wine. The former tradition, the Jerusalem form, is largely found in the Synoptics and John, the latter is in Paul's writings.[6] In any case, Lietzmann rejects Jewish influence on the origin of the Christian Eucharist. Instead, he states that the "simple nucleus" of the Jerusalem form was derived from "Hellenistic thought" that regards the Eucharist as a "'sacrifice,'" an idea which is "non-Jewish."[7] Regarding the Pauline Eucharist he states, "The meal is regarded as an analogue to the Hellenistic meals held as memorials to great men, founders of religious communities."[8] He denies any possibility of the Passover meal tradition in Jesus' Last Supper. His refutations are simple:

---

2. Despite its importance, however, the Eucharist is not often observed every Sunday in Protestant churches. Historically, the theology of the Eucharist has been controversial among Church fathers and theologians; Brandon, "Eucharist," 269; also see Bethune-Baker, *Introduction to the Early History of Christian Doctrine*, 393–96. It was this controversy that split Christianity into many factions. Ironically, although a different view of the Eucharist has broken the unity of Christianity, many doctrines of the Eucharist enrich the true meaning of the Eucharist itself. Clearly, interpretations of the Eucharist are important for Christian theology. This book attempts to contribute to the clarity of this issue by focusing on the Johannine Eucharist. I am convinced that early Christianity secured its identity through the Eucharist. However, since the Reformation, Protestants, except for a few denominations, have emphasized the Eucharist less than the Catholic churches and the Orthodox churches.

3. Lietzmann and Richardson, *Mass*.
4. Dix, *Shape of the Liturgy*.
5. Jeremias, *Eucharistic Words of Jesus*.
6. Lietzmann and Richardson, *Mass*, 204–8.
7. Lietzmann and Richardson, *Mass*, 204–5.
8. Lietzmann and Richardson, *Mass*, 205.

> The Passover meal has the following characteristics: (1) A lamb is eaten.—At the Lord's Supper there is no lamb. (2) The Midrash on the Exodus from Egypt and the wanderings in the desert is recited.—This is not the case at the Lord's Supper. (3) Only unleavened bread is eaten.—At the Lord's Supper leavened bread is eaten. (4) It is obligatory to drink four cups.—At the Lord's Supper there is only one cup. Thus at the Lord's Supper all the characteristic features of the Passover are lacking, and not only those which might naturally be omitted when the rite was celebrated weekly, or even more frequently, instead of once a year only . . . Neither the significance nor the ritual of this annual festival was identical with that of the Lord's Supper.[9]

Lietzmann confirms that the Lord's Supper is a pivotal part of the Christian Eucharist, and Richardson concludes that the Eucharist is developed "with varying degrees of legitimacy, from a breaking of bread which was practiced by Jesus with his disciples before, as well as on, the night in which he was betrayed."[10] Lietzmann's arguments are impressive in that he studies the Eucharist from what Jesus did and said in the context of Greek thought and Greek sacrifice, rather than from the Jewish Passover meal tradition, but he does not thoroughly survey John's Eucharist, especially John 6, as separate from the Synoptics and Paul.

Like Lietzmann, Dix provides a comprehensive study of the origin and development of Christian worship. Although his book focuses on the shape of the liturgy, most of its chapters deal with the Eucharist and point out that the Eucharist has importantly affected the development of the Christian liturgy. Dix insists that the Eucharist is "the heart and core of Christian worship and Christian living."[11] He states that the Eucharist was instituted at the Last Supper. Following John 13, Dix argues that the Last Supper was probably not the Passover meal, but "the evening meal twenty-four hours before the actual Passover."[12] He integrates John's Eucharist into the Synoptics and Paul, emphasizing the "four-action scheme" of the Eucharist: "(1) The offertory; bread and wine are 'taken' and placed on the table together. (2) The prayer; the president gives thanks to God over bread and wine together. (3) The fraction; the bread is broken. (4) The communion; the bread and wine are distributed together."[13] Following John's chronology of the Last

9. Lietzmann and Richardson, *Mass*, 172.
10. Lietzmann and Richardson, *Mass*, 693.
11. Dix, *Shape of the Liturgy*, 1.
12. Dix, *Shape of the Liturgy*, 50.
13. Dix, *Shape of the Liturgy*, 48. Here he states that the New Testament accounts of the Eucharist are called a "seven-action scheme": "Our Lord (1) took bread; (2) 'gave

Supper, Dix places the Johannine Eucharist in the middle of John (13–17) and disregards John 6.[14]

In contrast to Lietzmann and Dix, Joachim Jeremias sees the Last Supper as an actual Passover meal.[15] He argues several similarities between the Last Supper and the Passover meal. First, according to him, the Passover meal *"must be eaten within the gates of Jerusalem," "in a state of levitical purity"* at night.[16] Likewise, "the Last Supper took place in Jerusalem" (Mark 14:13, 26; John 18:1).[17] Second, "*the room for the meal* was made available to Jesus and his disciples without ado" (Mark 14:13–15) because the rooms of Jerusalem were open for the Passover without financial charge.[18] Third, like the Passover meal, the Last Supper was held at night (1 Cor 11:23 and John 13).[19] Jeremias enumerates all of the possibilities of the setting of the Eucharist from the Synoptics and John.[20] However, he does not focus on John 6 for this argument, because his argument mainly touches Paul and the Synoptics. Jeremias seems to think that John's eucharistic words (6:51–59) are supplementary, though he regards them as Johannine "eucharistic expressions."[21]

The massive works of Lietzmann, Dix, and Jeremias have investigated many areas of the Eucharist: its origin, development, function, ritual format, and historical debate on it. However, regarding the Johannine Eucharist, their interests are insufficient and unfair compared to their focuses on the Synoptics and Paul. Whether they see the eucharistic words in John 6 as supplementary to John 13 or the Johannine Eucharist as dependent on the explanation of the Synoptics and Paul, the unique literary structure and rhetoric of John demands further study. In this regard, it is necessary to explore some modern or current scholars' arguments on the Johannine Eucharist.

Raymond E. Brown, Cyril Vollert, and other Catholic scholars consider whether the eucharistic undertones are envisioned throughout the entire discourse or only in the latter part of John 6.[22] Vollert points out that Jesus is the true bread of life sent by God who satisfies human beings' hunger

---

thanks' over it; (3) broke it; (4) distributed it, saying certain words. Later He (5) took a cup; (6) 'gave thanks' over that; (7) handed it to His disciples, saying certain words."

14. Dix, *Shape of the Liturgy*, 50 and 266.
15. Jeremias, *Eucharistic Words*, 41.
16. Jeremias, *Eucharistic Words*, 43 and 49.
17. Jeremias, *Eucharistic Words*, 42.
18. Jeremias, *Eucharistic Words*, 44; italics original.
19. Jeremias, *Eucharistic Words*, 44.
20. Jeremias, *Eucharistic Words*, 20–26.
21. Jeremias, *Eucharistic Words*, 107–8.
22. Brown, *John I–XII*, 290; Vollert, "Eucharist," 404; Temple, "Eucharist," 442–52; Need, "Jesus the Bread," 194–200.

by giving higher nourishment.[23] Vollert, however, relates 6:48, "I am the bread of life" to 1 Cor. 11:24, "This is my body which is for you. Do this in remembrance of me," saying that it closely approaches "St. Paul's Eucharistic formula."[24] Thus, he declares that "The words 'flesh and blood' refer to Christ's sacrifice."[25]

It is clear that John 6 has influenced eucharistic doctrine; even the Lord's Supper has been interpreted in the light of John 6 by some scholars.[26] However, John 6:56, "He who eats my flesh and drinks my blood abides in me, and I in him" is so strong that it reminds one of cannibalism.[27] Although Catholic churches prefer the doctrine of transubstantiation to that of remembrance, which is preferred by Protestants, Catholics interpret this expression spiritually.[28] They focus on the phrase "abides in me and I in him." For both traditions, "to abide in Jesus" leads them to interpret flesh and blood as spiritual signs or metaphor.[29] However, Francis John Moore points out the problem of a spiritual interpretation. He says, "There is no further reference to the eating of the flesh and the drinking of the blood, not even at their last supper together before Passover."[30] If John 6 used "body" as in the Synoptics and 1 Cor 11, the spiritual interpretation may be acceptable. But why does John 6 replace "body" with "flesh"? This question will be examined later in this book.

Brown also presents the thesis of chapter 6 as a unity of midrashic exegesis and notes that recurrences of "bread from heaven" and "give" indicate a close connection to the Old Testament.[31] According to Moore, the use of the verb "to eat" implies the Jews taking ideas and principles into one's system.[32] For example, Jeremiah 15:16 says, "Thy words were found, and I ate them, and thy words became to me a joy and the delight of my heart" and Ezekiel 3:3 shows "Son of man, eat this scroll that I give you and fill your stomach with it." Thus, the eating of the flesh and drinking of blood become

---

23. Vollert, "Eucharist," 407.
24. Vollert, "Eucharist," 409.
25. Vollert, "Eucharist," 414.
26. Brown, *John I-VII*, 290; Moore, "Eating the Flesh," 70.
27. All quotations of the biblical text are from the RSV unless otherwise indicated.
28. The doctrine of transubstantiation explains that "at Eucharist the 'substance' of the bread and wine, changed into Christ's Body and Blood, while retaining their outward ('accidental') form of bread and wine, and it was elaborated in Middle ages. See Brandon, "Transubstantiation," 622; and Brandon, "Eucharist," 269.
29. Need, "Jesus the Bread," 194.
30. Moore, "Eating the Flesh," 72.
31. Brown, *John I-VII*, 282–90.
32. Moore, "Eating the Flesh," 73.

abstract, which emphasizes "abiding in Jesus." "He who eats me will live because of me" (John 6:57) is the same as "He who abides in me, and I in him, he it is that bears much fruit" (John 15:5). The flesh and blood here become a eucharistic understanding that Jesus is "offered in sacrifice for the sins of the world" as 1 Cor 11:23-25 describes.[33] These explanations of "flesh" and "blood" do not support a spiritual interpretation, but rather suggest certain other ideas from outside of the Old Testament. Although the rumor that the early Christians ate human "flesh" is not true, the pagans accused Christians based on the relationship between cannibalism and the Christian Eucharist. In this respect, it is appropriate to search for a prototype of the Johannine Eucharist in John 6. Where did it come from? Are there similar usages of "flesh" and "blood" in the Bible and in the first century Greco-Roman world? These questions will be argued in Chapter 4 of this book.

In his literary analysis, Joseph A. Grassi interprets John 6:51-59 in the perspective of a new Passover, similar to Brown's argument mentioned above.[34] First, Grassi mentions that to eat flesh and to drink blood do not appear throughout the whole Gospel. Second, he states that these verses are in the central portion of the Gospel which is related to "Jesus' death on the cross and the marriage feast at Cana."[35] Grassi accepts M. Girard's chiastic structure of the seven signs.[36]

Grassi maintains that the general correspondences found within John indicate that John 6 is the center of the seven signs.[37] In the cross, Jesus becomes the Passover lamb for his people, which rationally explains the strong expressions "eating flesh" and "drinking blood." Within the Passover setting, "the description of Jesus' death in terms of the sacrificed Passover lamb, whose flesh was to be eaten and whose blood was to bring life, is most significant."[38] Moreover, John the Baptist saw Jesus coming toward him, and said, "Behold, the Lamb of God, who takes away the sin of the world!"

---

33. Moore, "Eating the Flesh," 74.

34. Brown, *John I-VII*, 290-91.

35. Grassi, "Eating Jesus' Flesh," 24.

36. Grassi, "Eating Jesus' Flesh," 25. Grassi presents the structure of seven signs below:

A (2:1-22) The wedding feast at Cana
  B (4:46-54) The raising of the official's dying son
    C (5:1-16) The Sabbath healing at Bethesda
      D (6:1-71) The loaves' multiplication and the bread of life
    C' (9:1-41) The Sabbath healing of the blind man
  B' (11:1-41) The raising of Lazarus
A' (19:25-38) The hour of Jesus and the issue of blood and water

37. Grassi, "Eating Jesus' Flesh," 25.

38. Grassi, "Eating Jesus' Flesh," 28.

(John. 1:29). Thus, Grassi states, "Jesus' flesh and blood can be explained in terms of spirit and life."[39] Likewise, Brown and other scholars understand John 6 in the Jewish background; they are inclined to Paul's description in 1 Cor 11:23–25. Although Grassi points out that John 6 is related to the wine miracle of John 2 in chiastic struture, he misses important social and religious references in both John 2 and 6: Greco-Roman Sacred meals and the Dionysus cult.

John F. McConnell studied the relationship between the Eucharist and Greco-Roman mystery religions. His conclusion denies the possibility that the Christian Eucharist was influenced by mystery religions; however, ironically he lists eucharistic features of mystery religions and describes scholars' research on the connection between them. McConnell accepts that many scholars assert that "Paul borrowed the Eucharist from a concrete mystery religion," though he does not agree with them.[40] He says, "In this Dionysus-Zagreus cult, the crazed worshippers did at times rend and eat a living bull or goat, but there is not the slightest reason to believe that they did so with the idea that they were eating the god."[41] In another birth story, Dionysus was called Zagreus.[42] According to McConnell's interpretation, the worshippers eat living meat "in memory of Zagreus."[43] Even though his study mainly focuses on the Pauline tradition, to McConnell, "to eat flesh and to drink blood" in John 6:53 may be interpreted under "the Paschal lamb identified with Christ." Unlike other Catholic scholars, McConnell does not discuss the Eucharist of John 6. The main problem with McConnell's stance is that he disregards the differences between John's Eucharist and Paul's.[44]

While the above scholars relate John 6 to 1 Cor 11:23–25 and the Synoptic traditions, some scholars discern between them. For instance, Stephen W. Need and Gregory Riley observe the different settings of John 6, the Synoptics and 1 Cor 11:23–25.[45] In particular, Need raises an important question about whether or not John 6 actually intends to make a eucharistic

39. Grassi, "Eating Jesus' Flesh," 29.

40. McConnell, "Eucharist," 33.

41. McConnell, "Eucharist," 33.

42. Dionysus-Zagreus, who was killed by the Titans and, whose heart was rescued by Athena, was the son of Zeus and Persephone. After the rescue, Zeus ate Dionysus's heart and recreated him through Semele. In Carpenter and Gula, *Mythology*, 48.

43. McConnell, "Eucharist," 33.

44. Mircea Eliade states that "there is no reason to suppose that primitive Christianity was influenced by the Hellenistic mysteries," but some initiatory themes of the mystery religions "were taken over and revaluated by Christianity." Eliade, *Rites and Symbols of Initiation*, 118–21.

45. Riley, *I Was Thought to Be What I Am Not*, 19; Need, "Jesus the Bread," 194–200.

institution like that in 1 Cor 11.[46] He indicates that the setting of John 6 is different and does not follow the important eucharistic term "body," for John 6 is more interested in Jesus himself than the Eucharist itself.[47] Regarding the problematic terms "to eat flesh and to drink blood," Need asks, "Do these words actually refer to bread and wine, the elements of the Eucharist, or do they refer to Jesus himself?"[48] He states that the discourse is a metaphor so John 6 is not interested in receiving bread and taking wine, but focuses on Jesus himself, because Jesus is the Logos and the Logos becomes flesh (1:14).[49] However, not clearly explaining "flesh" in 6:63 creates another difficulty for Need when the "flesh" is a metaphor for Jesus.[50]

In 1 Cor 11, "Jesus on the night before Passover, at his last supper in an inner room with his closest associates" broke bread and took the cup saying, "Do this in remembrance of me" and "This cup is the new covenant in my blood. Do this, as often as you drink it, in remembrance of me." On the contrary, in John 6, everything is different. Even though John mentions that the Passover was at hand (6:4), the time is not the week of the Passover and the night as Paul describes.[51] Riley states: "No mention is made of eating flesh, or drinking blood, or, significantly, of eternal life for the consumer; there is only wine and bread during a meal [in the Synoptics and Paul] ... There is no Passover, no inner room, no ritual setting, no meal, no loaf of bread being broken for anyone, no cup to drink and no wine at all, no mention of a substitutionary death, no new covenant, and nothing to remember [in John]."[52]

Therefore, the interpretation of John 6 by Paul's description in 1 Cor 11 must be reconsidered, although both share the influence of the sacred meal tradition in Greco-Roman culture. Riley says, "Yet the Johannine passage is of a wholly different stamp from that of the four eucharistic texts of the Last Supper found elsewhere in the New Testament. The later Church

---

46. Need, "Jesus the Bread," 197.

47. Need, "Jesus the Bread," 195–97.

48. Need, "Jesus the Bread," 199.

49. Need, "Jesus the Bread," 200.

50. "Flesh" in John 6:53 and 6:63 are totoally different. I will argue this later in this book.

51. The setting that Jesus washed his disciples' feet is similar to that of Paul's Eucharist in John 13:1–18. It was the day before the Passover Festival (13:1). There were inner room at night (13:2), supper, and ritual setting. As Jesus explained the meaning of the bread and wine in the writing of Paul and the Synoptics, Jesus explained the meaning of the washing feet in John 13:12–17. After this ritual, Jesus mentioned who would betray him (13:18). In the same way Jesus said Judas would be a betrayer in the Synoptics.

52. Riley, *I Was Thought to Be What I Am Not*, 20.

interpreted them by means of the Johannine passage; in other words, the influence went in the other direction."[53]

If one accepts Riley's analysis, then there is a unique interpretation of the Eucharist in John 6, which is the shadow of the cult of Dionysus. I will examine this point in a later chapter of this book.

STATEMENT OF THE PROBLEM

John 6:53, "unless you eat the flesh of the Son of Man and drink his blood, you have no life in you" is one of the most difficult verses found anywhere in the Bible. In fact, John Chapter 6 has often been problematic for scholars. The chapter begins with feeding the five thousand (6:1-15), and presents Jesus' walking on the sea (6:16-24), bread from discourse (6:25-51a) discussion of Jesus' flesh and blood (6:51b-59), and the disciples' lack of faith and Peter's confession (6:60-71). It includes miracle stories, discourses, and controversial arguments. Because of these complicated structures and contents, many scholars have tried to interpret Chapter 6 in terms of the Eucharist or Christology.[54] Because the Eucharist and Christology are connected with each other, I will not deal with these topics separately here. Instead, I will look at not only Christology but also various subjects through the Eucharist. Although the eucharistic undertone is obvious in John 6, as Riley pointed out, the differences between the Eucharist discourses of the Synoptics and Paul's epistles make one hesitant to interpret this chapter in the eucharistic context of the Synoptics and Paul.

Although there are some differences, the Last Supper of Jesus appears in the Synoptics (Matt 26:26-29; Mark 14:22-25 and Luke 22:15-20), 1 Cor 11: 23-25, and the Gospel of John (6:51-59 and 13:1—17:26). John's Eucharist is different from the Synoptics's and Paul's, because John describes the Last Supper (13:1—17:24) without "Jesus' words about bread and wine."[55] Kurt Aland, however, places John 6:51-59 in parallel with the above Synoptics and 1 Cor 11:23-25.[56] Dennis E. Smith recognizes that John 6:53-54 contains "words of Jesus over bread and wine" in agreement with John 13:1—17:24.[57]

---

53. Riley, *I Was Thought to Be What I Am Not*, 19.

54. Moore, "Eating the Flesh," 70; Temple and Need see John 6 in terms of the Eucharist. Temple, "Eucharist," 442-52; Need, "Jesus the Bread," 194-201. Here, Need claims that John 6 must be understood in metaphor and John's eucharistic teaching has a Christological focus.

55. Davies and Allison, *Saint Matthew*, 274.

56. Aland, *Synopsis Quattuor Evangeliorum*, 436-37.

57. Smith, *Symposium to Eucharist*, 274.

10   THIS IS MY FLESH

The account of the Last Supper is difficult to trace in its tradition and history.[58] Paul's report must be the oldest version. Other writers of the scriptures might have known Paul's tradition of the Eucharist, but there is no agreement among scholars how much other scriptures would have adapted Paul's descriptions for their own purposes.[59] There are many parallels and "distinctivenesses"[60] between the Synoptics and Paul, which indicates that they communicated with each other. The Greek verses show them more clearly:

---

58. Davies and Allison, *Saint Matthew*, 465.

59. As I will argue further, Matthew adapts Mark, and Luke adapts Mark and Paul. However, the relationship between Paul and Mark is controversial. For example, Gregory Dix says, "This liturgical tradition must have originated in independence of the literary tradition in all its forms, Pauline or Synoptic." Dix, *Shape of the Liturgy*, 49.

60. According to Dennis R. MacDonald, distinctiveness pursues distinguishing characteristics between two texts. Its traits are "peculiar characterizations, or a sudden change of venue, or an unusual word or phrase." These rarities can be "flags for readers to compare the imitating texts with their models." MacDonald, *Homeric Epics and the Gospel of Mark*, 8–9. In this regard, distinctiveness may be considered the best test of dependence. See also MacDonald, *Does the New Testament Imitate Homer?*, 105–12.

1 Cor 11:23-25	Mark 14:22-25	Matt 26:26-29	Luke 22:15-20
23 Ἐγὼ γὰρ παρέλαβον ἀπὸ τοῦ κυρίου, ὃ καὶ παρέδωκα ὑμῖν, ὅτι ὁ κύριος Ἰησοῦς ἐν τῇ νυκτὶ ᾗ παρεδίδετο **ἔλαβεν ἄρτον** 24 καὶ *εὐχαριστήσας ἔκλασεν* καὶ *εἶπεν·τοῦτό μού ἐστιν τὸ σῶμα* τὸ ὑπὲρ ὑμῶν·τοῦτο ποιεῖτε εἰς τὴν ἐμὴν ἀνάμνησιν. 25 σαύτως καὶ τὸ ποτήριον μετὰ τὸ δειπνῆσαι λέγων·τοῦτο τὸ *ποτήριον* ἡ καινὴ διαθήκη ἐστὶν ἐν τῷ ἐμῷ αἵματι·τοῦτο ποιεῖτε, ὁσάκις ἐὰν *πίνητε*, εἰς τὴν ἐμὴν ἀνάμνησιν.	22 Καὶ <u>ἐσθιόντων αὐτῶν</u> ***λαβὼν ἄρτον*** εὐλογήσας ***ἔκλασεν*** καὶ ἔδωκεν αὐτοῖς καὶ ***εἶπεν·λάβετε. τοῦτό ἐστιν τὸ σῶμά μου.*** 23 <u>καὶ λαβὼν</u> **ποτήριον εὐχαριστήσας** ἔδωκεν αὐτοῖς, καὶ ***ἔπιον*** ἐξ αὐτοῦ πάντες. 24 καὶ εἶπεν αὐτοῖς·<u>τοῦτό ἐστιν τὸ αἷμά μου τῆς διαθήκης τὸ ἐκχυννόμενον ὑπὲρ πολλῶν.</u> 25 ἀμὴν λέγω ὑμῖν ὅτι οὐκέτι οὐ μὴ πίω ἐκ τοῦ γενήματος τῆς ἀμπέλου ἕως τῆς ἡμέρας ἐκείνης ὅταν αὐτὸ πίνω καινὸν ἐν τῇ βασιλείᾳ τοῦ θεοῦ.	26 Ἐσθιόντων <u>δὲ αὐτῶν</u> ***λαβὼν*** ὁ Ἰησοῦς ***ἄρτον*** καὶ **εὐλογήσας *ἔκλασεν*** καὶ δοὺς τοῖς μαθηταῖς ***εἶπεν·λάβετε*** φάγετε, ***τοῦτό ἐστιν τὸ σῶμά μου.*** 27 <u>καὶ λαβὼν **ποτήριον** καὶ **εὐχαριστήσας** ἔδωκεν αὐτοῖς</u> λέγων·***πίετε*** <u>ἐξ αὐτοῦ πάντες,</u> 28 <u>τοῦτο γάρ ἐστιν τὸ αἷμά μου τῆς διαθήκης</u> τὸ περὶ <u>πολλῶν ἐκχυννόμενον</u> εἰς ἄφεσιν ἁμαρτιῶν. 29 λέγω δὲ ὑμῖν, οὐ μὴ πίω ἀπ' ἄρτι ἐκ τούτου τοῦ γενήματος τῆς ἀμπέλου ἕως τῆς ἡμέρας ἐκείνης ὅταν αὐτὸ πίνω μεθ' ὑμῶν καινὸν ἐν τῇ βασιλείᾳ τοῦ πατρός μου.	15 καὶ εἶπεν πρὸς αὐτούς· ἐπιθυμίᾳ ἐπεθύμησα τοῦτο τὸ πάσχα φαγεῖν μεθ' ὑμῶν πρὸ τοῦ με παθεῖν·16 λέγω γὰρ ὑμῖν ὅτι οὐ μὴ φάγω αὐτὸ ἕως ὅτου πληρωθῇ <u>ἐν τῇ βασιλείᾳ τοῦ θεοῦ.</u> 17 <u>καὶ</u> δεξάμενος **ποτήριον εὐχαριστήσας εἶπεν·λάβετε** τοῦτο καὶ διαμερίσατε εἰς ἑαυτούς· 18 λέγω γὰρ ὑμῖν, [ὅτι] οὐ μὴ ***πίω*** ἀπὸ τοῦ νῦν ἀπὸ <u>τοῦ γενήματος τῆς ἀμπέλου</u> ἕως οὗ ἡ βασιλεία τοῦ θεοῦ ἔλθῃ. 19 <u>καὶ **λαβὼν ἄρτον** εὐχαριστήσας **ἔκλασεν** καὶ ἔδωκεν αὐτοῖς λέγων·**τοῦτό ἐστιν τὸ σῶμά μου** τὸ ὑπὲρ ὑμῶν</u> διδόμενον·τοῦτο ποιεῖτε εἰς τὴν ἐμὴν ἀνάμνησιν. 20 καὶ τὸ ποτήριον ὡσαύτως μετὰ τὸ δειπνῆσαι, λέγων·τοῦτο τὸ ποτήριον ἡ καινὴ διαθήκη ἐν τῷ αἵματί μου τὸ ὑπὲρ ὑμῶν ἐκχυννόμενον.
Italic type is parallels with 1 Corinthians	**Bold type** indicates parallels between the Synoptics	<u>Underline</u> points out the parallels in the Synoptics and 1 Corinthians	

Matthew's version follows Mark's vocabulary, order, and content almost exactly. More than 80 percent of Mark's descriptions can be found in Matthew's. Matthew modifies his version to add more explanation according to his unique theology. For instance, Matthew inserts "eat" (φάγετε) after "take" (λάβετε) in 26:26 as a counterpart to "drink" (πίετε),[61] and replaces Mark's "God" (θεοῦ) with "Father" (πατρός) in verse 29. Matthew also inserts "for the forgiveness of sins" (εἰς ἄφεσιν ἁμαρτιῶν) after "for many" (περὶ πολλῶν) in verse 28 because "forgiveness" is important for Matthew's community (6:12-15, 9:2-6, 12:31-32, and 18:21-35) where "Jesus' authority to forgive sins" transfers into that of Matthew's community.[62] Despite some of Matthew's modifications, Hans Lietzmann notes, "In any case—and this is of vital significance—we establish actual literary dependence of Matthew upon Mark, not merely kinship with the underlying tradition."[63]

Luke's version of the Eucharist shows the combination of Mark's and Paul's, though the order of explanation of "the fruit of the vine" is reversed. On the one hand, in Luke 22:15-19a, about 40 percent of Mark's phrases and vocabulary appear such as "in the Kingdom of God" (ἐν τῇ βασιλείᾳ τοῦ θεοῦ), "the fruit of the vine until" (τοῦ γενήματος τῆς ἀμπέλου ἕως), and "I tell you that … I shall not drink" (λέγω ὑμῖν ὅτι οὐκέτι οὐ μὴ πίω) Luke replaces Mark's λαβὼν into δεξάμενος and ἔδωκεν into διαμερίσατε when he/she describes taking a cup in 22:17. Both Luke's terms do not appear in Paul's eucharistic words (1 Cor 11:23-25). This indicates that Luke uses special source of the Eucharist. The order of the Eucharist is the same as Mark's. Here, the Lucan texts are dependent on that of Mark.[64] On the other hand, in Luke 22:19b-20, the influence of 1 Cor 11:24-25 on Lucan texts is apparent. Lietzmann also observes, "The second part is an analogue of the bread and wine sayings unmistakably dependent upon 1 Cor. XI 24-25."[65]

The Synoptics and Paul's writing share several important phrases, for instance: "This is my body" τοῦτό ἐστιν τὸ σῶμά μου,[66] "took bread" (ἔλαβεν ἄρτον[67] or λαβὼν ἄρτον),[68] "he had given thanks" (εὐχαριστήσας)[69] and

---

61. Lietzmann and Richardson, *Mass*, 175.

62. Schweizer, *Matthew*, 491; see Matthew's community and the role of forgiveness in Overman, *Matthew's Gospel and Formative Judaism*.

63. Lietzmann and Richardson, *Mass*, 175.

64. Lietzmann and Richardson, *Mass*, 176.

65. Lietzmann and Richardson, *Mass*, 175.

66. Mark 14:22, Matt 26:26, Luke 22:19, and 1 Cor 11:24. Actually, 1 Cor 11:24 is a little bit different, but almost identical.

67. 1 Cor 11:23b.

68. Mark 14:22, Matt 26:26, and Luke 22:19.

69. 1 Cor 11:24, Mark 14:23, Matt 26:27, and Luke 22:19.

"broke" (ἔκλασεν).⁷⁰ This indicates that the Synoptics and 1 Cor 11 share a common tradition and 1 Cor 11 might have affected Mark's Eucharist, though there is disagreement among scholars about whether 1 Cor 11 influenced Mark 14, or Mark 14 knew 1 Cor 11:23–25 when Mark wrote his eucharistic discourse.⁷¹

W. D. Davies and Dale C. Allison state similarities and differences among the Synoptics and 1 Corinthians:⁷²

Mark and Matthew	Paul and Luke
taking bread	taking/took bread
blessed	gave thanks
said	said/saying
take	____
this is my body	this is my body
____	which is (given) for you
____	do this in my remembrance
took a cup	and likewise the cup
gave thanks	____
this is my blood	this cup
of the covenant	the new covenant in my blood

Here, Davies and Allison show an affinity between Mark and Matthew, and between Luke and Paul. They also claim that Luke's account is more primitive than Mark's because Luke follows a certain influence of Paul.⁷³ Based on Marcan priority, however, the Eucharist of Matthew and Luke follow the Marcan Eucharist, imitating terms, order, and theology. Up to this point, Paul seems to preserve "the most primitive"⁷⁴ account of the Eucharist. It is quite likely that Mark and perhaps Luke know a similar version to Paul's account in 1 Cor 11:23–25. Dix also indicates that Paul shares "the same tradition of the Last Supper of Jesus as that followed by Mark."⁷⁵

As described earlier, the setting of the Synoptics and 1 Corinthians is that Passover is at hand in the inner room at night, which was before Jesus was betrayed by Judas Iscariot. Jesus' foretelling of his betrayal is before the

70. 1 Cor 11:24, Mark 14:22, Matt 26:26, and Luke 22:19.
71. Lietzmann and Richardson, *Mass*, 185.
72. Davies and Allison, *Saint Matthew*, 465–66.
73. Davies and Allison, *Saint Matthew*, 466.
74. Davies and Allison, *Saint Matthew*, 466.
75. Dix, *Shape of the Liturgy*, 185.

Last Supper in the Synoptics, but after the Last Supper in John Chapter 6. The setting of John 6 is that Passover is not immediate and the place of Jesus' teachings seems to be an open space in the synagogue at Capernaum, if one includes verse 59 as John's eucharistic discourse (6:59).[76] In addition, there is no inner room, and it is not night in John 6. Thus, some scholars do not include John 6 as the institution of the Eucharist. Instead, John 13 seems to follow the setting of the Last Supper of the Synoptics and 1 Cor 11, which shows the meal setting before Passover and the prediction of betrayal.[77] John 13 begins with "Now before the festival of the Passover." Although John 13 has "no references to words of Jesus over bread and wine," it includes the meal setting, which alludes to eating bread (13:18, 26) and drinking wine (13:26).[78] Smith relates John 6:53–54 to the scene of the Last Supper in John 13:1—17:26.[79] According to him, the enigmatic verses of John 6:53-54 are the words of the eucharistic institution. Like Bultmann, he thought that John 6:51b-57 "were added later and represent an imposition of a 'sacramental' tradition to the text of John."[80] Joachim Jeremias, unlike Bultmann, insists, "John 6.51c-58 does not originally belong to the discourse on the bread of life, but comes from a pre-Johannine Eucharistic homily."[81] According to Jeremias, because of hesitance to "disclose the sacred formula to the heathen," the author of John 6 omitted the words of the Eucharist.[82] However, as was already mentioned, John 6 is John's unique literary invention to explain the Johannine Eucharist. This unparalleled feature is clear in the Greek text comparing Mark, John, and 1 Cor 11:

---

76. Whether verse 59 is included in John's eucharistic discourse or not is debatable among scholars.

77. Smith, *Symposium to Eucharist*, 274.

78. Smith, *Symposium to Eucharist*, 274.

79. Smith, *Symposium to Eucharist*, 274.

80. Smith, *Symposium to Eucharist*, 274.

81. Jeremias, *Eucharistic Words of Jesus* (1955), 73.

82. Jeremias, *Eucharistic Words of Jesus*, 73.

Introduction

Mark 14:22-25	John 6:51-59	1 Cor 11:23-25
Καὶ ἐσθιόντων αὐτῶν λαβὼν <u>ἄρτον</u> εὐλογήσας ἔκλασεν καὶ ἔδωκεν αὐτοῖς καὶ εἶπεν·λάβετε, <u>τοῦτό ἐστιν</u> τὸ σῶμά μου. 23 καὶ λαβὼν ποτήριον εὐχαριστήσας ἔδωκεν αὐτοῖς, καὶ ἔπιον ἐξ αὐτοῦ πάντες. 24 καὶ εἶπεν αὐτοῖς· τοῦτό ἐστιν <u>τὸ αἷμά μου</u> τῆς διαθήκης τὸ ἐκχυννόμενον <u>ὑπὲρ</u> πολλῶν. 25 ἀμὴν λέγω ὑμῖν ὅτι οὐκέτι οὐ μὴ <u>πίω</u> ἐκ τοῦ γενήματος τῆς ἀμπέλου ἕως τῆς ἡμέρας ἐκείνης ὅταν αὐτὸ <u>πίνω</u> καινὸν ἐν τῇ βασιλείᾳ τοῦ θεοῦ.	51 **ἐγώ** εἰμι ὁ <u>ἄρτος</u> ὁ ζῶν ὁ ἐκ τοῦ οὐρανοῦ καταβάς· ἐάν τις φάγῃ ἐκ τούτου τοῦ ἄρτου ζήσει εἰς τὸν αἰῶνα, καὶ ὁ **ἄρτος** δὲ ὃν ἐγὼ δώσω ἡ σάρξ μού ἐστιν <u>ὑπὲρ</u> τῆς τοῦ κόσμου ζωῆς. 52 Ἐμάχοντο οὖν πρὸς ἀλλήλους οἱ Ἰουδαῖοι λέγοντες·πῶς δύναται οὗτος ἡμῖν δοῦναι τὴν σάρκα [αὐτοῦ] φαγεῖν; 53 <u>εἶπεν</u> οὖν αὐτοῖς ὁ **Ἰησοῦς**· ἀμὴν ἀμὴν λέγω ὑμῖν, ἐὰν μὴ φάγητε τὴν σάρκα τοῦ υἱοῦ τοῦ ἀνθρώπου καὶ πίητε αὐτοῦ τὸ αἷμα, οὐκ ἔχετε ζωὴν ἐν ἑαυτοῖς. 54 ὁ τρώγων μου τὴν σάρκα καὶ **πίνων** <u>μου τὸ αἷμα</u> ἔχει ζωὴν αἰώνιον, κἀγὼ ἀναστήσω αὐτὸν τῇ ἐσχάτῃ ἡμέρᾳ. 55 ἡ γὰρ σάρξ μου ἀληθής ἐστιν βρῶσις, καὶ τὸ αἷμά μου ἀληθής ἐστιν πόσις. 56 ὁ τρώγων μου τὴν σάρκα καὶ **πίνων** <u>μου τὸ αἷμα</u> ἐν ἐμοὶ μένει κἀγὼ ἐν αὐτῷ. 57 καθὼς ἀπέστειλέν με ὁ ζῶν πατὴρ κἀγὼ ζῶ διὰ τὸν πατέρα, καὶ ὁ τρώγων με κἀκεῖνος ζήσει δι᾽ ἐμέ. 58 <u>οὗτός ἐστιν</u> ὁ ἄρτος ὁ ἐξ οὐρανοῦ καταβάς, οὐ καθὼς ἔφαγον οἱ πατέρες καὶ ἀπέθανον·ὁ τρώγων τοῦτον τὸν ἄρτον ζήσει εἰς τὸν αἰῶνα. 59 Ταῦτα εἶπεν ἐν συναγωγῇ διδάσκων ἐν Καφαρναούμ.	23 Ἐγὼ γὰρ παρέλαβον ἀπὸ τοῦ κυρίου, ὃ καὶ παρέδωκα ὑμῖν, ὅτι ὁ κύριος **Ἰησοῦς** ἐν τῇ νυκτὶ ᾗ παρεδίδετο ἔλαβεν **ἄρτον** 24 καὶ εὐχαριστήσας ἔκλασεν καὶ εἶπεν· τοῦτό μού ἐστιν τὸ σῶμα τὸ ὑπὲρ ὑμῶν· τοῦτο ποιεῖτε εἰς τὴν ἐμὴν ἀνάμνησιν. 25 ὡσαύτως καὶ τὸ ποτήριον μετὰ τὸ δειπνῆσαι λέγων· τοῦτο τὸ ποτήριον ἡ καινὴ διαθήκη ἐστὶν ἐν τῷ ἐμῷ **αἵματι**·τοῦτο ποιεῖτε, ὁσάκις ἐὰν **πίνητε**, εἰς τὴν ἐμὴν ἀνάμνησιν.
<u>Underline</u> indicates parallels between Mark and John	**Bold type** indicates parallels between 1 Corinthians and John	

John uses similar terms to those that appear in the Synoptics and Paul. These common terms are: "bread," "eat," "said," "blood," "drink," and phrases "This is the bread" and "my blood." These similarities illustrate that although John does not show significant parallels with Paul and Mark, John might have known the account of Paul and Mark and developed a certain degree of dependence on them.[83] For example, Jesus' famous eucharistic words, "This is my body" in the Synoptics and Paul seem to disappear in John, but the connotation of these phrases appear in John's modification, "I am the living bread" ἐγώ εἰμι ὁ ἄρτος ὁ ζῶν (6:51).[84] Obviously, "This is my body" means "This bread is my body" in all cases. In addition, Heinz Schürmann states, "body" "σῶμα, like the Aramaic words biśrā and gûp, can indicate 'self.'" Therefore, "This is my body" can also mean "This [bread] is myself."[85] In addition to Schürmann's points, "This is the bread" οὗτός ἐστιν ὁ ἄρτος (6:58) clearly notes that "bread" is Jesus himself, which relates to Mark' "τοῦτό ἐστιν τὸ σῶμά μου." Robert Douglas Richardson states, "John's 'I am the bread of life' and 'My blood is drink indeed' are equivalents for Mark's 'This is my body' and 'This is my blood.'"[86] Moreover, Jeremias compares John 6:51c with 1 Cor 11:24b:[87]

John 6:51c	1 Cor 11:24b
The bread which I will give	This
is my flesh	is my body
for the life of the World	which is for you

Instead of 6:51a, taking 51c, Jeremias places "My flesh" and "My body," and "for the life of the World" and "for you" in parallel. He sees that "the structure and content of the sentence is the same." According to him, John does not clearly mention the institution of the Eucharist, but he inserts "the word of interpretation to the bread in the context of a discourse by Jesus."[88]

---

83. Lietzmann and Richardson, *Mass*, 287–88; Lightfoot, *History and Interpretation*, 164; and Creed, *Gospel according to Luke*, lvii–lviii., show that John was indebted to Luke; Dodd, *Interpretation*, 449, insists that John was influenced by the oral tradition of the Synoptics.

84. According to C. K. Barrett, ὁ ἄρτος ὁ ζῶν is related to ὕδωρ ζῶν (John 4:10) and ὕδατος τῆς ζωῆς (Rev 21:6; 22:1, 17). Barrett, *Gospel according to St John*, 246.

85. Schürmann, *Der Einsetzungsbericht, Lk 22, 19–20*, 107–10.

86. Lietzmann and Richardson, *Mass*, 296–97.

87. Jeremias, *Eucharistic Words*, 108.

88. Jeremias, *Eucharistic Words*, 108.

John's "My blood" μου τὸ αἷμα (6:54) is parallel to Mark (14:24), though John omits "the Marcan words '(blood) of the covenant shed for you.'"[89] In the case of the words over the cup, despite some variants of πίνω, John, Mark, and 1 Cor 11 share more commonality with regard to reference to the blood than the bread. In this aspect, John Martin Creed suggests that "both Paul and the narrative embodied in Mark represent a tradition" of John, and he indicates, "the Last Supper antedated the Passover."[90]

However, John never includes the typical eucharistic words that the Synoptics and Paul importantly share, which are "This is my body" τοῦτό ἐστιν τὸ σῶμά μου, "took bread" ἔλαβεν ἄρτον, "he had given thanks" εὐχαριστήσας, "cup" ποτήριον and "broke" ἔκλασεν. Instead, John mainly applies John's special terms and phrases such as "flesh" σάρξ, "life" ζωῆς, "the life of the world" τῆς τοῦ κόσμου ζωῆς, "he who eats my flesh" ὁ τρώγων μου τὴν σάρκα, "food or meat" βρῶσις, "drink" πόσις, and "the bread which came down from heaven" ὁ ἄρτος ὁ ἐξ οὐρανοῦ καταβάς. ζωῆς is also John's distinctive word,[91] but the Synoptic gospels and Paul never use it in the eucharistic discourses. Combining ὑπὲρ with τῆς τοῦ κόσμου ζωῆς, John constructs the ultimate purpose of the Eucharist: "for the life of the world," for which "no parallel in the New Testament" exists.[92] In comparison with the Synoptics and Paul, Jesus gives his body and blood for ὑπὲρ πολλῶν (Mark), περὶ πολλῶν (Matt), and ὑπὲρ ὑμῶν (Paul and Luke). It is particularly debatable why John uses σάρξ instead of σῶμά.[93] Therefore, the distinctiveness of John's Eucharist overwhelms commonness with the Synoptics and Paul. For this reason, the origin of John's Eucharist is more difficult to analyze than that of the Synoptics and Paul. Prior to investigation into the background of the Johannine Eucharist, a discussion of the methodology for this book is necessary.

METHODOLOGY

This book is based on literary research into Greco-Roman ancient texts, with an exegetical analysis of certain passages in the Johannine eucharistic

---

89. Lietzmann and Richardson, *Mass*, 297.

90. Creed, *Gospel according to Luke*, 261.

91. See John's usages of "life" in John 1:4; 3:15, 16, 36; 4:14, 36; 5:21, 24, 26, 29, 39, 40; 6:27, 33, 35, 40, 47, 48, 51, 53, 54, 63, 68; 8:12; 10:10, 11, 15, 17, 28; 11:25; 12:25, 50; 13:37, 38; 14:6; 15:13; 17:2, 3; and 20:31.

92. Barrett, *St John*, 246.

93. This question will be consistently asked throughout this book and possible answers will be discussed in this chapter 4.

discourses for exploring two fields: Greco-Roman religion and the early Christian ritual. Each academic area provides a specific idea for analysis and answers that are the crucial pieces of the puzzle that the Johannine eucharistic discourses represent. In an attempt to solve this puzzle, I will employ literary criticism and the history of ideas.

In New Testament study, broadly, literary criticism means "the effort to understand literature,"[94] focusing "the reasoned consideration of literary works and issues."[95] It uses the interests and methods of secular literary critics, such as I. A. Richards, T. S. Eliot, Northrop Frye, Seymour Chatman, and Gerard Genette.[96] Literary criticism applies "as a term, to any argumentation about literature, whether or not specific works are analyzed."[97] From ancient Greece to the Roman Empire, rhetoric functioned as literary criticism.[98] Narrowly, literary criticism is defined "as the analysis of the meaning of a written text by means of a style, and how that meaning is communicated by an author(s) to a reader(s)."[99] It emphasizes "the analysis of how form is related to meaning, and the aesthetic effects of language," away from "historical."[100]

Arthur O. Lovejoy's *The Great Chain of Being* provides another approach for this book, the history of ideas, which traces the origin of a certain idea or thought, dealing with the expression, preservation, and change of human ideas over time in history.[101] Lovejoy argues that "there is a great deal more that is common to more than one of these provinces than is usually recognized, that the same idea often appears, sometimes considerably disguised, in the most diverse regions of the intellectual world."[102] His argument importantly supports for tracing the background of the Johannine Eucharist from the Greco-Roman sacred meal tradition and the Dionysus cult. According to Lovejoy, the history of ideas "cuts into the hard-and-fast

---

94. Beardslee, *Literary Criticism*, 1; refer to Beardslee, *Literary Criticism*, 1–13.

95. *Encyclopædia Britannica Online*, s.v. "Literary Criticism."

96. See Richards, *Principles of Literary Criticism*; Eliot, *Points of View*; Frye, *Anatomy of Criticism*; Chatman, *Theory of Meter*; and Genette, *Figures III*.

97. *Encyclopædia Britannica Online*, s. v. "Literary Criticism."

98. Kennedy, *New History of Classical Rhetoric*, 3–10, especially 3–4; Plato's cautions against the risky consequences of poetic inspiration in his *Republic* are often regarded as the earliest important example of literary criticism. *Encyclopædia Britannica Online*, s. v. "Literary Criticism."

99. Spencer, "Literary Criticism," 245.

100. Spencer, "Literary Criticism," 245.

101. Regarding the method and aims of the study of the history of ideas, see Lovejoy, *Great Chain*, 1–21.

102. Lovejoy, *Great Chain*, 14–15.

individual systems and, for its own purposes, breaks them up into their component elements, into what may be called their unit-ideas,"[103] specifically concerning "the manifestations of specific unit-ideas in the collective thought of large groups of persons, not merely in the doctrines or opinions of a small number of profound thinkers or eminent writers."[104] In the case of the Johannine Eucharist, the idea of a sacred meal and "eating flesh and drinking blood" is the important unit of ideas that can be traced in the Greco-Roman culture and literature. Although some critics refute "the unit-ideas" for they consider it as "neither a useful analytical tool nor an applicable heuristic device" and "Even Lovejoy's defenders modify the concept through the idea of family resemblance,"[105] Lovejoy's methodology still remains important, evidenced by its regular citation and frequent analysis by many critics as well as followers.[106] The major concern of the history of ideas is "the study of meaning"[107] by tracking "a theory of culture."[108] Its broad application to the study of religion and Christian origins are found in Gregory Riley's books (*River of God*, *One Jesus Many Christs*, and *Resurrection Reconsidered*).[109] Therefore, by using literary criticism and the history of ideas as the fundamental tools for analysis, I will discuss the literary structure and meanings of the Johannine Eucharist.

CHAPTER OUTLINES

Inspired by Hans Lietzmann's *Mass and Lord's Supper*, which rejects any specific Jewish rite or ceremony as an explanation of the Christian Eucharist, I will analyze the Synoptic Gospels, Paul's writings, and Greek literature as the primary source materials relating to Johannine literature throughout this book.

In chapter 1, I have presented a historical overview of the Johannine Eucharist discussed by other scholars. How did other scholars approach it? What were their methodologies and perspectives for it? Then I have

---

103. Lovejoy, *Great Chain*, 3.
104. Lovejoy, *Great Chain*, 19.
105. Wilson, "Lovejoy's," 187.
106. Wilson, "Lovejoy's," 187; see complete bibliography of Lovejoy's writings and criticism in Wilson, *Arthur O. Lovejoy*; also see the review of reference works, *The Dictionary of the History of Ideas* and *New Dictionary of the History of Ideas*; Parsons, "Defining the History of Ideas," 683–99.
107. Bevir, *Logic*, 2.
108. Bevir, *Logic*, 1.
109. Riley, *River of God*; Riley, *One Jesus*; and Riley, *Resurrection Reconsidered*.

investigated the current problem of interpreting the Johannine Eucharist, especially John Chapter 6 as compared with the Synoptics and Paul, which prompted me to compose this book. Based on these problems and other scholars' research, I have selected my own methodologies for this book: literary criticism and the history of ideas.

In chapter 2, I will trace the background of the Johannine Eucharist in the conception of the Greco-Roman sacred meal and the Dionysus cult. To understand Christian religious meals properly, I will explain the phenomenon of sacred meals in the Greco-Roman world. I will also trace the significance of the sacrificial meal among Greco-Roman sacred meals, focusing on its elements and functions. Last, I will look into how hero cults influenced the Christian Eucharist in its functions and structure, then I will relate them to the Christian Eucharist to explain its origin and meanings.

I will also explore how the Dionysus cult is related to wine miracles and what function wine serves in its rituals as well as the general characteristics of Dionysus by surveying Greek and Jewish literature. In particular, I will analyze how the tearing to pieces, *sparagmos* (σπαραγμός) and the eating of raw flesh, *omophagia* (ὠμοφαγία) function in the ritual. For this chapter, Walter Burkert's *Greek Religion* will be used as a primary source because it provides a comprehensive understanding of Greco-Roman religion and Greek thought, as well as providing background information for sacred meals and the Dionysus cult.[110] Dennis E. Smith's *From Symposium to Eucharist* argues that the Eucharist was developed in the Greco-Roman banquet setting.[111] Smith states that "Early Christians celebrated a meal based on the banquet model found commonly in their world."[112] In *Dionysus: Myth and Cult*, Walter Otto analyzes various characteristics and theories of the Dionysus cult and its significance for religion.[113] These works will inform the arguments in this chapter.

In chapter 3, I will apply the idea of the sacred meal to interpret the Johannine Eucharist. I will trace Johannine meal customs from the feeding stories and Jesus' foot-washing story in which the Greco-Roman reclining custom and foot-washing custom appear. In addition, I will investigate the sacrificial features of John 1:29 and 6:51–59, comparing them with Greek sacrificial meal tradition, focusing on Jesus' suffering and death in the Johannine Eucharist.

---

110. Burkert, *Greek Religion*.
111. Smith, *Symposium to Eucharist*, 1–46.
112. Smith, *Symposium to Eucharist*, 279.
113. Otto, *Dionysus*.

In chapter 4, I will investigate how the Dionysus cult has influenced John's Eucharist concerning the similarity between Jesus and Dionysus in John's Gospel and the expressions of the characteristics of Dionysus (a wine god, a raw flesh eater, and a raw flesh giver) in early Christian literature, and specifically how it appears in John 2:1–11; 4:5–34; 6:16–19; and 15:1–11. In particular, I will try to interpret John 6:51–59 in light of of the Dionysus cult. Chapters 3 and 4 together function as an apogee of this book.

In the conclusion, I will summarize my arguments in order to substantiate my contention that the Johannine Eucharist is situated in the setting of the Greco-Roman sacred meal and the Dionysus cult, creating a synthesis of the two influences on the eucharistic discourses, especially in John 6. Finally, from the above arguments, I will offer an explication of the Dionysiac cannibalistic reading of the Eucharist for modern Christians.

2

Greco-Roman Background for the Johannine Eucharist

THIS CHAPTER WILL SURVEY the Greco-Roman background for the study of the Johannine Eucharist as well as for the eucharistic descriptions of Paul and the Synoptics. In fact, the term "Greco-Roman" contains such broad concepts that it needs to be limited for this book. I will study the Greco-Roman sacred meals and the Dionysus cult for the background of this book. Currently, scholars are primarily considering Greco-Roman sacred meals for the study of the Christian meal tradition, especially the Eucharist.[1] Throughout the Greco-Roman world, sacred meals are related to religious rituals in not only Christianity but also the mystery religions.[2] It is clear that Christianity, Greco-Roman religions and other oriental mystery religions shared "a common environment," and that non–Christians considered Christianity one of the mystery cults.[3] Indeed, the development of "Christian ritual" was indebted to the Greco-Roman mystery cults.[4] Thus, sacred meals in the Greco-Roman world importantly provided the commonalities between the mystery cults and the Christian ritual.

---

1. See Smith, "Meal Customs (Greco-Roman)"; Smith, "Meal Customs (Sacred Meals)"; Smith, *Symposium to Eucharist*.

2. Perrin and Duling, *New Testament*, 11–12.

3. Perrin and Duling, *New Testament*, 12.

4. St. John, "Sacred Meal," 58.

The Dionysus cult provides an important setting for John 6 and its related eucharistic discourses. I will argue that the nature of Dionysus as the god of wine offers clues for interpretation of Jesus' wine miracle in John 2:1–14, the dialogue between Jesus and the Samaritan woman in 4:5–34, the contextual meaning of Jesus' blood in 6:51–59, and the parable of a vine branch as Jesus in 15:1–12. In particular, the ritual of the Dionysus cult is closely related to the sacred meal setting where the participants eat the raw flesh of animals (*omophagia*) and the setting of the Greco-Roman hero cult in which Dionysus paradoxically appears to have both a divine character and a human one.

SACRED MEALS IN THE GRECO-ROMAN RELIGION

The term Eucharist comes from the Greek noun εὐχαριστία that means "thankfulness, gratitude, the rendering of thanks, thanksgiving," and "the observance and elements of the Eucharist."[5] As examined in Chapter One, the famous eucharistic passages are present in 1 Cor 11:23–25; Mark 14:22–25; Luke 22:15–20; and John 6:51–59. Before the Christian meal begins, participants perform rituals which include giving thanks to God, or blessing the bread and wine. Except for John's description, there is a common eucharistic phrase, "This is my body" τοῦτό ἐστιν τὸ σῶμά. In John 6:51, Jesus declares himself "I am the living bread" ἐγώ εἰμι ὁ ἄρτος ὁ ζῶν, which denotes that bread is Jesus himself or Jesus' body. Although John's eucharistic discourse is different from the Synoptics and Paul, it connotes that bread is Jesus' body and wine is his blood.

Although this book seeks the origin and meaning of the Johannine Eucharist, it does not search for the origin of the Christian Eucharist as a whole because each eucharistic tradition has unique origins deserving their own extensive studies. Scholars have investigated the Christian Eucharist from the influence of various traditions. In particular, the influence of the Jewish meal tradition has been studied, in which "the suffering and death of Jesus" is interpreted by "the passage concerning the suffering servant of God" in Isa 53:5–6.[6] Like a lamb at Passover, people eat Jesus for the sake of their deliverance. Christians especially seem to celebrate this tradition in the Christian sacred meal of "the sacrifice of an innocent victim for the sin of humankind."[7] However, the noted eucharistic formula of "This is my

---

5. Bauer, *Greek–English Lexicon*, 416.
6. Perrin, *New Testament*, 52.
7. Perrin, *New Testament*, 52.

body" (Matt 26:26; Mark 14:22; Luke 22:9; 1 Cor 11:24) is found nowhere in the Jewish tradition.

Thus, in order to understand Christian religious meals properly, I will explain the phenomenon of sacred meals in the Greco-Roman world. Furthermore, I will trace the significance of the sacrificial meal among Greco-Roman sacred meals, focusing on its elements and functions. Last, I will investigate how hero cults influenced the Christian Eucharist in its function and ritual, and then I will relate them to the Christian Eucharist to explain its origin and meanings.

The Greco-Roman Meal Custom

According to Dennis E. Smith, the Jews, Greeks, Romans and eventually Christians standardized meal customs during the Hellenistic and Roman periods (ca. 200 BCE to 200 CE).[8] The important common feature of meal customs was reclining. This custom originated from the Greeks. Plato and Xenophon describe this banquet custom in great detail.[9] For example, Plato describes it as "reclin[ing] on rustic beds" (*Rep* 372b) and "reclin[ing] on couches" (372e; 421b).[10] In detail, in the banquet, "Diners would all recline on the left elbow and eat with the right hand so that the placement of the recliners would be orderly."[11] David Noy studies Jewish meals in the Roman world, investigating useful information from the fourth century CE gold–glass and rabbinic references of second century CE.[12] According to his research, "diners were encouraged to wash their hands before eating, or at least the right hand, with which they were expected to eat as they would be reclining on the left elbow."[13] In the Jewish scholars' meals, "diners will recline for their meal after sitting for their aperitif and reclining is a synonym for dining."[14] Even in the Jewish traditional Passover meal, "Reclining for the meal was particularly important" because Jewish people considered that reclining was the most important custom for a formal meal in the Greco-Roman social context.[15] Thus, Noy quotes this custom from

8. Smith, "Meal Customs (Greco-Roman)," 650.
9. Xenophon, *Symposium*.
10. Plato, "Republic," 618–19, and 662
11. Smith, "Meal Customs (Greco-Roman)," 651.
12. Noy, "Sixth Hour," 134–44.
13. Noy, "Sixth Hour," 137.
14. Noy, "Sixth Hour," 138.
15. Noy, "Sixth Hour," 140.

Mishnah, *Pesahim* 10.1, "Even the poorest Israelite should not eat until he reclines at his table."[16]

Smith explains that sacred meals happened in everyday meals. Generally, everyday meals had customary religious components. He says, "Such formalities were especially pronounced at the formal evening meal, the *deipnon* or banquet."[17] *Deipnon* is used for the most important meal of the day and included "an evening's entertainment."[18] For this reason, the banquet consists of an eating part (banquet) and a drinking part (symposium).

Many important rituals of the banquet are from Greek tradition.[19] First, when the guests arrived, a servant led the guests to the dining room, where the guests' feet were washed by another servant.[20] Plato describes that the general banquet began after the religious ceremonies. *Symposium* 176a reports, "So Socrates drew up and had his dinner with the rest of them, and then, after the libation and the usual hymn and so forth, they began to turn their attention to the wine."[21] Furthermore, *Critias* 120a delineates that diners poured "the wine from the bowl in golden beakers"[22] over fire for the sake of people's solemn oath before they drank. Here the libation makes people take a vow so that they commit themselves to "the banquet and necessary business" that contributes to making ideal states (120b).[23] Xenophon also writes that the ceremonies occurred in transition from the supper to the symposium in the banquet; servants cleaned the table and diners offered libation and paean (*Symposium* II.1).[24] Homer's *Iliad* also describes the libation to Athena before a meal: "when they [Achaeans] had bathed and anointed themselves richly with oil, they sat down to a meal, and from the full mixing bowl they drew off honey-sweet wine and poured it to Athene" (*Il.* 10.575–579).[25]

The Greco-Roman meal custom appears through the New Testament banquet custom (Matt 15:35; Mark 6:40; Luke 11:37, 14:10, 16:22, 17:7; John

---

16. Noy, "Sixth Hour," 140.
17. Smith, "Meal Customs (Sacred Meals)," 653.
18. Smith, *Symposium to Eucharist*, 21.
19. "Some of the dining practices described in rabbinic texts would have been quite familiar to well-to-do non–Jews, and in some respects non-Jews would have felt quite at home dining with Rabban Gamaliel. However, there would also have been unfamiliar elements such as the blessing of the food and drink, the absence of women, and of course the nature of the food being eaten." Noy, "Sixth Hour," 141.
20. Smith, *Symposium to Eucharist*, 27.
21. Plato, "Symposium," 530.
22. Plato, *Critias*, 1223.
23. Plato, *Critias*, 1223.
24. Xenophon, *Symposium*, 31.
25. Homer, *Iliad Books 1–12*, 10.575–79.

6:10, 13:23), especially in the eucharistic meal (Luke 22:14; John 13:12).[26] In the Old Testament and Apocrypha, there are also examples of the reclining custom.[27] In Amos 6:4, the prophet criticizes the luxurious meal, saying that "Lying upon beds of ivory, stretched comfortably on their couches, they eat lambs taken from the flock, and calves from the stall!" Tobit also shows that reclining is a usual eating custom; "Then on our festival of Pentecost, the feast of Weeks, a fine dinner was prepared for me, and I reclined to eat" (2:1) and "when they had bathed and reclined to eat" (7:9). Judith 12:15–16 says that "Meanwhile her maid went ahead and spread out on the ground for her in front of Holofernes the fleece Bagoas had furnished for her daily use in reclining at her dinner. Then Judith came in and reclined on it." As I mentioned earlier, there are two major courses in a formal banquet: the *deipnon* (eating part) and the *symposion* (drinking part). This form is reflected in the Lord's Supper traditions in the New Testament where the wine is drunk "after supper" (Luke 22:20; 1 Cor 11:25).[28]

As Joachim Jeremias has stated, Paul's account of the Eucharist is the oldest of the five biblical texts, and the written date is 54 CE.[29] Here Paul describes that he received this Eucharist from the Lord saying that before his betrayal, Jesus took the bread, gave thanks, and broke it (1 Cor 11:23–24). As Plato describes the banquet ritual, the major eucharistic descriptions of the New Testament include a certain ritual before or during eating or drinking such as "blessing" and "offering thankfulness."[30] Jeremias mentions, "the pre-Pauline formula has the eucharistic words linked with the grace before and after the meal" in 1 Cor 11:23b–25.[31] This pre-Pauline formula, though Jeremias assumes "a table fellowship," is the grounding and structure of the Eucharist in 1 Corinthians and the Synoptics, which is inherited from the meal custom of the Greco-Roman world.[32]

Sacrificial Meals

Observers can find strong evidence of sacred meals within the sacrificial meals because "any banquet in the Greco-Roman period could have been

---

26. See ἀναπίπτω in Bauer, *Greek–English Lexicon*, 70.
27. Both Bible verses are from NAB.
28. I will specifically look into Johannine meal custom in next chapter.
29. Jeremias, "This Is My Body," 198.
30. Matt 15:38; 26:27; Mark 8:6; 14:23; Luke 22:17, 19; John 6:11, 23; Acts 27:35; 1 Cor 10:16; 11:24.
31. Jeremias, "This Is My Body," 198.
32. Jeremias, "This Is My Body," 196–97.

Greco-Roman Background for the Johannine Eucharist 27

connected with a sacrifice in some way."[33] Sacrifice was "a primary form" of religious ritual in the ancient world.[34] From prehistory and the Minoan-Mycenaean Age, animal sacrifice was an important element of ancient festivals.[35] In Greek religion, the basic form of sacrifice (*thysia*) included "the slaughter, butchering and burning of a portion of the animal at the altar,"[36] then the deity, the priest or temple, and the worshippers received the rest of the portions of the animal.[37] Walter Burkert also states that although the form of the animal sacrificial ritual varies according to local custom, "the fundamental structure is identical and clear" because it precedes "a meat meal."[38] During this process, the priest pours the blood onto the ground or an altar.[39]

The term *thysia* (θυσία,) means "act of offering," "sacrifice," or "sacrificial meal."[40] The *thysia* in which both humans and gods received something to eat points to this sacrifice. It includes a common meal for both gods and mortals, or a meal among mortals preceded by food to the gods. According to David Gill, in the fullest form of the *thysia* that appear in Homeric literature and other ancient writings, "the god's portion, the thigh bones wrapped in fat and other selected pieces of meat, was consumed on the altar, while the worshippers ate the rest of the sacrificial animal in a sacred meal"[41] (*Il*. 1.458–474; 2.420–431; and compressed in *Il*. 7.327–330). Both examples in *Il*. 1.458–474 and 2.420–431 show that worshippers first offered a burnt offering to the god and then feasted on the equal portions. All three references indicate the term of *daitos eises*, which means equal meal or equal banquet.[42] Sion M. Honea studies this term and concludes that *daitos eises* "originates in the cult of Paleolithic hunters who desired to ensure the equal distribution of responsibility for the killing."[43] This term describes the "symbolic value" of responsibility and esteem among worshippers, which established strong interrelationships within communities.[44]

---

33. Smith, *Symposium to Eucharist*, 85.
34. Smith, "Meal Customs (Sacred Meals)," 654.
35. Burkert, *Greek Religion*, 13 and 34.
36. Smith, *Symposium to Eucharist*, 67.
37. Smith, "Meal Customs (Sacred Meals)," 654.
38. Burkert, *Greek Religion*, 57.
39. Burkert, *Greek Religion*, 56.
40. Bauer, *Greek–English Lexicon*, 462.
41. Gill, *Greek Cult Tables*, 11.
42. Honea, "Homer's *Daitos Eises*," 53–58.
43. Honea, "Homer's *Daitos Eises*," 66.
44. Honea, "Homer's *Daitos Eises*," 67.

In the sacrificial meal, although the human portions were much larger than those of the deity, sometimes the blood and considerable portions of the meat from the sacrificial animal were assigned to the gods at the table in the *thysia*. Gill indicates, "Usually the cult official who performed the *thysia* also took care of the table of the god."[45] These portions were called *trapezomata*. The term itself is nowhere to be found in Homer, but the practice is present at the sacrifice in the house of Eumaios in *Odyssey* 14.418–438.[46] After Eumaios burns some of the meat wrapped in fat for the gods, he places the rest of the cooked meat on the table. Next Eumaios divides the cooked meat into seven portions, one for the Nymphs and Hermes and the other six for himself and his guest, Odysseus (lines 434–436). His story shows a constitution of the *thysia* and the practice of assigning *trapezomata*. In *thysia*, the deity receives a gift that is the animal at the altar, and consumes the burned portion. Adding *trapezomata* to *thysia* emphasizes that the deity is invisibly present and eats his/her portions of meat with his/her worshippers. In addition, the term of equal portions appears when Eumaios divides the meat into seven parts and offers one to the gods, which gives considerable support for *daitos eises*. Through sharing the symbolic value of responsibility and esteem not only with worshippers, but also with the deities, the ritual highlights the presence of the deity at sacred meals so that worshippers experience communion with their deities as well as strong interrelationship between themselves.

In emphasizing the remembrance of the death and suffering of Jesus in the Eucharist, one can regard Jesus as the sacrificial animal on the altar in *thysia* that was offered to God for many people (Heb 9:23, 26; 10:12). The practice of *trapezomata* provides the Christian Eucharist with Jesus' presence among the participants. The notion of *daitos eises* may have influenced the openness and equality of the Eucharist, although Paul harshly accused some Corinthian church members of abusing the Eucharist to break up this openness and the equal sharing of food (1 Cor 11:19–22).

As mentioned above, the sacred meal was commonly held in a sacrificial ritual. John St. John states that the sacred meal is the root of Christian ritual because the features of the sacred meal and the Eucharist share similar components.[47] For instance, the bread and the wine are laid on the altar. This action equates Jesus' flesh and blood with the slaughtered animal presented to the gods as a gift. The priest consecrates these two elements using prayer and singing just as the meats are consecrated when the worshipper offers the

---

45. Gill, "*Trapezomata*," 126.
46. Gill, "*Trapezomata*," 134.
47. John, "Sacred Meal," 60.

god's portion in *thysia*. Furthermore, when the priest slaughters the sacrificial animal, he pours out its blood to purify people's defilement "by defiling themselves with other blood,"[48] or he sprays its blood over the seats for purifying the assemblies.[49] Jeremias also points out in the Jewish sacrifice that the animal's blood is poured out on "the altar of burnt-offering"[50] just as Moses sprinkled the blood over the people, saying that "this is the blood of the covenant" (Exod 24:8).[51] Jeremias' point demonstrates how the Jewish sacrifice is similar to the function of the Greek animal sacrifice. However, Jeremias' statement does not explain that the Jewish law does not allow either eating the meat with the blood, or drinking blood only, because the Jewish people, unlike the Greek, have "a universal blood taboo."[52] Moreover, Aeschylus describes the oath of seven heroes who slaughter a bull and dip their fingers in the bull's blood, which makes a covenant between them and the gods (*Sept.* 43–44).[53]

Burkert vividly illustrates how the animal blood is used in the ritual: "An ox is felled by a blow with an axe, and then the artery in the neck is opened. The blood is collected in a basin and sprayed over the altar and against the sides; to stain the altar with blood (*haimassein*) is a pious duty."[54] Here Burkert shows the sacrificial use of the blood. Likewise, Jesus' blood is mentioned as the sacrificial purpose because his blood is "the covenant which is poured out for many for the forgiveness of sins" (Matt 26:28), "blood of the covenant, which is poured out for many" (Mark 14:24), "poured out for you is the new covenant" (Luke 22:20), and "the new covenant" (1 Cor 11:25).

Mark 14:24 and 1 Cor 11:24 use the "imagery of sacrificial meals," "connecting the ceremony with a sacrificial interpretation of the death of Jesus."[55] The concept of ingesting the deity similarly exists in John's Eucharist (6:53–57).[56] The notion of communion with the gods also appears throughout the New Testament eucharistic discourses, though this concept has not existed in the Jewish Passover meal tradition. In addition, Christians have

48. Burkert, *Greek Religion*, 80.
49. Burkert, *Greek Religion*, 81.
50. Jeremias, "This is My Body," 202.
51. Jeremias, "This is My Body," 202.
52. Burkert, *Greek Religion*, 59.
53. Aeschylus, *Seven Against Thebes*, 34.
54. Burkert, *Greek Religion*, 56.
55. Smith, "Meal Customs (Sacred Meals)," 654.
56. John's Eucharist supports the notion of transubstantiation in the history of Christian doctrine.

adopted the presence of the deity in the sacred meal into the presence of the Lord in various ways such as "memorial" (1 Cor 11:24), "eschatological proclamation" (1 Cor 11:26), "symbolic representation" (1 Cor 10:16), and "community identity" (1 Cor 10:17).[57] Paul uses the idea of the *thysia* sacrifice when he explains the Eucharist in 1 Cor 10:16–21, especially verses 18, 20, and 21. The Greek verses show this clearly.

> 18 βλέπετε τὸν Ἰσραὴλ κατὰ σάρκα· οὐχ οἱ ἐσθίοντες τὰς θυσίας κοινωνοὶ τοῦ θυσιαστηρίου εἰσίν; 19 Τί οὖν φημι; ὅτι εἰδωλόθυτόν τί ἐστιν ἢ ὅτι εἴδωλόν τί ἐστιν; 20 ἀλλ' ὅτι ἃ θύουσιν, δαιμονίοις καὶ οὐ θεῷ [θύουσιν]·οὐ θέλω δὲ ὑμᾶς κοινωνοὺς τῶν δαιμονίων γίνεσθαι. 21 οὐ δύνασθε ποτήριον κυρίου πίνειν καὶ ποτήριον δαιμονίων, οὐ δύνασθε τραπέζης κυρίου μετέχειν καὶ τραπέζης δαιμονίων (emphasis added).

After Paul mentions that the cup of blessing (ποτήριον τῆς εὐλογίας) and bread (ἄρτον) are the blood (αἵματος τοῦ Χριστοῦ) and body of Christ (σώματος τοῦ Χριστοῦ) in 1 Cor 10:16, like the people of Israel who ate the meat at the *thysia* sacrifices (οἱ ἐσθίοντες τὰς θυσίας κοινωνοὶ), Christians eat bread and wine when they participate in *thysia* to God (θεῷ [θύουσιν]). Paul also contrasts the "*thysia* to demons" (θύουσιν, δαιμονίοις) with "*thysia* to God" (θεῷ [θύουσιν]) and "the cup of the Lord" (ποτήριον κυρίου) with "the cup of the demons" (ποτήριον δαιμονίων) as well as the "table of the Lord" (τραπέζης κυρίου) with "the table of demons" (τραπέζης δαιμονίων). Here, Paul closely relates the *thysia* to the Eucharist, which demonstrates that Paul understands the Eucharist in the structure and function of the *thysia* sacrifice: the animal sacrifice and the sacred meal.

Like some cases in the older Roman religions, eating the food is eating the deity in the sacred meal.[58] For instance, in the Dionysus cult, the worshippers eat the raw flesh of a bull for this reason. By eating the god, the worshippers can experience direct communion with the deity. Gregory Riley indicates, "A central feature of the mysteries of Dionysiac religion was the ritual and symbolic consumption of the flesh and blood of the god;"[59] it reenacts "the rending and eating of the baby Dionysus by the Titans" and brings "inspiration and possession by the god Dionysus himself."[60] Riley states that the Dionysus cult inspired early Christians to understand "the Eucharist as sharing in the body and blood of Christ" and "made this type of

---

57. Smith, "Meal Customs (Sacred Meals)," 654.
58. See Thomas, "Sacred Meal."
59. Riley, *One Jesus Many Christs*, 128.
60. Riley, *One Jesus Many Christs*, 186–87.

slander, about the eating of a baby."⁶¹ In addition, the Dionysus cult features drinking wine in its banquet and ritual. In the Dionysus tradition, wine was often considered the blood of Dionysus,⁶² which means that drinking wine intakes Dionysus himself for participants who experience ecstasy and are unified with the god. One needs to attend that the Christian Eucharist includes wine in its celebration. Although the Christian Eucharist, unlike the Dionysus cult, changed flesh into bread, it continues to use wine in its ritual. Like the case of excessive wine drunkenness of the Dionysus cult, people mocked that Christians were filled with new wine at daytime (Acts 2:13). Riley also indicates that owing to drunkenness in Christian eucharistic celebrations, Paul warned the members of the Corinthian church because wine "led occasionally to abuses" in the context of the "love feast."⁶³ Even Romans criticized the Christian banquet for immorality. These intoxications show that the Dionysus tradition and the Christian eucharistic ritual shared a certain degree of similarities. Furthermore, the flesh and the blood of Dionysus are redolent of John's eucharistic discourse in chapter 6 where Jesus says that he is the living bread and encourages people to eat his flesh and drink his blood (John 6:51–59). For this reason, I will explore the important characteristics of the Dionysus cult.

Hero Cult

The Greeks considered that "heroes fulfilled the same role as gods," and they felt a closer relationship with heroes than gods.⁶⁴ According to Gunnel Ekroth's study, in the four best-preserved sacrificial calendars from classical Attica, "Of the 170 or so sacrifices listed in these texts, 40 percent were performed to heroes, while the amounts of money spent on the victims for these sacrifices was around 38 percent of the budget."⁶⁵ This indicates that almost 40 percent of budget and numbers of the sacrifices were dedicated to the hero cult. Plato describes heroes as "half gods" or "demigods,"⁶⁶ the heroes were "the offspring of the union between divine and human females."⁶⁷ Hesiod identifies heroes as "a god-like race who are called demi-gods,"

---

61. Riley, *One Jesus Many Christs*, 187.
62. Burkert, *Greek Religion*, 164.
63. Riley, *One Jesus Many Christs*, 188.
64. Ekroth, "Heroes and Hero-Cults," 108.
65. Ekroth, "Heroes and Hero-Cults," 108.
66. Plato, "Cratylus," 436.
67. Riley, *One Jesus Many Christs*, 39.

ἀνδρῶν ἡρώων θεῖον γένος οἱ καλέονται ἡμίθεοι (159).[68] Accoring to Riley, "The heroes were simply examples of mingled races, with strengths of the gods and weaknesses of humans, as any child of different races might mix the characteristics of each parent."[69] Because of their devine origin, heroes are often called the sons of gods. In many cases, heroes die at the peak of their lives. Ekroth states, "Many mythic and epic heroes and heroines perished violently at a young age."[70] Riley understands Jesus in the characteristics of Greek heroes who have a divine origin in their birth, learn many things through suffering (*pathei mathos*), die in the midst of life, and gain immortality because of "their divine ancestry and their suffering."[71] He defines the meaning of a hero as "a person of distinguished courage, admired for bravery and noble character; and one of such qualities who stands as an ideal and an example."[72] Although heroes inherited immortality from their divine fathers (or mothers) and later became gods, they experienced all sorts of human agony, difficulty, and death as normal human beings did.[73] Riley points out, "So the heroes were the models, high as ideals, but based in real life and accessible situations" for normal people.[74] Because of "the sense of being recognized as such," they are worshipped in the hero cult.[75] The Greeks even worshipped their enemies' heroes. Margaret Visser states that enemy heroes become "powerful protectors instead of hated enemies" after their deaths.[76] Whether the heroes are their enemies or their friends, people were encouraged not to forget the heroes because they would become angry for lack of attention.[77]

Because heroes were thought to have human experience and were connected with specific locations, they were regarded as intimate helpers for human beings rather than high and noble gods.[78] Riley also indicates that the dead hero becomes a "protector of the living" and "judge" for the living.[79] Justin Martyr wrote an apologetic letter to a Roman emperor, explaining

---

68. Hesiod, "Works and Days," 15.
69. Riley, *I Was Thought to Be What I Am Not*, 11.
70. Ekroth, "Heroes and Hero-Cults," 105.
71. Riley, *One Jesus Many Christs*, 91.
72. Riley, *One Jesus Many Christs*, 36.
73. Riley, *I Was Thought to Be What I Am Not*, 11.
74. Riley, *One Jesus Many Christs*, 206.
75. Nock, "Cult," 143.
76. Visser, "Worship Your Enemy," 403.
77. Visser, "Worship Your Enemy," 417.
78. Ekroth, "Heroes and Hero-Cults," 105.
79. Riley, *One Jesus Many Christs*, 94.

that Jesus Christ, who was crucified, died, rose again, and ascended into heaven, was no different from the sons of Zeus.[80] Justin compared Jesus with one of Zeus' sons who were famous heroes, too (such as Asclepius, Hermes, Dionysus, Dioscure, Perseus of Danae, and Bellerophon).[81] The stories of the sons of Zeus were "paradigms for the early church in its understanding of Jesus."[82] In this point, the hero tradition gives a hint to interpret Jesus' Last Supper or the institution of the Eucharist.

Although "Meals for deities without worshipper participation were also characteristic of the cult of the heroes, in which they are probably an extension or continuation of the meals that were held at the graves of the dead" to ease the dead heroes' "journey into the next world," the sacred meals were eaten among worshippers in the hero cult.[83] These ceremonies consisted of "holocaust on low hearth-altars, libations of the blood in pits, and the offering of prepared meals."[84] More than others, the highlight of the hero cult is held in the term of *thysia* at which the worshipers eat the meat.[85] Ekroth insists that at the standard *thysia* sacrifice, the participants drink animal blood as they eat the meat.[86] Another example of usage of the blood at the hero cult is briefly mentioned by Pindar (*Olympian* 1.90–93).[87] The *thysia* sacrifices to Pelops at Olympia show that the hero cult initiates by "a pouring out of blood, *haimakouria*," which seems to function as "a means of contacting and inviting the hero and ensuring his presence at the sacrifice."[88]

Usually, the assembly of the hero cult was held at night.[89] As the Bacchic cult was "secret and nocturnal rites,"[90] "the Eucharist is celebrated behind a screen" and the eucharistic meals were also secret in Eastern Christianity, which is traced in the eucharistic discourse of the Synoptics and Pauline writings.[91] In the hero cult, the dead hero god received "only a libation and the guests consumed the rest."[92] Thus, the cups that were used in libation

80. Justin, "First Apology," 255.
81. Justin, "First Apology," 255.
82. Riley, *One Jesus Many Christs*, 19.
83. Gill, "*Trapezomata*," 121; Coldstream, "Hero Cults in the Age of Homer," 8.
84. Ekroth, "Heroes and Hero-Cults," 106.
85. Ekroth, "Heroes and Hero-Cults," 106.
86. Ekroth, "Heroes and Hero-Cults," 107.
87. Pindar, *Odes of Pindar*, 13.
88. Ekroth, "Heroes and Hero-Cults," 107.
89. Nock, "Cult," 148.
90. Riley, *One Jesus Many Christs*, 184.
91. Riley, *One Jesus Many Christs*, 186.
92. Nock, "Cult," 149.

were hallowed by heroes' names. "In the modern literature on Greek sacrifice, meals for the gods and heroes have frequently been called by the general term *theoxenia*."[93] Ekroth also states, "Apart from regular animal sacrifices, the heroes also received *theoxenia*, offerings of food of the kind eaten by humans."[94] This statment shows that the sacred meal is the central part of the hero cult. Through the sacred meals, the participants share "the table fellowship with the heroes."[95] According to Ekroth, the purpose of the *theoxenia* is to bring the heroes closer to the worshipers and to invite the worshipers as honored guests of the heroes.[96] The important thing in the hero cult is to remember the hero who now becomes the protector and judge of the people.[97] In particular, in the Dionysus cult, eating the flesh stands for the god's suffering and drinking wine signifies the blood of Dionysus. Dionysus was an important Greek hero, and later became the god of wine.[98]

THE DIONYSUS CULT IN THE GRECO-ROMAN WORLD

General Characteristics of Dionysus

Dionysus (or Dionysos) [Διώνυσος] is a foreign origin deity perhaps from Asia Minor who showed up relatively late in Greece and overcame "determined resistance in various parts of Greece."[99] In Euripides' *Bacchae*, Dionysus is called Bromius (Βρόμιος) or Evius (Εὔιος).[100] Walter Otto states that Dionysus perhaps came from Thrace into Greece as "a foreigner."[101] Based on recent archaeological evidence, however, some scholars indicate that "the name and the cult of Dionysus" come from Mycenaean origin because Dionysus's name has appeared on "Linear B tablets from Pylos in the Peloponnese."[102] For this reason, I prefer Clifford Herschel Moore's

93. Gill, "Trapezomata," 122. Here Gill sees that *theoxenia* and *theodaisia* are synonyms, though there are some minute differences.

94. Ekroth, "Heroes and Hero-Cults," 107.

95. Nock, "Cult," 148.

96. Ekroth, "Heroes and Hero-Cults," 107.

97. The hero cult may provide the important background for the Eucharist of the Synoptics and 1 Cor 11 in which the authors of the Gospels and Paul emphasize the remembrance of Jesus Christ.

98. I will investigate the Dionysus cult in the next section in detail.

99. Hard, *Routledge Handbook*, 170; also refer to Otto, *Dionysus*, 63.

100. Βρόμιος means "sounding" or "boisterous" and Εὔιος comes from the cry, εὐοῖ. See Liddell, *Greek–English Lexicon*.

101. Otto, *Dionysus*, 52.

102. Hard, *Routledge Handbook*, 170 and see Burkert, *Greek Religion*, 162; regarding

assertion that the cult of Dionysus came into "Greece by more than one wave of immigration."[103] Concerning the name, the first syllable of "Dionysus" (the genitive of Zeus's name) seems to indicate Zeus, but the rest of the meaning is uncertain. It might come from a "word nysos (akin to Latin *nurus* or Greek) meaning 'child' or 'son,'" or from the name "connected with the legendary Nysa."[104] Therefore, the possible meanings of "Dionysus" are "Son of Zeus" or "the Nysa of Zeus," though the exact meaning is still unclear.[105] In general, scholars agree that the name of Dionysus is "a sacred and unfathomable symbol."[106]

Although he barely mentions Dionysus, Homer is an important witness for "the great age of the Greek Dionysus."[107] In Book 6 of the *Iliad* (130ff), Homer mentions Dionysus, and the term "maenad" appears in *Iliad* 22.461. According to Otto, "Homer, then, not only knows Dionysus, but he alludes to almost everything which is characteristic of the myth and cult of Dionysus," and "In Delphi the worship of Dionysus could be considered older than that of Apollo."[108]

The *Homeric Hymns to Dionysus* gives some evidence of Dionysus. Showing the conflicting traditions about the birthplace of Dionysus,[109] the hymn affirms that Dionysus was born in "Nysa, a mountain most high and richly grown with woods, far off in Phoenice, near the streams of Aegyptus" (line 8–9) and he inspired "frenzied women" (line 17–18).[110] According to Hesiod, Dionysus's mother is Semele, daughter of Cadmus, and his father is Zeus. Hesiod emphasizes that a mortal woman bore an immortal son (line 940–942).[111] While emphasizing that "the one of the essentials of the myth of Dionysus" is "the mortality of the mother,"[112] Otto further states, "Semele's cult and memory are associated throughout with the memory of her great son . . . In Magnesia a marble altar was dedicated 'to Dionysus and Semele' . . . Thus the human mother of the divine son was crowned

an introductory explanation of Linear B, see Chadwick, *Linear B and Related Scripts*.

103. Moore, *Religious Thought*, 47.
104. Hard, *Routledge Handbook*, 170.
105. See Otto, *Dionysus*, 61–62.
106. Mayerson, *Classical Mythology*, 249.
107. Otto, *Dionysus*, 53; Philip Mayerson indicates that even the worship of Dionysus is earlier than that of Zeus. Mayerson, *Classical Mythology*, 248.
108. Otto, *Dionysus*, 53 and 57.
109. Hard, *Routledge Handbook*, 171–72.
110. Homer, "Homeric Hymn I to Dionysus," 287.
111. Hesiod, "Theogony," 149.
112. Otto, *Dionysus*, 70.

with immortality and received her share of cultic honors."[113] The passage of *The Homeric Hymn VII to Dionysus* also describes Dionysus as "the son of glorious Semele" (line 1).[114] In this story, Hera, the wife of Zeus is jealous of Semele. She plots to kill Semele and she disguises herself as an old crone to convince Semele that she will ask Zeus to reveal his identity. Seeing his immortal glory, Semele is immediately burned by the god's radiance and Zeus rescues a fetal Dionysus. Herodotus also mentions that Zeus brings the new-born Dionysus, who has been sewn in his thigh, to Nysa in Ethiopia (2.146).[115] Actually, there are several different versions of the Dionysus birth story.

Nonnos at Panopolis in Asia Minor in fifth century CE introduced another version of Dionysus's story in *Dionysiaca* that was based on Orphic Hymns.[116] Nonnos wrote Dionysus was born of Zeus and Persephone, the queen of the Greek underworld, Hades.[117] A jealous Hera sent Titans to kill the baby. After luring the baby with toys, Titans ripped Dionysus to pieces.[118] When Zeus repelled Titans away with his thunderbolts, Titans ate everything but Dionysus's heart. Zeus took the heart and put it in the womb of Semele to recreate Dionysus. A slightly different legend claims that Zeus gave Semele the heart to eat to impregnate her.[119] The several different birth stories of Dionysus emphasize rebirth after violent death as Jesus' stories emphasizes resurrection or eternal life after his crucifixion.

Furthermore, Dionysus's birth stories show that he is a suffering son of God. According to Nonnos, Dionysus was killed by his enemies and his body cut to pieces by knives.[120] Otto indicates, "Dionysus, himself, is a suffering, dying god who must succumb to the violence of terrible enemies in the midst of the glory of his youthful greatness."[121] Although Dionysus was a son of Zeus, his enemies persecuted him and eventually killed him. His cult often confronted resistance and persecution. According to Otto, he was "the persecuted god, the suffering and dying god" loving to "share his tragic fate."[122] For instance, Euripides vividly portrays the suffering Dionysus by

113. Otto, *Dionysus*, 68.
114. Homer, "VII to Dionysus," 429.
115. Herodotus, *Herodotus*, 453–54.
116. See Athanassakis, trans., *Orphic Hymns*.
117. Nonnos, *Dionysiaca I*, 225.
118. Nonnos, *Dionysiaca I*, 227–29.
119. Frazer, *New Golden Bough*, 353.
120. Nonnos, *Dionysiaca I*, 229 (v.225).
121. Otto, *Dionysus*, 103.
122. Otto, *Dionysus*, 49.

the hand of Pentheus, a king of Thebes, in the *Bacchae*. Indeed, Euripides describes "the most influential and most sublime portrayal of the Dionysian world" in the fifth century BCE.[123] Here, Pentheus unjustly persecutes Dionysus, the son of his aunt, Semele. Pentheus first bans women from following Dionysus by bounding and shackling them in chains in the town prison (line 528-33).[124] In his introduction, Alan Shapiro describes the persecution of Pentheus:

> Pentheus's first lines on the stage (254—88) define the issues of his conflict with Dionysos: the city's control of women, sexuality, and the reinforcement of restraints and boundaries. He dwells on the seductive effects of the new cult on women and pays particular attention to the erotic attractions of the young Lydian Stranger (see 273-77). He will imprison the bacchants in the city, hunt down and put in chains those on the mountain, and have the Stranger's head, with its tossing hair, severed from his body.[125]

Then Pentheus arrests Dionysus and puts him into prison. Although Pentheus's persecution seems not to succeed in the end, as a mortal, he plays an important role in resisting the god. Hard also mentions, "Some of the most characteristic myths of the mature Dionysos are those in which he suffers persecution from mortals who refuse to acknowledge his divinity and try to suppress his rites when he first introduces them into their land."[126] According to Friedrich Nietzsche:

> the suffering of Dionysus was the sole subject of the earliest form of Greek tragedy and for a long time there was no other available stage hero than Dionysus himself. And we may maintain with equal assurance that up to the time of Euripides Dionysus remained the tragic hero, and that all the famous figures of the Greek stage, Prometheus, Oedipus, and so on, are only masks of that original hero Dionysus.[127]

From ancient times, Dionysus has acquired the position of the suffering son of god as a peerless tragic hero. For this reason, Arthur Evans argues, "The most obvious influence of Euripides' *Bakkhai* on Christian mythology lies in its concept of Dionysos as the suffering Son of God."[128]

123. Burkert, *Greek Religion*, 162.
124. Euripides, *Bakkhai*, 59.
125. Shapiro, "Introduction," 19.
126. Hard, *Routledge Handbook*, 173.
127. Nietzsche, *Birth of Tragedy*, 59.
128. Evans, *God of Ecstasy*, 146.

The image of Dionysus, however, goes far beyond "suffering son of god," because the portrait of Dionysus is complicated. Otto illustrates Dionysus as "a god of paradox."[129] He explains, "The cult of Dionysos is very ancient in Greece, and yet it is seen to be in a process of continual change."[130] Dionysus wears different masks and reveals himself in different ways at different times to his worshipers.[131] Plutarch says that the Greeks thought Dionysus was the master of wine and the lord of "the nature of every sort of moisture" and consecrated eggs as "a symbol of that which produces everything and contains everything within itself" to the rite of Dionysus.[132] Clifford Herschel Moore observes that Dionysus came as "the god of all living things, of plants, trees, the lower animals, as well as of man." He further explains the various living features of Dionysus:

> In short he was a nature divinity whose death was seen in the dead vegetation of winter and whose rebirth appeared with the revival of spring. His orgiastic rites no doubt were originally, in part at least, intended to recall the dead god to life. But in all such religions there is the tendency to see in the rebirth of the dead god the warrant of man's future life. The hope is easily awakened that as the vegetation, whose life disappears in the ground, is revivified in the spring, so man, whose body also is laid in the earth, may be recalled to new life. The Dionysiac myth set forth the story of the god's death and rebirth. It was natural then that men should feel that if they could secure union with the god, lose themselves in the divine, they too might attain immortality.[133]

Dionysus's death in winter and rebirth in spring seem to relate to the Demeter cult.[134] Otto mentions that "Mysterious dedications called him the Lord of Souls."[135] Jocelyn M. C. Toynbee also argues that "life, death, and afterlife" are the significantly continuing themes in the mosaics of the House of Dionysos at Paphos which is one of "the most important mosaic sites of Greek-speaking Roman Cyprus."[136] She points out that the mosaic pictures

---

129. Otto, *Dionysus*, xix.
130. Burkert, Greek Religion, 290.
131. Faraone, "Introduction," 2.
132. "Isis and Osiris," 87.
133. Moore, *Religious Thought*, 48–49.
134. Plutarch, *Plutarch's Moralia XV*, 103 (frag. 24).
135. Otto, *Dionysus*, 49.
136. Toynbee, "Life, Death, and Afterlife on Roman-Age Mosaics," 211.

clearly show "symbols of the love of divinities for mortals in this life and of the union after death of mortals with their gods."[137]

Another important characteristic of Dionysus is madness. Dionysus is the mad god and his ardent followers, the maenads, are also mad.[138] Likewise, in the *Phaedrus*, Socrates says, "in reality the greatest blessings come byway of madness."[139] He praises madness because "the prophetess at Delphi" and other prophets are able to prophesy on behalf of "individuals in Greece" when they are mad as well as "greatest of arts" are connected with madness.[140] Dodds categorizes Plato's descriptions of madness in the four types: "1) Prophetic madness, whose patron god is Apollo. 2) Telestic or ritual madness, whose patron is Dionysus. 3) Poetic madness, inspired by the Muses. 4) Erotic madness, inspired by Aphrodite and Eros."[141] Although Dionysus bestows madness on his enemies, indeed Dionysus empowers his followers to use the blessing of madness as Plato describes above. In the Dionysiac ritual, the participants experience "mental healing" in "collective or congregational" madness.[142] Compared to Apollo's reason and moderation, Friedrich Nietzsche also insists that Dionysus is the god of emotion and madness in *Birth of Tragedy*.[143] Burkert explains that madness in the Dionysus cult increases "an experience of intensified mental power" which is achieved by "mass phenomenon."[144] This mental power offers "freedom" for his worshipers.[145] Perceptions of Dionysus as a "mad god" are strengthened by his primary characteristic, his connection to wine.[146]

---

137. Toynbee, "Life, Death, and Afterlife on Roman-Age Mosaics," 211.
138. Otto, *Dionysus*, 135.
139. Plato, *Phaedrus*, 491 (244A).
140. Plato, *Phaedrus*, 491 (244A–244D).
141. Dodds, *Greeks*, 64.
142. Dodds, *Greeks*, 69.
143. Nietzsche, *The Birth of Tragedy*, 19 and 76.
144. Burkert, *Greek Religion*, 162.
145. Dodds, *Greeks*, 76. I will further investigate "freedom" of madness in the ritual of the Dionysus cult section.
146. Dodds mentions that "the two great Dionysiac techniques" are "the use of wine and the use of the religious dance" in Dodds, *Greeks*, 69.

Dionysus as a Wine God

Dionysus can simply be defined as "the god of wine" and of "intoxicated ecstasy."[147] Hesiod also describes Dionysus as the god of wine.[148] The major effect of wine is to change grief and misery into happiness and joy. With wine, "the poor man feels himself rich, the slave free, the weak strong and powerful."[149] Plutarch wonderfully says that wine "frees the soul of subservience."[150] Intoxicated by wine, human beings feel liberated from all kinds of social, psychological, spiritual, and economic bondage. Even one of the Old Testament books speaks of it: "Give strong drink unto him that is perishing, and wine unto the distressed in soul: Let him drink and forget his misery and remember his sorrow no more!" (Prov 31:6). Furthermore, wine has been a medicine from ancient to modern times. In 1 Timothy 5:23, the author encourages to use wine as an internal medicien for infirmities (ἀσθενείας) and in Luke 10:34 for surgical treatment.[151] Another important usage of wine is to provide human beings with present joy, psychological release, and social freedom. Wine not only helps people to overcome their difficulties by forgetting their current problems, but also heal their illness physically and internally.

Thus, wine has a religious value as well as medical one.[152] Ancient Greeks thought Dionysus performed miracles in connection with wine. Albert Henrichs says, "He is first and foremost the god of wine,"[153] and Otto indicates that "the epiphany of Dionysus was accompanied by wondrous streams of wine" in many cases.[154] In Euripides' *Bacchae*, one Baccante drove her fennel in the ground, and "it struck the earth, at the touch of god, a spring of wine poured out"[155] (lines 705–707). Indeed, many ancient descriptions about Dionysus and his pictures show that Dionysus loves to drink wine and encourage his followers to be intoxicated by it.

---

147. Burkert, *Greek Religion*, 161.

148. Hesiod, "Works and Days," 614.

149. Otto, *Dionysus*, 148–49.

150. Otto, *Dionysus*, 149.

151. "No longer drink only water, but use a little wine for your stomach's sake and your frequent infirmities" (1 Tim 5:23 NKJV) and "So he went to him and bandaged his wounds, pouring on oil and wine; and he set him on his own animal, brought him to an inn, and took care of him" (Luke 10:34 NKJV).

152. Mayerson, *Classical Mythology*, 251.

153. Henrichs, "He Has a God," 14.

154. Otto, *Dionysus*, 97.

155. Euripides, *Euripides V*, 185.

There are other stories about wine connected to Dionysus. According to the passage from Pausanias, the priests of Dionysus brought empty jars into a temple and sealed them. The next day when the priests opened the jars, they found that the jars miraculously filled with wine.[156]

Campbell Bonner shows that water changing into wine is similar to the Dionysus cult through his investigation of "the peculiar structural features of a temple at Corinth."[157] He conjectures that the temple was used in the "practice of some sort of pious fraud."[158] He thinks that the priests might have secretly hidden a person in the tunnel and then locked the temple. That person might have poured wine into the empty jars so that the priests would be able to demonstrate the changed wine.[159] This story elucidates a key feature of Dionysus. He had made water into wine before Jesus changed water into wine in John chapter 2. A similar miracle was reported on the Island of Andros where the Dionysiac festival took place. During the festival, "a stream of wine flowed in the temple of Dionysus there," and when people took out the wine from the temple, it immediately transformed to water.[160] This story shows that wine also can be turned into water just as water turns into wine.

These descriptions show that the Dionysus cult is closely related to the wine miracle mentioned above which represents the importance of the "chthonic aspects of Dionysus himself."[161] With the gift of wine, Dionysus is believed to bring about changes in the "personality of the human recipient."[162] When the worshipers of Dionysus drink wine, they believe that they take the god Dionysus within themselves.[163] In particular, together with using music and dance, drinking wine is "to put individuals or whole companies into direct communication with the spirits or into union with a god."[164] By doing so, they feel that the spirit of Dionysus controls and dwells in themselves. This phenomenon is a religious ecstasy where the mortal can experience immortality in this world.

In the process of making wine, the crushed grapes signify the dismemberment of Dionysus.[165] Wine itself stands for the blood of Dionysus.

---

156. Pausanias, "Elis II," 157; Meyer, ed. *Ancient Mysterie*, 95.
157. Bonner, "Dionysiac Miracle," 368.
158. Bonner, "Dionysiac Miracle," 371.
159. Bonner, "Dionysiac Miracle," 373.
160. Otto, *Dionysus*, 98.
161. Bonner, "Dionysiac Miracle," 374.
162. Henrichs, "He Has a God," 19.
163. Evans, *God of Ecstasy*, 148.
164. Moore, *Religious Thought*, 50.
165. Seaford, *Dionysos*, 74 and 127.

Richard Seaford mentions the notion of death and resurrection of Dionysus, indicating that "Conceivably psychic wholeness induced by wine was associated with the restoration to wholeness of Dionysos dismembered in the making of the wine."[166] In addition, "The mysterious process of the fermentation and ripening of wine still has the power today" to evoke one of the powers of Dionysus.[167] Definitely, the color of wine vividly gives a lifelike quality to Dionysus's blood. In "the Eating of Flesh I" which explains the Pythagorean or Orphic abstention from animal flesh, Plutarch interprets Dionysus's suffering and dismemberment at the hands of the Titans in the perspective of "rebirth." In other words, he concludes that "all this is a myth which in its inner meaning has to do with rebirth" (996B and C).[168]

On top of this point, Plutarch insists that Dionysus was another name of Osiris, (364E)[169] and he was identified by the Greeks with Osiris (356B; 362B).[170] It is Osiris who has impacted the Christian notion of resurrection and afterlife. Martin Nilsson states that the Zagreus-Dionysiac mystery is "a copy of the Osiris myth."[171] Osiris' death and survival show a "paradigm that is the basis of hope"[172] because he was "the embodiment of the fertility of the earth and plants"[173] and later became "the god of the after-life and resurrection."[174] Such characteristics of the Zagreus-Dionysiac mystery ensure people of their eternal life after their death.[175] These features remind one of Jesus' emphasis on "eternal life" (John 6:47) and "resurrection" (John 6:39, 44, 58), which will be discussed later in this book. One important basic fact is that Christianity began in the fertile field of Greco-Roman Religion, especially in the Dionysus cult. Both Burkert and Nilsson attest that "The wine god became exceedingly popular in sixth century Attic vase painting,"[176] and Dionysiac mysteries were widely spread "in the Hellenistic

---

166. Seaford, *Dionysos*, 74.

167. Otto, *Dionysus*, 147.

168. Plutarch, "The Eating of Flesh I," 559.

169. Plutarch, "Isis and Osiris," 89.

170. Plutarch, "Isis and Osiris," 35 and 69.

171. Nilsson, *Dionysiac Mysteries*, 2 and also refer to Frazer, *New Golden Bough*, 351.

172. Griffiths, "Great Egyptian," 50.

173. Posener, *Egyptian Civilization*, 201.

174. Posener, *Egyptian Civilization*, 202; also see Eliade, *Rites and Symbols of Initiation*, 112.

175. Although the Orphics did not eat meat, many features shared with the Dionysus cult. Evans says, "The Orphics changed Dionysian religion by introducing the concept of moral purification as the essence of spirituality." Evans, *God of Ecstasy*, 158.

176. Burkert, *Greek Religion*, 166.

Greco-Roman Background for the Johannine Eucharist 43

age" and "Roman times."[177] Unlike Jewish people who were not interested in spreading their faith over the Greco-Roman world, Christians were passionate to promulgate their belief. Rainer Riesner states that a pre-Christian Jewish mission was inactive.[178] While "the consciousness of a universal mission to the Gentiles was part of the early Christian belief of living in the times of Messianic fulfillment," Jewish consciousness of mission was passively accepting those who came to Judaism.[179] This Christian mission mindset naturally led them to use these rich religious soils as their host field. Moore observes how Christians interpreted the Greco-Roman myths:

> Christianity knew its saviour and redeemer not as some god whose history was contained in a myth filled with rude, primitive, and even offensive elements, as were the stories of Attis, of Osiris, and to a degree of Dionysus. Such myths required violent interpretation to make them acceptable to enlightened minds. . . Christianity showed a superior power of adaptation to every class; it was a practical guide of life for all, a guide which was soon recognized by its opponents to be of the highest ethical value.[180]

In particular, Christians found that Dionysus and Jesus shared many commonalities, though some Church fathers tried to deny them. One early Church Father, Justin Martyr, complained that Dionysus disguised himself as Jesus to delude Christians.[181] In "Dialogue with Trypho," he said,

> I am established in the knowledge of and faith in the Scriptures by those counterfeits which he who is called the devil is said to have performed among the Greeks . . . For when they tell that Bacchus, son of Jupiter, was begotten by [Jupiter's] intercourse with Semele, and that he was the discoverer of the vine; and when they relate, that being torn in pieces, and having died, he rose again, and ascended to heaven; and when they introduce wine into his mysteries, do I not perceive that [the devil] has imitated the prophecy announced by the patriach Jacob, and recorded by Moses?[182]

---

177. Nilsson, *Dionysiac Mysteries*, 147.

178. McKnight, *Light Among the Gentiles*, 62–66.

179. Riesner, "Pre-Christian Jewish Mission?," 249–50.

180. Moore, *Religious Thought*, 357.

181. Justin, "Dialogue with Trypho," 233, (Chapter 69); Justin Martyr also complains that other mystery religions, especially the mysteries of Mithra, wickedly imitate Christian Eucharist. Justin, "First Apology," 286–87.

182. Justin, "Dialogue with Trypho," 233.

The ritual of the Dionysus cult will lead one to understand detailed information of it. I will look into it next.

The Rituals of the Dionysus Cult

The worshipers of Dionysus engaged in certain rituals which were described as "orgies" and "revels."[183] According to Plutarch, another epithet of Dionysus was "Reveller,"[184] and people celebrated "his mystic festival on sacred nights" with "common revellings."[185] The orgy was a solemn act of honor to the god, in which the worshipers could be in communion with the god and transformed into different beings.[186] The rituals were completely different from that of other Olympian gods.[187] Dodds understands that "the blessings of madness" control early Dionysiac ritual: "Its social function was essentially cathartic, in the psychological sense: it purged the individual of those infectious irrational impulses which, when dammed up, had given rise, as they have done in other cultures, to outbreaks of dancing mania and similar manifestations of collective hysteria; it relieved them by providing them with a ritual outlet."[188]

Essentially, the wide range of the Dionysian rituals enables people to set them free because Dionysus appears "Lusios, 'the Liberator'" here. Hard explains the unique madness of the Dionysian rituals:

> Under his influence his devotees, mostly women, in divine madness left their homes and daily tasks to roam the wild mountainside, clad no longer in their ordinary dress but wearing the skins of wild beasts, their flowing hair bound with ivy and wild bryony. In their excitement they were unconscious of time and place, unfettered by the normal limitations of human powers and sensibilities. Wild music stimulated their orgiastic dance; in frenzy they tore living creatures limb from limb, and devoured the raw dripping flesh, calling meantime on the god by name. This mad revel was continued until the participants fell exhausted to the ground (Chapter 69).[189]

---

183. Mayerson, *Classical Mythology*, 250; Plutarch, "Reply," 266 (1119F).

184. Plutarch, "Reply," 266 (1119F). See footnote g.

185. Plutarch, "Reply," 266 (1119F). See footnote g; Plutarch, "Whether the Affections," 391 (501F).

186. Mayerson, *Classical Mythology*, 250.

187. Moore, *Religious Thought*, 49.

188. Dodds, *Greeks*, 76.

189. Moore, *Religious Thought*, 49.

Greco-Roman Background for the Johannine Eucharist 45

Here, as Euripides' *Bacchae* also shows that "the women play a dominant role" in this ritual.[190] Otto states, "At the center of the cults and myths of Dionysus stand the forms of the frenzied deity and the women, swept along by his wildness, who have taken in the newborn child, have reared him and are, therefore, called his nurses."[191] Actually, the nature of Dionysus himself is intimately related to women worshippers because "This feminine world is confronted by the radically different masculine world of Apollo."[192] According to Burkert, however, "a man, a foreigner no less, admitted" for Bacchic initiation.[193]

Drinking wine is a crucial activity throughout the Dionysus ritual, for wine is the most important "sacramental intoxicant."[194] By doing so, the worshippers believe that divinity has entered into them; deity and devotee become one.[195] Wine accelerates ecstasy for the orgiastic devotee, by which "the soul, escaping from the body during the Dionysiac frenzy, might unite itself with god, might indeed become a god."[196] The unity of the god is a craving desire of ancient people. It promises a religious ecstasy which is a pre-taste of the happiness in the afterlife, escaping from mundane agony. Dodds highlights that the aim of the Dionysian rituals is ecstasy—"which again could mean anything from 'taking you out of yourself' to a profound alteration of personality."[197] Burkert also indicates that the Dionysiac initiation provides people with "liberation from former distress and from the pressures of everyday life, an encounter with the divine through an experience of the force and meaning of life."[198] Furthermore, he points out two sources of true ecstasy in the Dionysiac ritual, "which cannot have been missing even in the secret celebrations: alcohol and sexual excitement, the drinking of wine and phallus symbolism."[199] Sexual initiation also importantly considers the unity of two participants, and it definitely connotes sexual ecstasy. Actually, the myth of Dionysus does not much emphasize sexual activity; however, it, along with drinking wine, seems to continue in some areas in this cult.[200]

---

190. Otto, *Dionysus*, 126.
191. Otto, *Dionysus*, 54.
192. Otto, *Dionysus*, 142.
193. Burkert, *Greek Religion*, 291.
194. Mayerson, *Classical Mythology*, 251.
195. Mayerson, *Classical Mythology*, 250 and see Griffiths, "Great Egyptian."
196. Moore, *Religious Thought*, 51.
197. Dodds, *Greeks*, 77.
198. Burkert, *Greek Religion*, 293.
199. Burkert, *Greek Religion*, 292.
200. Burkert, *Greek Religion*, 292.

The climax to the Dionysiac orgy was the tearing to pieces, *sparagmos*, and the eating of raw flesh, *omophagia*. Particularly, as Burkert indicated, *omophagia* is "the gruesome high point of Dionysiac frenzy."[201] In the *Bacchae*, first, a woman tears (σπαράγμοσιν) a fat calf with her bare hands (line 734–740), and second, Agave and a whole horde of Bacchae tear off Pentheus's body, not through their own strength, "for the god had put inhuman power" in their hands (line 1125–1137).[202] Dodds finds that Euripides discreetly speaks of *omophagia* (ὠμοφαγία) twice, in the *Bacchae* 138 and *Cretans* 472.[203] Euripides describes that Dionysus himself "delights in the raw flesh" (*Bacchae* 138).[204] The *omophagia* is thought to commemorate the day when the infant Dionysus was himself torn to pieces and devoured."[205] For this reason, Otto indicates that this ritual is "a so-called sacramental sacrifice, which was supposed to bestow upon its participants the power of the god who had been killed and eaten."[206] Mayerson expounds that the ritual of *omophagia* and *sparagmos* makes the worshippers experience Dionysus's "divinity and his own life drama."[207] Thus, the functions of *omophagia* and *sparagmos* are to remember Dionysus's death and resurrection as well as to intake his divinity because ancient people considered the rent animals to be "the incarnation of Dionysus."[208] The sacramental eating of the bleeding flesh gave to the participant the vital powers of Dionysus.[209] In addition, Dodds indicates that the raw flesh diet expects "the homoeopathic effects" to the participants, by reasoning "if you want to be like god you must eat god . . . And you must eat him quick and raw, before the blood has oozed from him: only so can you add his life to yours, for 'the blood is the life.'"[210] Here *omophagia* also functions as a strong union with the god and the participant.

The most common victim was a bull because it symbolized the epiphany of Dionysus.[211] Ancient literature and works of art depict Dionysus as

201. Burkert, *Greek Religion*, 291.
202. Euripides, *Euripides V*, 204.
203. Dodds, ed. *Euripides Bacchae*, xvii; Dodds, *Greeks*, 277.
204. Euripides, *Euripides V*, 160.
205. Dodds, ed., *Euripides Bacchae*, xvii.
206. Otto, *Dionysus*, 107.
207. Mayerson, *Classical Mythology*, 252.
208. Mayerson, *Classical Mythology*, 252.
209. Dodds, ed., *Euripides Bacchae*, xvii–xviii.
210. Dodds, *Greeks*, 277.
211. Mayerson, *Classical Mythology*, 252; Dodds, ed., *Euripides Bacchae*, xviii; Frazer, *New Golden Bough*, 352; See Moore, *Religious Thought*, 51.

"either with horns on his head or even in the form of a bull."²¹² For example, in Euripides' *Bacchae*, Dionysus is described as "the bull-horned god" (ταυρόκερων θεόν) who "was born of Zeus" (100) and "bull" (1017 and 1159).²¹³ In addition, Pentheus says to Dionysus that "You are a bull who walks before me there. Horns have sprouted from your head. Have you always been a beast? But now I see a bull" (920–923).²¹⁴ Nonnos also describes that Dionysus was rent by his enemies in the form of the bull. According to him, "Then the bold bull collapsed: the murderers each eager for his turn with the knife chopt piecemeal the bull-shaped Dionysos" (*Dionysiaca* 205).²¹⁵ For this reason, Plutarch describes that "many of Greeks make statues of Dionysus in the form of a bull; and the women of Elis invoke him, praying that the god may come with the hoof of a bull; and the epithet applied to Dionysus among the Argives is 'Son of the bull.'"²¹⁶ The Orphic Hymns also refers to Dionysus as "bull-faced god."²¹⁷ Furthermore, the bull was a "symbol of fertility and prolific generation" and "the spirits of nurturing and fertilizing streams" for ancient people.²¹⁸ Frazer emphasizes the ritual of *omophagia* and *sparagmos*, stating, "Indeed, the rending and devouring of live bulls and calves appear to have been a regular feature of the Dionysiac rites."²¹⁹

The specific ritual of the Dionysus cult is complicated and secretive.²²⁰ Burkert points out these features of the ritual, "Whereas the literary mythology and the iconography of the god found their classical forms towards the end of the fifth century, beneath this exterior the god and his activity remain mysterious and incomprehensible."²²¹ Ismene Lada-Richards explains one of the Dionysiac rituals which is a "symbol of a chthonic entrance"²²² to the cave or pit or vault "where the Dionysiac *thiasoi* would have been enacting their mystic initiation rites: having experienced the terrors of death through

---

212. Sandys, ed. *Bacchae of Euripides*, 106. Also refer to page 201 and 208.
213. Euripides, *Euripides V*, 159, 200, and 205.
214. Euripides, *Euripides V*, 195–96.
215. Nonnos, *Dionysiaca*, 229.
216. Plutarch, "Isis and Osiris," 85 (364F). Frazer also quotes Plutarch's description of the bull in Frazer, *New Golden Bough*, 354.
217. Athanassakis, trans., *Orphic Hymns*, 43 and 63.
218. Otto, *Dionysus*, 165.
219. Frazer, *New Golden Bough*, 355.
220. Eliade, *Rites and Symbols of Initiation*, 110.
221. Burkert, *Greek Religion*, 167.
222. Lada-Richards, *Initiating Dionysus*, 78.

his/her submergence in the cave."²²³ However, *omophagia* and *sparagmos* are extremely important and repeated in the Dionysus cult. For instance, Dodds reports that *omophagia* and *sparagmos* are attested in "the regulations of the Dionysiac cult at Miletus in 276 BC."²²⁴ Even one of the Church Fathers, Clement of Alexandria says, "The raving Dionysus is worshipped by Bacchants with orgies, in which they celebrate their sacred frenzy by a feast of raw flesh."²²⁵

SUMMARY

In many cases, the origin of the Eucharist has been traced from the Passover meal tradition, but it does not persuasively explain the famous eucharistic formulae in the Gospel of John. The Greco-Roman sacred meals, however, freshly illuminate the Christian Eucharist. As Smith argues, Greco-Roman meal custom provides the fundamental background of the Christian meal custom such as reclining, giving thanks, praying, and drinking wine. In this regard, the standardized Greco-Roman meal custom influenced Jewish and Christian meal custom of the first century. The Greek animal sacrifice showed that there were frequently sacred meals among worshippers who ritually invited the deity or were being invited by the deity in the sacrifices. The *thysia* sacrifice also explains the equal portion idea (*daitos eises*) and God's presence with the worshippers when adding *trapezomata* to *thysia*. Therefore, the Greek sacrificial meal establishes strong union not only with worshippers, but also with the deity. Although the Jewish animal sacrifice contained similar ritual forms as that of the Greeks, unlike the Greek sacrifice, it considered drinking blood a taboo. Furthermore, in the Dionysus cult, eating the food was eating the god's flesh and drinking the wine was ingesting the god's blood, which never appeared in the Jewish tradition.

The characteristics of heroes give us an insight as to how Jesus was understood in early Christianity. Particularly, the hero cult was accompanied with the *thysia* sacrifice where participants ate the sacrificial meat and often drank animal blood. As the ritual of the hero cults emphasizes remembrance of heroes, the eucharistic tradition of the New Testament firmly commands Christians to remember Jesus by eating bread and drinking wine. In this regard, the important idea of the hero cult is associated with the sacrificial meal in the Dionysus cult. Perhaps, in order to avoid the rumor that Christians were eating babies in their ritual, the early Christians

---

223. Lada-Richards, *Initiating Dionysus*, 78–79.
224. Dodds, *Greeks*, 276.
225. Clement, "Exhortation to the Greeks," 31.

selected bread and wine instead of flesh and blood for the Eucharist. John's eucharistic discourse in Chapter 6 shows this in detail. Naturally, one reason that the early Christians were persecuted was due to a certain report that Christians practiced the Eucharist as cannibalism. Riley points out: "Christians were persecuted and killed not because the Eucharist was perceived as a new Passover, but because, to the world that heard of it, it was cannibalism, the eating of the flesh and blood of Jesus."[226]

Most eucharistic discourses in the New Testament are colored by the setting of the sacrificial meal. In particular, John Chapter 6 is influenced by the meal of the Dionysus cult among other sacrificial meals. In any case, the Dionysus cult influenced the construction of the famous eucharistic formulae of the New Testament because it included important elements of the hero cults that shed fresh insight into Jesus' death for human sins and the sacrificial meal that explains the meaning of eating the deity, by connoting "This is my body." Therefore, I have dealt with the Dionysus cult in this Chapter's following section.

As a foreign origin deity, perhaps from Asia Minor, Dionysus confronted a great deal of resistance in Greece. The name of Dionysus is still unclear, but scholars agree that his name contains "a sacred and unfathomable symbol." Homer importantly witnesses the great age of Dionysus. *Homeric Hymns* and the writings of Hesiod, Euripides, Plutarch and *Orphic Hymns* provide ample evidence of the myth of Dionysus and his cult. Dionysus was born of Zeus and mortal Semele under persecution of Hera. The myth of Dionysus highlights the mortality of Semele. In particular, Euripides provides the image of Dionysus as the suffering son of the god. Later, in fifth century CE., inspired by Euripides and *Orphic hymns*, Nonnos describes another version of the birth story of Dionysus where Titans sent by Hera rent and killed the baby Dionysus, but Zeus resurrected the baby. Because of Euripides' *Bacchae*, Dionysus acquired the position of the suffering son of god as an incomparable tragic hero, and later he may have influenced the understanding of Jesus' innocent suffering and death as "the suffering Son of God." Justin Martyr parallels Jesus's crucifixion and Dionysus's death. Actually, he says, "If somebody objects that he [Jesus] was crucified, this is in common with the sons of Zeus."[227] In this perspective, Dionysus's twice birth stories remind one of Jesus' resurrection and eternal life after his violent death.

In his connection to wine, Dionysus is perceived as a "mad god." As a fact, Dionysus is a wine god, and his epiphany is closely related to wine

---

226. Riley, *One Jesus Many Christs*, 151.
227. Justin, "First Apology," 256.

miracles in many places. Wine has a crucial religious value in creating a path to communion with the god, providing religious ecstasy. By doing so, the worshipers comfortably feel that Dionysus dwells in mortals so that they can experience immortality in this world. As wine provides two characteristics, happiness and madness of human beings, Dionysus brings the blessing of afterlife for his followers and destruction for his enemies. The process of making wine signifies Dionysus's suffering and dismemberment at the hands of the Titans, and the fermentation and ripening of wine evokes the power of Dionysus. Because of his popularity in both ancient and early Christian times, his mysterious myth and cult were associated with other deities such as Osiris, Demeter, Zagreus, and Persephone. In particular, relating with Osiris and Orpheus, Dionysus became the god of afterlife and influenced the notion of resurrection of Christian belief.

The unique ritual of the Dionysus cult was held in orgy where the participants tore and ate the raw flesh in order to commemorate the violent death of baby Dionysus and to intake the god's power. Although the ritual was complicated and secretive, the main parts were *omophagia* and *sparagmos* whose usual victim was a bull, because ancient Greeks thought that Dionysus was killed in the form of the bull by the Titans. Although Church Fathers harshly denied an influence of the Dionysiac ritual on the Christian Eucharist, ironically their denials revealed the resemblance between the feast of the raw flesh in the Dionysus cult and the Christian Eucharist.[228] Justin Martyr obviously metaphysically replaces flesh and blood with the bread and the cup to erase any influence of the Dionysus cult:

> Now it is evident, that in this prophecy [allusion is made] to the bread which our Christ gave us to eat, in remembrance of His being made flesh for the sake of His believers, for whom also He suffered; and to the cup which He gave us to drink, in remembrance of His own blood, with giving of thanks.[229]

The homoeopathic effects of the flesh and blood link the Dionysiac ritual and the eucharistic ritual, particularly appearing in John 6:51–59. Both rituals emphasize that the participants have close communion with their God by eating raw flesh and drinking blood. Furthermore, the fact that the sacred ritual of the Dionysus cult was usually held at night provides a secret mood to the ritual as the Synoptic tradition of the Eucharist does.

Therefore, broadly, the sacred meal tradition explains many aspects of the sacrificial meal, the hero cult, and the Dionysus cult. Particularly, the

---

228. Justin, "Justin Martyr, Irenaeus," 233; Origen, "Against Celsus," 445.
229. Justin, "Justin Martyr, Irenaeus," 234.

Dionysus cult includes the detailed rituals of the hero cult and of the sacred meal, by focusing *theoxenia*. For this reason, in remembering the hero, the Dionysus cult is important not only for the interpretation of the Synoptic tradition, but also for the interpretation of John Chapter 6 when one studies the Christian Eucharist in the New Testament. Thus, this book will specifically investigate how the sacred meal tradition and the Dionysus cult influence the formation of the Johannine Eucharist in the next two chapters.

3

Greco-Roman Sacred Meals in the Johannine Eucharist

DENNIS E. SMITH STATES that meals in the Gospels reflect "typical elements of the Greco-Roman banquet and/or symposium tradition."[1] He says in further detail:

> These include such features as reclining (Mark 2:15; 6:39; 8:6; 14:3 14:18 [and synoptic parallels]; Luke 7:36; 11:37; 14:7; 24:30), washing of the feet prior to reclining (Luke 7:44; John 13:3–5), anointing the head with perfumes (Mark 14:3), saying prayers before the *deipnon* (Mark 6:41; 8:6–7; 14:22), ranking at the table (Luke 14:7) and at the symposium (Mark 14:23), sharing a wine libation around the table (Mark 14:23), discourse on appropriate themes during the symposium (Luke 14:7–24), ending the meal with a hymn (Mark 14:26).[2]

In this chapter, however, I will mainly apply the sacred meals tradition of the Greco-Roman world to the interpretation of the Gospel of John.[3] While continuing to focus on John 6, I will argue Johannine meal customs and the sacrificial meal tradition throughout Johannine literature. Because

---

1. Smith, *Symposium to Eucharist*, 222.
2. Smith, *Symposium to Eucharist*, 222.
3. Smith argues that the Greco-Roman banquet tradition and ideology influence all meals in the Gospels. See Smith, *Symposium to Eucharist*, 219–87.

Greco-Roman Sacred Meals in the Johannine Eucharist 53

John 6 contains a significant description of the eucharistic words in 6:51–59 and this discourse is tightly woven into other discourses in John chapter 6, I will critically interpret each pericope of it. For this reason, first, I will briefly review the literary unit of the Gospel and the structure of John 6.

John's Gospel does not describe the words of the Eucharist in the scene of the Last Supper (John 13:1—17:26); instead, it puts them in John 6:51–59. This is John's unique literary invention that closely relates chapters 2, 4, and 13 with chapter 6 to reinforce the ingesting metaphor as well as the allusion of the Dionysus cult.[4] In particular, chapters 6 and 13 are resonant with each other in several themes such as Jesus' death, betrayal, and resurrection.[5] For example, in John 6:64, Jesus knew from the first who would betray him, and Jesus said that one of his disciples would betray him in 13:21. Bultmann also points out that the editor of John adopts "a critical position with regard to cultic sacramental piety" and "reference to the Eucharist" in John 6 and 13.[6]

Furthermore, the author of John repeats this ingesting theme throughout the Gospel with a subtle angle of emphasis on each pericope. Bultmann sees that the current chapter order does not follow the original order, so he puts Chapter 6 between 4 and 5; he says, "So the original order must have been chs. 4, 6, 5, 7."[7] Using his transposition theories, he also rearranges several pericopes by scattering into the current order of the Gospel of John.[8] In the case of John 6, he puts 6:60–71 after 8:30–40 under the title of "The Mystery of the Death of Jesus: 12:20–33; 8:30–40; 6:60–71."[9] Moreover, he firmly attests that verses 6:51b–58 "have been added by an ecclesiastical editor."[10] Unlike Butmann, scholars who use narrative criticism to study the Gospel of John consider it as a complete literary work; it is unnecessary to trace the original work. In this point of view, all chapters of the Gospel of John are correctly numbered sequentially, contain a structure according to literary theme and function so that each chapter sustains the overall integrity.

The literary structure of John 6 is more complicated than other chapters. Its own structure and location are closely connected to John 2, 4, 13, and 21. In order to understand properly John's literary scheme in the eucharistic discourse in John 6 and 13, I will examine not only the chapter's own

4. Regarding the allusion of the Dionysus cult in the Gospel of John, I will argue next chapter.

5. Webster investigates these issues by using narrative criticism in Webster, *Ingesting Jesus*, 65–89 and 101–24.

6. Bultmann, *Gospel of John*, 220.

7. Bultmann, *Gospel of John*, 209.

8. See Bultmann, *Gospel of John*, 209.

9. Bultmann, *Gospel of John*, 419–51.

10. Bultmann, *Gospel of John*, 219.

structure but also the relationship between other chapters or units. Regarding the structure of John 6, Johannes Beutler states:

> The discourse on the Bread of Life with its narrative framework has turned out as a coherent and well-structured literary unit. The two miracle stories at the beginning (vv.1–15, 16–21) along with the double narrative about the consequences of the discourse (vv.60–65, 66–71) form a double frame into which the discourse itself (vv.22–59) seems to be integrated.[11]

Beutler considers verse 35 as "the center of the chapter and the first self-proclamation of Jesus" that is "the turning point of the discourse."[12] Seeing verse 35 as "the axle and climax," Petrus Martiz and Gilbert Van Belle also present the Bread discourse in "a concentric six part chiasm."[13] For them, it is verse 35 where "the whole discourse stands in service of the Christology and the Eucharist."[14] The explanations of Beutler, Martiz and Belle primarily focus on John 6, though they do not explain why the author of John maintained the current order. Unlike them, Webster presents the structure and literary unit of John 6 by relating with other chapters so that she argues John's tightened literary unit in the theme of "Ingestion." Eventually, all aspects of the structure of John 6 and other chapters show that John's literary units and each chapter's structure may present various spectrums according to the literary interests of the author. Considering the Gospel of John as a complete literary work, I will explore the specific chapter or pericope relating to the Johannine Eucharist.

---

11. Beutler, "Structure of John 6," 126; also see 122.
12. Beutler, "Structure of John 6," 118.
13. Martiz and Belle, "Imagery of Eating and Drinking in John 6:35,"), 335. The chiasm is like:

A 6:22–27[1]
  B 6:28–29[2]
    C 6:30–33[3]
      D 6:35
    C' 6:34–40[4]
  B' 6:41–51[5]
A' 6:52–59[6]

14. Martiz and Belle, "Imagery of Eating and Drinking in John 6:35," 336.

JOHANNINE MEAL CUSTOMS

Reclining Custom

Most Christians' image of the Last Supper is probably dependent on the way many painters have portrayed the biblical scene since the fourth century. Most people think of the meal customs of the New Testament as similar to modern dining customs that require sitting, not reclining at the meal. In Leonardo da Vinci's most famous painting of the 1490s, "The Last Supper," in which he represents the last meal shared by Jesus with his disciples before his arrest and death, he portrays Jesus and his disciples sitting on chairs before the table. It shows no reclining customs at the meal. I mentioned earlier, however, that reclining customs seemed to be standardized in the Greco-Roman world until the third century because "the ancient meal, or more particularly the banquet, was a social institution that was shared in common throughout the culture regardless of the social or ethnic distinctiveness that a group might otherwise have."[15] Smith argues that in the Gospels, in "all descriptions of meals, Jesus is reclining," and "This is even true of the miraculous feedings that take place outdoors."[16] In this chapter, I will investigate how these Greco-Roman meal customs appear in the Gospel of John.

In fact, Johannine literature includes a lot of imagery of eating and drinking as well as a "special emphasis on food" that Jesus provides both on earth and in heaven.[17] The Gospel of John describes several meal settings in which "eating and drinking ostensibly occur, collectively referred to here as 'meals'" (2:1-11; 4:32-34; 6:1-71; 7:37-39; 8:51-52; 12:1-8, 24; 13:1-30; 15:1-7; 18:11; 19:28-37; 21:1-25).[18] Smith examines how Jesus uses the banquet metaphor to integrate his ministry, though the world is not ready to take "the food of the gods."[19] Because the world is not ready, Jesus replies "'my time has not come,' when asked to provide for the wedding banquet (2:4) or attend the festival (7:8)."[20] After the feeding story of John 6:1-15, when people sought Jesus, he told them, "Truly, truly, I say to you, you seek me, not because you saw signs, but because you ate your fill of the loaves" (6:26). In the context of the entire collection of ingesting stories of John 6,

---

15. Smith and Taussig, *Many Tables*, 21; For further information of the Greco-Roman meal customs, see Smith, *Symposium to Eucharist*, 13-46.
16. Smith, *Symposium to Eucharist*, 219.
17. Smith, *Symposium to Eucharist*, 273.
18. Webster, *Ingesting Jesus*, 2.
19. Smith, *Symposium to Eucharist*, 273.
20. Smith, *Symposium to Eucharist*, 273.

Jesus intends to teach "the time of the heavenly banquet, the banquet of Jesus," through miraculous feeding, the bread from heaven (6:31–40), and the eucharistic words (6:51–59).[21] However, the crowd, especially Jews, were concerned only with earthly food. So Jesus patiently advises them, "Do not labor for the food which perishes, but for the food which endures to eternal life" (6:27a). The food that Jesus will give them is indeed the food of life that "God the Father set his seal" on the Son of Man (6:27). He is discussing two types of food: "the physical, daily food that the disciples fetch; and the spiritual food of Jesus, doing the will of him who sent him and fulfilling the work that he was commissioned to do."[22] Through the food imagery, Jesus teaches the disciples what they must seek in this world. In this aspect of the heavenly banquet, according to Smith, "Indeed, Jesus goes away to prepare a place for the banquet (14:2–4)" and "Meanwhile, the disciples are to 'feed the sheep' (21:15–17; see also 6:1–14)."[23] Jane S. Webster also indicates that "The prevalence of eating and drinking language, the references to food and drink, and the narrative context of meals establishes ingestion as a significant literary motif in the Gospel of John."[24]

Unlike the Synoptic Gospels, the Gospel of John does not describe the words of institution in the scene of the Last Supper in John 13:1–30. Instead, it explains that John's meal custom reflects the Greco-Roman meal customs. Just before the Passover, Jesus knew that his death was near so he wanted to eat his last meal with his disciples (13:1). This meal was a formal evening meal which was called *deipnon* (δεῖπνον) (13:2 and 4). Importantly, the Greeks and Romans used this term widely when they referred to the formal evening meal which usually consisted of an eating part (banquet) and a drinking part (symposium). John chapters 13–17 are the farewell discourse of Jesus. After Jesus ate the meal and performed the foot washing ceremony (13:2–12), he began a long discourse (symposium) with his disciples (13:13—17:26). John describes the custom of reclining (ἀνακείμενος) that is an important feature of the Greco-Roman meal customs in John 13:12 and 13:24. The Greek texts show it more clearly:

> Ὅτε οὖν ἔνιψεν τοὺς πόδας αὐτῶν [καὶ] ἔλαβεν τὰ ἱμάτια αὐτοῦ καὶ **ἀνέπεσεν πάλιν**, εἶπεν αὐτοῖς· γινώσκετε τί πεποίηκα ὑμῖν (13:12); ἦν **ἀνακείμενος** εἷς ἐκ τῶν μαθητῶν αὐτοῦ ἐν τῷ κόλπῳ τοῦ Ἰησοῦ, ὃν ἠγάπα ὁ Ἰησοῦς (13:23; emphasis added)

---

21. Smith, *Symposium to Eucharist*, 273.
22. Martiz and Belle, "Imagery of Eating and Drinking in John 6:35," 344.
23. Smith, *Symposium to Eucharist*, 273.
24. Webster, *Ingesting Jesus*, 2.

Walter Bauer investigates ἀναπίπτω in detail. In the Greco-Roman world, ἀναπίπτω primarily means "lie down," or "recline" at a meal and secondly means "lean" or "lean back."[25] As I demonstrated in chapter 2, the New Testament and other early Christian literature often show this reclining custom. However, most English Bibles mistranslate this term. For instance, they translate ἀνέπεσεν into "was set down" (KJV), "returned to his place" (NIV), "sat down" (ASV, NLT, DYB, and Webster), "resumed his place" (RSV), and "returned to the table" (NRSV). NASB translates it into "reclined [at the table] and YLT as "having reclined (at meat)." The adverb πάλιν points out that this reclining is not a one-time action, but a repeated and continual one. In the case of ἀνακείμενος in 13:23, the Bible translators follow the original meaning of the term because the verb ἀνακείμαι not only means "always of reclining at table," but also the translators intend to describe the close relationship between Jesus and the beloved disciple.[26] Most English Bibles translate ἀνακείμενος into "leaning" (KJV, NKJV, WEB, Webster, Douay), "reclining" (NIV, ASV, NASB, NRSV, and YLT), "lying" (RSV), "sitting" (NLT), and "resting his head on" (BBE). Therefore, the description of the Johannine Last Supper proves that the Greco-Roman reclining custom influenced the Johannine meal custom.

This word ἀναπίπτω is also used in Jesus' feeding stories in John 6:10–11 and Mark 6:40.[27] Here, John seems to follow Mark's version. This feeding story in John 6:1–15 includes the eucharistic elements such as "took the loaves" (**ἔλαβεν οὖν τοὺς ἄρτους**) and "gave thanks" (**εὐχαριστήσας**) before eating as well as the reclining custom. Both Mark and John describe the eucharistic words and actions of Jesus, which remind one of the Last Supper.[28] Ernst Haenchen indicates that John 6:11 is "an allusion to the Lord's Supper."[29] The Greek text of 6:10–11 shows these elements more clearly:

> 10 εἶπεν ὁ Ἰησοῦς· ποιήσατε τοὺς ἀνθρώπους **ἀναπεσεῖν**. ἦν δὲ χόρτος πολὺς ἐν τῷ τόπῳ. **ἀναπεσεῖν** οὖν οἱ ἄνδρες τὸν ἀριθμὸν ὡς πεντακισχίλιοι. 11 ἔλαβεν οὖν τοὺς ἄρτους ὁ Ἰησοῦς καὶ **εὐχαριστήσας** διέδωκεν τοῖς **ἀνακειμένοις** ὁμοίως καὶ ἐκ τῶν ὀψαρίων ὅσον ἤθελον (emphasis added)

Although the geographical setting of this story is the mountainside on the far shore of the Sea of Galilee (6:1–3), this story describes that when the

---

25. Bauer, *Greek–English Lexicon*, 70.
26. Bauer, *Greek–English Lexicon*, 65.
27. Matthew also modified Mark's story in 15:35.
28. Barrett, *St John*, 230.
29. Haenchen, *John 1*, 272.

multitude eats bread and fish, five thousand people perform the reclining custom not inside a room, but in an exterior space. In addition, this story demonstrates that the reclining custom is combined with the eucharistic customs such as taking bread and giving thanks to God.

Foot Washing

The full story of Jesus' washing the disciples' feet appears only in the Gospel of John (13:1–17). Luke describes that when Jesus ate the meal with Pharisees (7:36), a woman who was called a sinner kissed Jesus' feet, washed them with her hair, and anointed them with ointment (7:44–46). In Luke 12:35–48, the author also briefly alludes to foot washing and suggests that the master will serve his faithful and watchful servants who have been waiting for their master. Here Luke does not identify the master as Jesus. Although Luke's story focuses more on the proper attitude of the faithful servants, it contains the reclining custom in Luke 12:37: "Blessed are those slaves whom the master shall find on the alert when he comes; truly I say to you, that he will gird himself [to serve,] and have them recline [at the table,] (ἀνακλινεῖ) and will come up and wait on them" (NASB). The original meanings of ἀνακλινεῖ are "cause to lie down," "recline," "lie down" at a meal, or "recline at a meal," though many translations prefer "sit."[30] Unlike Luke's story, John's story is interested in the role of Jesus as a voluntary servant. Before the Passover, knowing it was his last time to serve them, Jesus wanted to love his people at the end, rising from supper, pouring water into a basin, and washing the disciples' feet. After that he wiped their feet with a towel (13:4–5). The washing process is detailed and even vivid. The interpretation of Jesus' act follows in 13:13–16, whose meanings parallel Luke 22:24–28 where Jesus taught the disciples true service.

As I discussed earlier, in the Greco-Roman meal customs, foot washing by servants is an important element for starting the banquet and symposium. Likewise, John's Last Supper shows that Jesus clearly observes this tradition. Smith points out that here "the meal utilizes a motif from the banquet tradition for its symbolic reference" and "the motif is the washing of the feet of the guests by a servant before the meal is to begin."[31] This scene symbolically indicates "an interpretation of the death of Jesus" (13:6–9) and "a model of servanthood for the disciples to follow" (13:12–16).[32] Thus, Webster concludes that "the Last Supper in John 13 is the most well-developed meal

30. Bauer, *Greek–English Lexicon*, 65.
31. Smith, *Symposium to Eucharist*, 274.
32. Smith, *Symposium to Eucharist*, 274.

narrative in the Gospel . . . This feast is anticipated in the footwashing and, elsewhere, in the miraculous meal events in John 2, 6, and 21."[33]

THE IDEA OF THE SACRIFICIAL MEAL IN THE GOSPEL OF JOHN

In the New Testament, there is no description of actual sacrifice, but "the idea of sacrifice" is abundant, especially appearing in "the whole earthly life of Jesus."[34] In John's Gospel, this idea is closely woven with "the metaphors of 'hunger' and 'thirst', of 'drinking' and 'eating,'" which are connected to "the metaphors of 'bread' and 'water' and these furthermore to 'flesh' and 'blood.'"[35] Royden Yerkes argues that the sacred meal was the important element in early development of sacrifice because it is natural that "the meal should become ceremonious."[36] According to him, "The word sacrifice, which means 'to make a thing sacred' or 'to do a sacred act,' was used in Latin to describe various rites which arose from the common meal."[37] His argument may be compared to other scholars' approach that sacrifice generates the sacred meal rather than vice versa. The connotations of sacrifice appear in Jesus' title "Lamb of the God" (1:29, 36) and the whole imagery of eating and drinking in the Bread of Life discourse (6:1–71).

Jesus as a Sacrificial Lamb

One of the unique descriptions of Jesus is "the Lamb" in Johannine literature.[38] It appears one time in 1 Peter (1:19), two times in John (1:29, 36) and twenty-four times in Revelation. While John and 1 Peter take ἀμνός, "sheep one year old," all appearances in Revelation uses ἀρνίον which indicates "a sheep any age."[39] When Jesus appears as the image of the judge at the end of the world, he is naturally supposed to be a full-grown sheep instead of the one-year lamb so that Revelation may prefer ἀρνίον. In particular, "the Lamb of God" ὁ ἀμνός τοῦ θεοῦ is John's single usage. In the Gospel of John, John

33. Webster, *Ingesting Jesus*, 121.
34. Aulén, *Eucharist and Sacrifice*, 148.
35. Martiz and Belle, "Imagery of Eating and Drinking in John 6:35," 352.
36. Yerkes, *Sacrifice*, 20.
37. Yerkes, *Sacrifice*, 25.
38. John 1:29, 36; Rev 5:6, 8, 12–13; 6:1, 16; 7:9–10, 14, 17; 12:11; 13:8; 14:1, 4, 10; 15:3; 17:14; 19:7, 9; 21:9, 14, 24, 27; 22:1, 3. In addition, John 21:15–17 describes lamb as the Christian community. See Bauer, *Greek-English Lexicon*, 133.
39 Bauer, *Greek-English Lexicon*, 54 and 133.

the Baptist plays the important role of introducing Jesus; he is a witness to testify about Jesus (1:6–8), and he is the desert voice to straighten the way for Jesus (1:23). Now when John the Baptist sees Jesus, he calls out, "Behold, the Lamb of God, who takes away the sin of the world!" (1:29) which is found nowhere in the New Testament except here. Webster observes the significance of the title "Lamb of God" because it incites the disciples of John the Baptist to leave their master, instead they follow Jesus and stay with him (1:36–40).[40] Barrett mentions difficulty in interpreting this verse (1:29): "It is certain that this phrase has an Old Testament background, less certain what that background is."[41] For example, Webster categorizes scholars' arguments regarding the lamb: as "(1) the Passover lamb, (2) the Suffering Servant in Isaiah, (3) the Lamb who comes at the end of the world, (4) the replacement of Isaac who was willing to be sacrificed, or (5) the daily temple offering."[42] Although she briefly introduces each position, she prefers the first interpretation. According to her, John's Gospel puts this verse "within the context of the Passover" because, unlike the Synoptics, John's Jesus is crucified on the Day of Preparation of the Passover (John 19:14 and 42) so the time of Jesus' death is parallel with that of the slaughter of the Passover lambs.[43] Furthermore, she indicates that both the bones of the Passover lamb and Jesus are not broken (Exod 12:46; John 19:33, 36; Num 9:12; Ps 34:20).[44] Indeed, John 19:37 says, "For these things took place that the scripture might be fulfilled, 'Not a bone of him shall be broken,'" which may explain that the lamb and Jesus are identical. Therefore, the Lamb of God means that Jesus is the true paschal lamb in John 1:29 and 1:36.[45] In the broad point that "Jesus' death saves people from sin" and the paschal lamb implies delivery of people from death, the lamb and Jesus share commonality.[46] In the specific point, however, in fact, the function of the paschal lamb and the Lamb of God in John 1:29 are different, though the Greek term ἀμνός is used for the Passover lamb and "Sacrificial lamb without blemish" in early Christian literature.[47] Thus, the author of 1 Peter clearly says ἀμνός in the context of sacrificial lamb: "You know that you were ransomed from the futile ways inherited from your fathers, not with perishable things such

---

40. Webster, *Ingesting Jesus*, 34–35; also see Cullmann, *Early Christian Worship*, 64.
41. Barrett, *St John*, 146.
42. Webster, *Ingesting Jesus*, 27.
43. Webster, *Ingesting Jesus*, 31.
44. Webster, *Ingesting Jesus*, 32.
45. Barrett, *St John*, 147; Webster, *Ingesting Jesus*, 30–34.
46. Webster, *Ingesting Jesus*, 34.
47. Bauer, *Greek-English Lexicon*, 54.

as silver or gold but with the precious blood of Christ, like that of a lamb (ἀμνός) without blemish or spot" (1:18–19). Haechen properly points that "the paschal lamb of course does not remove sin, although its blood causes the angel of death to pass over."[48]

John 1:29 is also reminiscent of Lev 16:7–10 where the scapegoat is sent away into the wilderness in order to take away sins. The critical problem is that the animal is not a lamb, but a goat.[49] In addition, this verse also notes the lamb of Isa 53:7 in which the suffering servant of God is compared to a lamb that is supposed to be slaughtered.[50] As Bultmann indicates, however, the servant of God would not be substituted to "bear the sins."[51] Instead, as 1 John 2:2 indicates, Jesus becomes "the expiation (ἱλασμός) for our sins, and not for ours only but also for the sins of the whole world."[52] In his exegesis on John 1:29, Wilbert F. Howard asserts that interpreters rightly see this verse "in the light of several references in 1 John" in which Jesus and his blood will cleanse humans from all sin and unrighteousness (1:7, 9); Jesus is the expiation both for human sin and the sin of the world (2:2); and he "appeared to take away sins" (3:5).[53] Throughout several cases of the interpretation of John 1:29, the Lamb of God lacks the specific reference to the Old Testament. Instead, it alludes to the sacrificial animal which people offered to God for their sin in Greek religion. Oscar Cullmann insists that the writer of John interprets the lamb as "the sacrificial lamb which bears away sin (αἴρειν) rather than the Suffering Servant who bears it (φέρειν)."[54] Bultmann also points out that here "the lamb is thought of as the sacrificial lamb."[55] As mentioned above, however, the complication is that although the language of 1:29 is sacrificial, "nowhere in the Pentateuch is a lamb spoken of as bearer of the people's sin."[56] Therefore, the concept of the sacrificial lamb of God is John's unique invention that combines the symbol of the paschal lamb and the Greek *thysia* sacrifice.

In the study of religion, "some appreciation of the function of sacrifice" is critical because "most religious systems function (to a greater or lesser

---

48. Haenchen, *John 1*, 152; also see Barrett, *St John*, 147.
49. Haenchen, *John 1*, 152; Howard and Gossip, "St. John," 484.
50. Cullmann, *Early Christian Worship*, 65.
51. Bultmann, *Gospel of John*, 96, especially see footnote 3.
52. ἱλασμός means "appeasement necessitated by sin." Bauer, *Greek-English Lexicon*, 474.
53. Howard and Gossip, "St. John," 483–84.
54. Cullmann, *Early Christian Worship*, 64.
55. Bultmann, *Gospel of John*, 96.
56. Howard and Gossip, "St. John," 484.

extent) by means of sacrificial activity."⁵⁷ Henri Hubert and Marcel Mauss define that the purpose of sacrifice serves as "an intermediary between the sacrifier, or the object which is to receive the practical benefits of the sacrifice, and the divinity to whom the sacrifice is usually addressed."⁵⁸ Bruce Chilton states that "Sacrifice, for Hubert and Mauss, functions essentially to mediate the arrival or the departure of the divine."⁵⁹ Eventually, sacrifice makes the god and humans connected. In this regard, the verse "the Lamb of God, who takes away the sin of the world!" (1:29) forces one to pay attention to the intention of sacrifice. In other words, as a sacrificial lamb, Jesus makes a bridge between human beings and God by removing "the sin of the world." The author of Hebrews witnesses that Jesus sacrifices himself to "put away sin" (ἀθέτησιν [τῆς] ἁμαρτίας διὰ τῆς θυσίας αὐτοῦ).⁶⁰ In John and Hebrews, sin is a major obstacle between the world (human beings) and God. The Greek text of John 1:29b (ἴδε ὁ ἀμνὸς τοῦ θεοῦ ὁ αἴρων τὴν ἁμαρτίαν τοῦ κόσμου) shows that the lamb of God lifts up or takes away the sin (ἁμαρτίαν), but does not provide forgiveness (ἄφεσιν) for the sin.⁶¹ In the aspect of function only, the lamb of God looks like the scapegoat in Lev 16:7–10. Unlike the sacrificial lamb, however, the scapegoat is not killed. Furthermore, the notion of sin of "the world" is different between John and Leviticus. While sin in Leviticus is primarily related to Israel and God of the Old Testament, sin in John deals in the Greco-Roman world. Broadly, "sin" signifies "a departure from either human or divine standards of uprightness" in the Bible.⁶² Surpassing the boundary of the sin of the Old Testament, John insists that Jesus carries away sin of the world (ἁμαρτίαν τοῦ κόσμου).

In this aspect, one may observe the notion of sin by the Greeks is slightly different from that of the Jews whose notion of sin is related to "the sense of a breach in a personal relationship with God."⁶³ Even the modern term of "sin" has no equivalent in either Greek or Latin. Sin can be denoted by different terms such as Greek *adikia* (ἀδικία wrongdoing, injustice), *anomia* (ἀνομία lawless conduct), *hamartia* (ἁμαρτία failure, fault), or

57. Chilton, *Temple of Jesus*, 3.

58. Hubert and Mauss, *Sacrifice*, 11.

59. Chilton, *Temple of Jesus*, 11.

60. Heb 9:26, "for then he would have had to suffer repeatedly since the foundation of the world. But as it is, he has appeared once for all at the end of the age to put away sin by the sacrifice of himself." In several places, Hebrews mentions "sacrifice" (*thysia*) in 5:1, 3; 7:27; 8:3; 9:9, 23, 26; 10:1, 3, 8, 11, 12, 26; 11:4; 13:11, 15, 16.

61. ἄφεσιν is also used in the eucharistic word of Matthew 26:28 for "the act of freeing from an obligation, guilt, or punishment." See Bauer, *Greek–English Lexicon*, 155.

62. Bauer, *Greek–English Lexicon*, 50.

63. LaCocque, "Sin and Guilt," 8405.

miasma (μίασμα defilement). Among them, *miasma* relates more to "sin" as "a prime source of religious danger."[64] Robert Parker describes that although *miasma* is primarily related with dirt, it is also implied in "connection with contagious religious danger."[65] In many cases, defilement and sin appear together because, until today, "the defilement of sin" has maintained the important "dualistic view of reality" that consists of purity and impurity.[66] In the Greek world, people saw 'impurity' as a cause and symptom of disease. Walter Burkert notes that a concept of sin is developed from the "figure of impurity."[67] Thus, the notion of sin originates from *miasma* in Greek culture. The result of sin and pollution has a common lineage.[68] There is a common mythological schema as seen in the story of Oedipus, where pollution causes plague, crop-failure, and infertility of women and of animals. Such pollution pushes people to change the situation by using the process of purification.[69] Thus the threat of pollution encourages action to put right the disorder, which establishes "harmonious triangular links among the individual, the cosmos, and the social structure."[70] Likewise, the result of sin, in the Bible, brings the similar spell of misfortunes such as diseases.[71] The threat of sin also expects a process of forgiveness for restoration of God's broken law, otherwise the bad omen is perpetuated. Thus, if Jesus lifts up (or carries away) sin as the lamb of God, he is supposed to play an active role as a priest as well as a sacrificial victim to purify defilement of the world.[72]

In the aspect of focusing on the true communion with God, sacrifice requires the removal of the sin. The emphasis on union with God does not appear in the Jewish sacrifice in which God's forgiveness and blessing are dominant. Through the *thysia* sacrifice, the Greeks seek this communion with the god by eating the sacrificial meal not only with the deity, but also with the worshippers. In fact, Jewish religion also shows this animal sacrifice. Like the Greek *thysia* sacrifice, Bernhard Lang describes that normal Jewish animal sacrifice also includes a sacrificial meal: "Jews took a lamb or a goat, went to the Jerusalem Temple, and presented themselves to a priest who then

---

64. Parker, *Miasma*, 2.

65. Parker, *Miasma*, 5.

66. LaCocque, "Sin and Guilt," 8403; *Encyclopædia Britannica Online*, s. v. "Purification Rite."

67. Burkert, *Greek Religion*, 77.

68. Parker, *Miasma*, 236–39.

69. Preston, "Purification: An Overview," 7507.

70. Preston, "Purification: An Overview," 7503.

71. Parker, *Miasma*, 236–37.

72. This concept appears in Hebrews in which Jesus is the High priest and the sacrificial lamb.

saw to it that the animal was slaughtered, and certain parts burned on the altar. A feast was then arranged for the sacrificer and the latter's guests."[73] In many cases, the Jewish sacrifice and the Greek sacrifice share some common parts in its process. While the former emphasizes God's mercy and forgiveness rather than communion with God, because Jews think that mere human beings cannot share God's realm by communing with God, the latter aims at the union with God throughout the *thysia* sacrifice.

The fact that the paschal lamb is eaten by people supports at least that the sacred meal is an important element for the Passover. In addition, if the lamb in John 1:29 indicated that Jesus was the paschal lamb, the metaphor of eating would be obvious. By doing so, the author of John may smoothly highlight the suffering of Jesus like the paschal lamb. In the *thysia* sacrifice, however, participants also eat the sacrificial lamb so that the metaphor of eating is also dominant. Modern biblical scholars think that the Gospel of John was written at the end of the first century or at the first part of the second century. Under the command of the future emperor Vespasian, the Roman army marched to Galilee in 67 and quickly defeated the Jewish resistance. Then Titus, the son of Vespasian, laid siege to Jerusalem in 70 CE. F. J. Foakes-Jackson reports that the daily sacrifice ceased on August 5, 70 CE.[74] Josephus describes it in detail: "Titus now ordered the troops that were with him to raze the foundations of Antonia and to prepare an easy ascent for the whole army. Then, having learnt that on that day—it was the seventeenth of Panemus—the so-called continual sacrifice had for lack of men ceased to be offered to God."[75] Then, the Roman soldiers totally destroyed the temple on August 30, 70 CE.[76] Josephus realistically reports this disastrous scene:

> While the temple blazed, the victors plundered everything that fell in their way and slaughtered wholesale all who were caught. No pity was shown for age, no reverence for rank; children and greybeards, laity and priests, alike were massacred; every class was pursued and encompassed in the grasp of war, whether suppliants for mercy or offering resistance. The roar of the flames streaming far and wide mingled with the groans of the falling victims; and, owing to the height of the hill and the mass of the burning pile, one would have thought that the whole city was ablaze . . . The Romans, thinking it useless, now that the temple

---

73. Lang, "This is My Body," 190.
74. Foakes-Jackson, *Josephus and the Jews*, 211.
75. Josephus, *The Jewish War* 6.93–94.
76. Foakes-Jackson, *Josephus and the Jews*, 212.

was on fire, to spare the surrounding buildings, set them all alight, both the remnants of the porticoes and the gates... They further burnt the treasure-chambers.[77]

The official Jewish sacrifice was diminished. Instead, rabbianic Judaism began following 70 CE. As the center of Jewish faith, the system of synagogue replaced the role of the temple. Meanwhile the sacrifice of Greco-Roman religions officially continued to be observed until the fourth century, such as the sacrifice of Fortune (Tyche), Mithra, Demeter, Zeus, Dionysus, etc.[78]

One of the important reasons that Christianity rapidly spread throughout the Greco-Roman world was due to Paul's mission to Gentiles, proclaiming the Gospel beyond the Jewish people.[79] From 333 BCE, Alexander the Great and his successors hellenized all of the ancient Mediterranean world. Without a doubt, the Roman Empire was built on this foundation of Hellenism. The Jewish people were not excepted from the influence of Hellenism. When the New Testament mentions "Jews" or "Jewish people," they are hellenized Jews who translate their canon into Greek, and systematize their faith with Greek philosophy. In particular, since the destruction of the Jerusalem temple and Roman occupation caused Jews to be scattered over all over the Greco-Roman world, the Jewish sacrificial system became less influential among Gentile Christians. Royden Yerkes describes how the Greek idea of sacrifice applied to the Christian Eucharist in this phenomenon in detail:

> Within a hundred years after St. Paul the Greek word *eucharistia* had become a name of the Banquet and of the Bread and Wine which constituted it. This word we remember as in use for at least two centuries before Christ as a technical term to describe an elaborate act of thanksgiving culminating in a thusia [thysia]. By the year 200 the Christian Church was composed chiefly, if not wholly, of Greek-thinking Gentiles who had no hesitancy in applying the word *thusia* [thysia] to describe best the Christian worship which by that time was widespread in the Roman

---

77. Josephus, *Jewish War* 6.271–282.

78. Emperor Julian resumed the State sacrifice during his reign because he believed that "restoration of the public cult was the condition for the restoration of the Empire and the definition of the State." Belayche, "Sacrifice and Theory of Sacrifice," 107, also see 101–26.

79. According to Acts Chapter 10, Peter begin to evangelize Cornelius, a centurion of the Italian Regiment, and his families, most gentile mission is conducted by Paul in Acts. Paul himself is confident that he is an apostle to the Gentiles (Rom 1:5; 11:13; Gal 2:8; also see 1 Tim 2:7); see the role of Paul in spreading Christianity over the all world in Bornkamm, *Paul*.

Empire. When Christian thought was translated into Latin, *sacrificium* was the normal word to express this idea. From this comes our word *sacrifice*.[80]

Here, he argues the *thysia* sacrifice influenced the Christian Eucharist.

According to Bauer, the New Testament authors favor using *thysia* when they literally or imaginatively describe sacrifice (Matt 9:13, 12:7; Mark 9:49, 12:33; Luke 13:1; Heb 5:1; 8:3; 9:9, 23; 10:1, 5, 8, 11–12; 11:4; 13:15–16; Rom 12:1; 1 Pet 2:5).[81] Actually, this term does not appear in the Gospel of John, but the idea of sacrifice is observed.

The Idea of Sacrifice in John 6

John 6 contains the most extensive idea of Greek sacrifice in "the ingesting motif."[82] The image of the sacrificial meal appears in John 6:51–59, however, as the structure of John 6 shows, the whole of John 6 is literally woven with the idea of sacrifice. John Crossan argues that "the general theme of 'bread' appears as early as 6:5 and as late as 6:58 and thus dominates the chapter."[83] Jesus says to the crowd, "I am the bread of life; he who comes to me shall not hunger, and he who believes in me shall never thirst" (6:35), which implies that the bread is Jesus's flesh and blood, which is supposed to be eaten by those who are hungry and by those who are thirsty for "life," ζωήν (6:53). Yet the description of the bread for the hungry and thirsty (6:35) is awkward because the bread cannot be drunk. Charles H. Dodd observes that "within the limits of Jewish eschatological beliefs," the author of John describes Jesus as a second Moses who "gave the people both water from the rock and 'bread from heaven.'" Dodd describes Jesus as "the Giver of bread" in 6:27–34 and as "the Giver of water" in 4:10–15.[84] His explanation seems to be persuasive, for verse 35, the center of John 6, implies that the bread and water consist of Jesus himself (his flesh and blood).[85] Crossan suggests a relationship between "Jesus and Crowds" (6:1–15 and 6:22–59), and "Jesus and Disciples" (6:16–21 and 6:60–71) in the structure of John 6.[86] His point indicates that

---

80. Yerkes, *Sacrifice*, 214.

81. Bauer, *Greek-English Lexicon*, 462–63.

82. Webster, *Ingesting Jesus*, 65. Here, Webster argues that whole chapter of John 6 develops the "ingesting motif positively and substantially."

83. Crossan, "It is Written," 4.

84. Dodd, *Interpretation*, 338–39.

85. Dodd's Moses typology is questionable because Jesus surpasses Moses in John 6. Unlike Moses, Jesus is "equal to God" (5:18). See Dodd, *Interpretation*, 340.

86. Crossan, "It is Written," 4. Crossan also indicates that "a precise inclusion

the literary unit of John 6 is solid: "narratives and the following discourse are thus drawn together into one unified piece."[87] In addition, it shows that Jesus' feeding story is related to the eucharistic words in 6:51–59.

The story of the feeding of the multitude in 6:1–15 happens around the time of Passover on a mountainside (6:3–4). Using a boy's two small fish and five barley loaves, Jesus wants to feed the people who are coming to him (6:6), thus, he takes the loaves, gives thanks and distributes them (6:11). Although there are no eucharistic words (such as "This is my body"), verse 11 reminds one of the eucharistic actions which appear in the Synoptics. Scholars agree that the eucharistic idea and undertone are pervasive in the multiplication and its following discourses in John 6.[88] Brown says that John's story of the multiplication adapts "the scene of the institution of the Eucharist," though John does not report the actual scene.[89] As Webster explains, Jesus' multiplication of the bread in 6:1–15 recalls "God's provision both in the wilderness in the past, on this mountain in the present, and at the messianic banquet in the future."[90] Just as the people of Israel ate plenty of food in the wilderness that God provided, the crowd eats plenty of food that Jesus miraculously supplies. The author of John emphasizes the size of the crowd four times, using phrases such as "great crowd" πολὺς ὄχλος (6:2, 5), "five thousand men in number" (6:10), and "so many" τοσοῦτος (6:9). The size of the multitude indicates a great quantity of food. Thus, comparing the food (βρῶσιν) of Jesus in 4:32, Webster observes that "The distinguishing feature of the food in John 6:1–15 is its quantity" because "Jesus transforms a small amount of food into enough for many people with plenty leftover."[91] Here, Jesus' power to make a surplus of food with two fish and five barley loaves suggests his ability to endow people with an eternal life when they take Jesus' flesh and blood (6:53–54). As the miracle worker who surpasses Moses' miracles, through this multiplication, Jesus also predicts his sacrificial death that atones for all the sins of humanity.[92] This sacrificial offering becomes specific in 6:51–59, which reminds one of past images of animal sacrifice, the present sacrifice of Jesus, and the future sacrifice of participation in the Eucharist. Markus Barth points out that "In

---

between the handling of the Disciples in 6:1–15 and the Twelve in 6:67–71."

87. Webster, *Ingesting Jesus*, 66. See also Crossan, "It is Written," 4.

88. Dodd, *Interpretation*, 425. Rudolf Schnackenburg also states that there is "the presence of Eucharistic undertones." Schnackenburg, *Gospel according to St. John*, 16.

89. Brown, *John I-VII*, 247.

90. Webster, *Ingesting Jesus*, 69.

91. Webster, *Ingesting Jesus*, 70.

92. Hebrews 10:8 says the similar notion, "But when Christ had offered for all time a single sacrifice for sins, he sat down at the right hand of God."

John 6:52–58 Christ reveals himself as a sacrifice; he completes the imagery of *flesh* and *blood* by speaking of a sacrificial meal in which flesh and blood are consumed."[93] When Jesus insists that he is the bread that comes from heaven (6:35–40), the Jews challenge Jesus' origin from heaven, asking, "Is not this Jesus, the son of Joseph, whose father and mother we know? How does he now say, 'I have come down from heaven'?" (6:42). This challenge prompts Jesus' further explanation of his origin from heaven and his ability to raise people at the last day (6:44–46). Jesus continues to reiterate that he is the bread of life that came down from heaven (6:48–51a). Then, he suddenly states that this living bread that came down from heaven is his flesh (6:51c): "I am the living bread which came down from heaven; if any one eats of this bread, he will live forever; and the bread which I shall give for the life of the world is my flesh." Consequently, the Jews again challenge him, wondering how he can give them his flesh to eat (6:52). They hear Jesus' shocking response: "Truly, truly, I say to you, unless you eat the flesh of the Son of man and drink his blood, you have no life in you" (6:53). Webster interprets this verse as a matter of condition: "Eating the flesh and drinking the blood of Jesus are made a condition for eternal life."[94] Since presenting the multiplication of fish and bread and the discourse of the bread of life, Jesus gradually but firmly reinforces "the language of eating," insisting that the crowd must eat his flesh and drink his blood (6:53).[95] In order to provide his flesh and blood, like a sacrificial animal, Jesus must first die before "he is available as the substance of food" for the life of the world (6:51c).[96] Bultmann emphasizes Jesus' necessary death, which is a crucial step that must precede the ingestion of Jesus's flesh and blood:

> If this flesh is described as the flesh which was given for the life of the world, clearly this has Jesus' submission unto death in mind, which in the early Christian view was a death . . . Moreover the reason why the passage speaks not of Jesus' ψυχή (=life), which would be specifically Johannine, but of his σάρξ, is that it refers to the eating of his flesh (and the drinking of his blood) in the Lord's Supper, which he instituted by his submission unto death.[97]

---

93. Barth, *Lord's Supper*, 93.
94. Webster, *Ingesting Jesus*, 82.
95. Webster, *Ingesting Jesus*, 83.
96. Webster, *Ingesting Jesus*, 83.
97. Bultmann, *Gospel of John*, 234–35.

Bultmann indicates that by using σάρξ, John brings out "Jesus' submission unto death," which intends to give life to the world throughout the institution of the Eucharist.

In John 6:51–53, no actual sacrifice appears, but John's construction and assumption of the eucharistic words seem to refer to a sacrifice. Through the "proclamation of his sacrificial death," Jesus further claims that he will give eternal life for those who eat his flesh and drink his blood and he will raise them on the last day (6:54).[98] By using Jesus' sacrificial death through the ingesting motif, the author relates Jesus' death with the institution of the Eucharist. In order to understand the eating of Jesus' real flesh and blood, Bultmann also suggests that John uses a "sacramental dualism of the mysteries" because "the sacrament alone is real, true nourishment," which provides life.[99] Indeed, John frequently uses ingesting language and the metaphor of sacrifice, which directs his/her audience to understand Jesus' sacrificial death. However, the people understand Jesus' sayings about ingesting his flesh and blood in a literal way, and thus, they become confused (6:52, 60). In fact, Jesus says that he is the living bread from heaven (6:51), not actual bread. Here, the actual bread is just a symbol of his sacrificial death. Yet the multitude does not understand its meaning, so Jesus tells them, "you seek me, not because you saw signs, but because you ate your fill of the loaves" (6:25). Jesus wants the multitude to understand signs, but they fail to comprehend what Jesus says to them. Here, John uses the imagery of flesh and blood to make his readers vividly conceptualize blood sacrifice. This would resonate with them because of their cultural intimacy to Greek notions of sacrifice, especially those of the Dionysus cult.[100] Through the controversy between Jesus and the multitude, John reiterates the ignorance of the multitude in order to emphasize Jesus' sacrificial death for the sin of the world.

Although he separates the Eucharist from the sacrifice of Christ in John 6:51–59, Barth further comments on John's use of this imagery of sacrifice: "Only the imagery that is used in John's Gospel is unique. The

---

98. Barth, *Lord's Supper*, 92.

99. Bultmann, *Gospel of John*, 236.

100. Barth argues that eating flesh and drinking blood not only come from other pagan cults (Mithras), but also come from Paul's statement in 1 Cor 10:19–21. Barth, *Lord's Supper*, 92. In next chapter, I will investigate the relationship between the Dionysus cult and the Gospel of John in detail; The ancient Greeks uses blood sacrifices as "rites of absorptive purification, transferring defilement to despised animals." Various kinds of animals are dedicated as "scapegoats in ritual sacrifices." While human sacrifice mostly disappeared, "its symbolic form" has been preserved in Jesus' suffering and sacrificial death, where Jesus carries over the "sins of the world" to be "perfect offering." See Preston, "Purification: An Overview," 7509.

same is true of John 19:34: the water (of life!) and the blood (to be drunk as the carrier of life) flow out of the body of Christ crucified. He who died on the cross is the source of the life-giving water."[101] On this point, Dodd states that "the issue of the blood and water" in John 19:34 is undoubtedly a sign (σημεῖον) and symbolically indicates "the life-giving stream."[102] In this regard, the First Epistle of John 5:6–8 describes that Jesus came by "water and blood" as well as the Spirit. It is worthy of quotation: "This is he who came by water and blood, Jesus Christ, not with the water only but with the water and the blood. And the Spirit is the witness, because the Spirit is the truth. There are three witnesses, the Spirit, the water, and the blood; and these three agree." The water and the blood from Jesus function in a similar way to the sacrificial victim on the altar. Unlike descriptions of sacrifice in Hebrews, in which Jewish sacrificial features appear alongside the features of Greek *thysia* sacrifice, John's imagery of sacrifice (eating flesh and drinking blood) is not influenced by the Jewish animal sacrificial tradition.[103] Barth indicates that "Under all circumstances, the consumption of flesh in which there still is blood is prohibited (Gen. 9:4; Lev. 3:17; 7:27; 17:10–14; Deut. 12:23; cf. 1 Sam 14:33)" in the Old Testament sacrifices.[104] Although Bultmann posits that "an ecclesiastical editor," inserted John 6:51–59 into the current position, a reading with which I do not agree, his interpretation of these verses brings out "the idea of the sacramental union," especially in verse 56.[105] Bultmann rightly observes that the typical Johannine formula, "he in me and I in him" with regard to the ingestion of Jesus indicates the Lord's Supper because it unites people with Jesus in "a mysterious way."[106] According to Bultmann, the author of John uses of the idea of union with

---

101. Barth, *Lord's Supper*, 94.

102. Dodd, *Interpretation*, 425 and 428.

103. Barth introduces a reference of the eating of flesh and the drinking of blood in the Bible: "To a sacrificial meal of the end time, which will take place on the mountain of Israel, God invites, or compels, the birds of the air and all the animals of the field. There they shall eat the flesh and drink the blood–not of the usually consumed rams and lambs, goats and bulls and fatted Bashan cows, but of "might men," "all kinds of warriors," and "the princes of the earth" (Ezek 39:17–20). In short, the victory over Israel's enemies is to be celebrated by a ghastly meal in which human beings are devoured and their blood is gulped. The same imagery recurs in the New Testament: in Revelation 16:6; 17:6, 16; and 19:17–18 the victory that enemies have seemingly gained over the members of the church is celebrated in festival demonstrations and actions; the reputed victors eat the flesh or drink the Christians' blood. Obviously, heinous celebrations of this kind cannot have provided the background for the imagery used in John 6:51–59." Barth, *Lord's Supper*, 92–93.

104. Barth, *Lord's Supper*, 93.

105. Bultmann, *Gospel of John*, 236.

106. Bultmann, *Gospel of John*, 236.

Jesus in 5:21, 26 "to describe the living power of Jesus, which is the basis of the power of the sacrament": Jesus attests that "I live because of the Father, so he who eats me will live because of me" (6:57).[107] The imagery of flesh and blood becomes powerful only when people can connect that imagery to the actual models: Greek sacrifice. Unfortunately, except for the twelve disciples, the crowd continually fails to recognize this imagery because after they see and eat the bread and fish, they try to make Jesus their king by force (6:15), and they sternly argue among themselves, saying, "How can this man give us [His] flesh to eat?" (6:52), when Jesus talks about his flesh. Even some of his disciples do not perceive the meaning of Jesus' discourse: they say that his teaching is difficult and leave him (6:60, 66). As I mentioned above, ironically, the ignorance of the multitude and some disciples alludes to Jesus' sacrificial death, which is highlighted in the prediction of Judas' betrayal (6:64 and 13:11). By doing so, John explains why Jesus must die, what the purpose of his death is, and the meaning of true discipleship for his readers.[108]

Because of the people's literal understanding of eating flesh and drinking blood, and their consequent complaints that Jesus' teachings are hard (σκληρός ἐστιν ὁ λόγος οὗτος 6:60), Jesus corrects their misunderstanding about the flesh, saying: "It is the spirit that gives life, the flesh is of no avail; the words that I have spoken to you are spirit and life" (6:63). Literally, 6:63 seems to oppose verse 6:53: "unless you eat the flesh of the Son of Man ... you have no life in you"; for "if John is referring to the eucharist in vv. 51c ff., v. 63 must have a similar reference."[109] However, Howard and Gossip state that Jesus' flesh and blood in 6:53 may symbolize "the Word of God."[110] In fact, the word of God indicates Jesus himself. For example, in 1:14, John has already declared that the word became flesh (ὁ λόγος σὰρξ ἐγένετο). Thus, although I do not agree with this Christological interpretation of Jesus' flesh and blood in 6:53, I agree that the flesh in verse 53 and 63 denotes a different meaning. For Bultmann, the σάρξ in verse 63 is directed to the

---

107. Bultmann, *Gospel of John*, 236.

108. Throughout the Gospel of John, the author of John is specifically aware of his readers. For example, in 20:31, he says, "these are written that you may believe that Jesus is the Christ, the Son of God, and that believing you may have life in his name." Bultmann states that "The Evangelist, after his manner, expressly emphasized in a note the knowledge of Jesus (v. 65v), and in an anticipation of that which was to follow he drew attention at the same time to Jesus' foreknowledge of the extremest possibility of unbelief, that of the betrayal." Bultmann, *Gospel of John*, 447.

109. Dunn, "John 6," 334.

110. Howard and Gossip, "St. John," 575.

σὰρξ in 1:14 in to a certain degree.¹¹¹ In this regard, although he postulates that the offence (6:61) arises from the ambiguity of the flesh (σὰρξ) in John's Gospel, Bultmann sees that the setting of 6:60–71 is different than that of 6:1–59, such that he relocates 6:60–71 after 8:30–40.¹¹² Unlike Bultmann, many scholars refute this relocation. In the different approach to the "hard saying" of Jesus, Günther Bornkamm argues that σκληρός ὁ λόγος does not refer to ingesting Jesus, but it refers back to Jesus' talk of the Son of Man's descent (καταβαίνειν) in 1:51.¹¹³ His point, however, fails to explain why John suddenly brings out his descent here; what is the purpose? Unlike Bornkamm's argument, Jesus seems to show that his ascension in verse 62 is one of the strong examples of his sign. Barth interprets verse 63 in the context of Jesus' sacrificial death, stating that "In its present context, John 6:63 stands in close relationship to the preceding discourses on Christ's incarnation and sacrificial death, specifically to Christ's ascension, mentioned in verse 62."¹¹⁴ Therefore, one can observe that the idea of sacrifice dominates the entirety of John 6 because Jesus' ascension implies the preceding passion and the sacrificial death of Jesus.¹¹⁵

Up to now, the above scholars have supposed that John 6, especially 6:51–59, deals with the Eucharist as closely related to John 13. However, as I discussed regarding the historical survey of John 6 in chapter 1, many scholars agree with the eucharistic undertone of John 6, but some scholars still object to the eucharistic reading of John 6. James Dunn is one of the pioneers for this position. First, Dunn accepts that John 6 represents the Johannine Eucharist as a "most redoubtable stronghold."¹¹⁶ However he suggests that a new reappraisal on John 6 is necessary.¹¹⁷ He calls into question G. Bornkamm's argument that verses 60–63 cannot refer back to verses 51c–58. In particular, the hard saying of verse 60 refers back to "Jesus' talk of the καταβαίνειν of the Son of Man (not to the idea of eating his flesh and drinking his blood)."¹¹⁸ Dunn also makes the criticism that "Bultmann and Lohse have overstated the contrast between what goes before vi. 51c and what follows it."¹¹⁹ From this point, Dunn also points out that all references

---

111. Bultmann, *Gospel of John*, 446.
112. Bultmann, *Gospel of John*, 443–51, especially 446.
113. Bornkamm, "Die eucharistische Rede im Johannes-Evanglium," 166.
114. Barth, *Lord's Supper*, 98.
115. Howard and Gossip, "St. John," 575.
116. Dunn, "John 6," 328.
117. Dunn, "John 6," 328.
118. Dunn, "John 6," 329.
119. Dunn, "John 6," 329.

regarding the σάρξ incorporate the idea of Jesus' sacrificial death: "in particular the sacrificial connotations of the phrase 'flesh and blood' cannot be ignored."[120] According to him, the unacceptable saying (σκληρός ὁ λόγος) therefore is related to the "talk of Jesus' incarnation *and his death.*" Dunn further states:

> When we see this, the connection between *vv.* 62 and 63… becomes clear, and we realize that *vv.* 62–3 together meet the objection of *v.* 60 and, by expanding the thought implicit in the talk of eating his flesh and almost explicit in *v.* 51c, answer the yet unanswered question of *v.* 52 … Jesus has said that he will give his flesh for the life of the world and that life comes from eating the flesh of the Son of Man who descended from heaven. He now explains more fully that this will be possible because the Son of Man will ascend to where he was before, and as the climax and result of his ascension and glorification will give the Spirit. The life-giving consumption of the Son of Man really refers to the reception of the Spirit of the exalted Jesus. For it is the *Spirit* who gives life (*v.* 63).[121]

Thus, Dunn designates that the σάρξ in verse 63, like manna that descends from heaven, does not give life, but the σάρξ in 51–58, as in 1:14, gives life to the world.[122] In all of Jesus's discourses in John 6, the focus is Jesus himself and the "accent is on the need to believe in him (*vv.* 29, 35, 36, 40, 47, 64, 49)."[123] Dunn objects to any interpretation of John 6, especially 6:51–59, as the eucharistic elements. He firmly states:

> Those who distinguish the bread of the earlier verses from the flesh and bread of *vv.* 51c–58, by equating the former with divine revelation and the latter exclusively with the eucharistic elements, are wrong. There is no such distinction. Jesus himself is central throughout—not his revelation (as distinct from himself) and not the sacramental elements. The manna and the bread of the miracle are contrasted with and are symbols of Jesus, not of the Lord's Supper … vi. 35 also makes it clear that the 'eating' and 'drinking' is simply a vivid metaphor, highly appropriate in the circumstances, for coming to and believing in Jesus.[124]

120. Dunn, "John 6," 331.
121. Dunn, "John 6," 331.
122. Dunn, "John 6," 331–32.
123. Dunn, "John 6," 333.
124. Dunn, "John 6," 333.

He avers that "eating flesh" and "drinking blood" are a metaphor for Jesus himself without any eucharistic connotation. In addition, he insists that if John 6:51–59 is interpreted as "eucharistic language for its metaphorical value," 6:63 must be understood as offering the same perspective. His point is clear that any interpreter retains the consistent application to the σάρξ so that according to verse 63, "the actual reception" of "the eucharistic elements are of no avail—they play no part; in the event it is the Sprit who gives life, and he does so primarily through the words of Jesus."[125] His Christological approach to John 6 helps one to refute the "false literalism" that interprets the σάρξ in verse 53 and 63 from the same perspective.[126] However, although he interprets the flesh to imply Jesus' death, and there is an idea of sacrifice in 6:51–70, Dunn overstates the Christological interpretation of John 6. If manna and the miraculous bread represent Jesus, how is the symbol addressed? If the Eucharist mainly focuses on the remembrance of Jesus' death and resurrection as well as a true union with God, it is natural that Jesus is the center in the Eucharist, whether it is held in a ritual setting or controversial situation.

As I mentioned earlier in chapter 1, Christology and Eucharist are inseparable. For instance, John M. Perry argues that the author of John weaved "his community's high Christology (6:38)" into his community's "eucharistic theology (6:50)."[127] In the development of the Johannine Eucharist, Perry states that "the Fourth Evangelist introduced the passion-oriented interpretation of the bread and wine into chap. 6 by adding 6.51b–58."[128] He slightly objects to Bultmann's discussion that "a sacramentalizing redactor" added 6:51b–58 at a later time.[129] Instead of the redactor, he sees that the Fourth Evangelist added 6:51b–58. By doing so, the Evangelist alters the early Johannine tradition of the Eucharist, which is "a symbol of the life-giving presence of the Risen Lord," into the "passion-oriented interpretation of the bread and wine" in John.[130] Actually, unlike Perry, this book does not trace back to the development of the Johannine community and the evolution of its Eucharist. In a certain degree, however, I agree with Perry's arguments that the Forth Evangelist includes the sacramental elements as well as Christological and that 6:51b–58 clearly focuses on Jesus' death (for me, it is Jesus' sacrificial death.). Thus, it is unnecessary to separate the Eucharist

---

125. Dunn, "John 6," 335.
126. Dunn, "John 6," 334.
127. Perry, "Evolution," 27.
128. Perry, "Evolution," 32.
129. See his footnote 27, Perry, "Evolution," 32.
130. Perry, "Evolution," 32–35.

from the Christology. In particular, when Christology itself concentrates on the suffering and death of Jesus, it overlaps the elements of the Eucharist. By using many symbols and metaphors of ingestion, John describes Jesus' sacrificial death in John 6, which is highlighted in the Eucharist. Because John's eucharistic discourse has a more sophisticated literary structure and the ingestion motif, it is different from the words of institution of the Synoptics. Indeed, Dunn properly points out that "while all the NT version of the words of institution have σῶμα and not σάρξ," John does not.[131] Like the eucharistic institution of the Synoptics, John's Eucharist also implies a sacrificial death of Jesus. The critical question, however, arises: why does John omit σῶμα? Why does the author add σάρξ in the eucharistic discourse? In the next chapter, motivated by these questions, I will investigate another element of the Johannine Eucharist.

SUMMARY

In order to trace the unit of ideas for the Johannine Eucharist, in chapter 2, I have investigated Greco-Roman background that mainly includes the characteristics of sacred meals and the Dionysus cult. Then, in this Chapter, I have argued that the Gospel of John interlaces Greco-Roman meal customs and the idea of Greek sacrificial meals with the Johannine Eucharist. As I mentioned several times, most scholars have privileged the Jewish influence on the Johannine Eucharist. For this reason, the unique characteristics of the Johannine Eucharist have not been illuminated in the ritual or in New Testament studies.

On the one hand, literary analysis of the Gospel of John shows that the author of John is a skillful writer. Like a trained scribe for the kingdom of heaven in Matthew 13:52 who "brings out of his treasure what is new and what is old," the author dexterously weaves the old source (Jewish background) and the new source (Greco-Roman background) for his/her literary theme. As T. S. Eliot says that "Immature poets imitate; mature poets steal ... The good poet welds his theft into a whole of feeling which is unique, utterly different from that from which it was torn," the author of John acts like a thief, which seems to present a subtle puzzle for modern readers.[132] Unless the readers recognize the idea of sacrifice and the model of Dionysus in the Johannine Eucharist, they fail to understand the problematic phrase "eat my flesh and drink my blood." In his mimesis criticism, Dennis MacDonald shows that ancient authors "broadcast their

131. Dunn, "John 6," 334.
132. Eliot, *Sacred Wood*, 125.

imitations by supplying intertextual flags to alert readers."[133] However, when modern readers are inclined to favor Jewish literature and religion, "[W]hat was overt to them often is covert to us."[134] Because both ancient Jews and Christians, such as Philo and Origen, imitated the Homeric epics and other Greek literature in their writings, the Greco-Roman background proves an important hermeneutical tool for the Johannine Eucharist.[135]

The study of Greco-Roman background shows that the Gospel of John has as strong an affinity with Greco-Roman culture as Jewish culture. The reclining custom at the meal is a standard phenomenon in the New Testament, though many English Bible translations omit or mistranslate this custom. Jesus' foot washing story also demonstrates that Greco-Roman banquet custom infiltrates into Jewish and Christian meal customs, especially Jesus' Last Supper.

The idea of the sacrificial meal abundantly appears in the Gospel of John in the ingesting motif. It is important in explaining the origin of the sacrifice. The meal itself generates sacred ritual, rather than the sacrifice generating the meal (Yerkes). Although unlike the Old Testament, the New Testament never includes any actual sacrifice, the connotation of sacrifice is dominant. One of the famous examples is Jesus' title "Lamb of God" (John 1:29, 36), which is John's unique description throughout the Bible. Scholars have struggled to define the meaning of "lamb," but most of them have preferred the Paschal lamb. However, unlike the Lamb of God in John, the Paschal lamb does not remove sin. In addition, the scapegoat model cannot apply to the Lamb of God because the scapegoat is not killed, but just let go into the wilderness. Instead, Bultmann and Cullmann state that the Lamb of God is the sacrificial lamb which may include the symbol of the Paschal lamb and the Greek *thysia* sacrifice.

In any religion, sacrificial activity is widespread because it connects human beings and the divine. The sacrificial idea of the Lamb of God functions to bridge humans and God by putting away sin of the world, rather than forgiving sin, which implies that John's notion of sin was affinity to Greek *miasma* from which the concept of sin arises. Although the Jewish sacrifice and the Greek *thysia* sacrifice share some commonalities, their functions are different: While the Greek sacrifice emphasizes communion with the god, the Jewish one indicates that humans cannot be united with God, but just passively receive God's mercy and forgiveness. The Jewish people might have known both the Jewish and Greek sacrifice at that time,

---

133. MacDonald, *Imitate Homer?*, 149.
134. MacDonald, *Imitate Homer?*, 149.
135. See MacDonald, *Imitate Homer?*, 150.

but historical events pushed them closer to the Greek sacrifice: While the official Jewish sacrifice ended when the Jerusalem temple was totally destroyed by Roman army in 70 CE., the *thysia* sacrifice continued until the fourth century, which might have influenced Hellenized Jews.

This idea of sacrifice mostly appears in John 6 with the ingesting motif. The whole structure of John 6 contains the bread of life discourse (6:1–15, 22–50) and the following Eucharist discourse (6:51–71). Both discourses are closely related to ingesting and the sacrificial motif. Eating bread and fish implies eating Jesus' flesh and blood. As John alludes in 6:51–59, to eat Jesus' flesh, like the sacrificial animal, Jesus must first die. Thus, the death of Jesus parallels the death of the sacrificial animal, especially the sacrificial lamb. Jesus reveals himself in a sacrifice in which people eat his flesh and drink his blood for eternal life. Through σάρξ, the words of the Eucharist in John 6:51–59 importantly imply the idea of sacrifice and the sacrificial meal. At the same time, John shows that some disciples and the multitude understood σάρξ literally, which is compared to Jesus' conception of the *imagery* of flesh and blood. Due to their misunderstanding, some left Jesus, and one of his disciples, Judas, would betray him (6:64, 13:11). By doing so, John reminds his readers that Jesus must die and offer his flesh and blood to cleanse the sin of the world.

Because of the discrepancy of the meaning of σάρξ in John 6:51–59 and 63, scholars have tried to interpret John 6 as either Eucharist or Christology; however, the separation of Christology and the Eucharist in John 6 solves only one part of the difficulty. From the perspective of literary criticism and the idea of sacrifice, Christology and the Eucharist are inseparable. Emphatically and slightly ironically, scholars' arguments show that John 6 is still a "hard teaching" of Jesus, and a new approach is needed when one consistently contemplates why John uses σάρξ instead of the σῶμα. The Greco-Roman background of the Johannine Eucharist may be a novel solution to this problem because of its bountiful connotation of sacrifice. Furthermore, academically, New Testament studies and ritual studies should strike a balance between the Jewish and the Greek tradition in order to provide Christians with varieties of exegetical tastes for their spiritual journey.

4

The Dionysus Cult and John's Eucharist

AS A FOREIGN GOD to Greeks and the god of wine, Dionysus also shares many features with "the cults of Phrygian Kybele, who was likewise celebrated with ecstatic dancing to percussive music, and Egyptian Osiris, a chthonian vegetation god who experienced dismemberment and resurrection."[1] Dionysus and his cult are so complicated that one cannot describe them in a word; for the characteristics of Dionysus himself are various and his cult overlaps in ritual with other religions. As a later religion, Christianity seems to share important features with the Dionysus cult, and Jesus looks like Dionysus in many ways. Jennifer Larson writes about how much Dionysus and Christianity share with each other:

> Dionysos has attracted a great deal of criticism attention because a profound theology, analogous to certain Christian doctrines, can be extracted from his myths and cults in a way that is not true of the other Olympian gods. A suffering god, an ecstatic religious experience in which worshipers are united with the deity, the consumption of wine as part of the ritual, and the belief in the god's ability to offer salvation from death: all these elements have contributed to theories that Dionysiac religion

---

1. Larson, *Ancient Greek Cults*, 126.

was co-opted by Christianity, on the one hand, and attempts to recast the pagan Greeks as Christian precursors, on the other.[2]

Early Christian writers were aware of the similarity between Christianity and the Dionysus cult.[3] Justin Martyr (100–165 BCE) claims that the wicked demons deceive human race with the story of Greek myths. He states that the demons imitate the story of the Old Testament in explaining the myth of Dionysus (*Apology* 1.54).[4] He further says, "So when the demons heard these prophetic words they made out that Dionysus had been a son of Zeus, and handed down that he was the discoverer of the vine (hence they introduce wine in his mysteries), and taught that after being torn in pieces he ascended into heaven" (1.54).[5]

Despite Church Fathers' accusation of the Dionysiac cult, its influence frequently informed Christian writers. Gregory of Nazianzus, bishop of Constantinople in the fourth century CE., wrote *The Passion of Christ*, using Euripides' *Bacchae* as a model. His writing was quite late, since the Gospel of John was written around the first part of the second century. Although the authorship and written date of *The Passion of Christ* are still under discussion among some scholars, André Tuilier affirms that it was written by Gregory of Nazianzus in the fourth century which is far earlier than the twelfth century.[6] Through offering a critical Greek text, he examines its style, and its historical and theological dependence on Gregory of Nazianzus.[7] Whether *The Passion of Christ* was written in the fourth or twelfth century, it is important evidence of the influence of Dionysus over Christianity. Since the edict of Milan in 313, Christianity had become a legitimate religion in the Roman Empire, and it became the official religion of the Roman Empire in 380, which means Christianity had begun to be a dominate religion. Because Christianity was developing its own power, it is important that Gregory of Nazianzus or an anonymous author of twelfth century instead composed his Christian apologetic writing by imitating a pagan literature.[8] This imitation significantly shows the influence of Dio-

2. Larson, *Ancient Greek Cults*, 126–27.
3. Seaford, *Dionysos*, 126.
4. Richardson, ed., *Christian Fathers*, 277.
5. Richardson, ed., *Christian Fathers*, 278.
6. Tuilier, ed., *Passion du Christ*, 38 and 58.
7. Tuilier, ed., *Passion du Christ*, 58.
8. Christianity between the sixth and eleventh century exercised an absolute power over all European society, which was negatively called "dark age." Broadly, after fall of the Roman Empire, Europe was "one large church–state, called Christendom" in which the pope wielded supreme authority over European society in the first and the emperor in the second. Although some historians trace the origin of Renaissance in the twelfth

nysus and Greek literature on Christianity in his time. For instance, he narrated the life, death, and resurrection of Jesus Christ using a large number of direct quotations from the *Bacchae*.[9] Following Tuilier's position, Evans further states the Dionysiac influence on the Christian writings:

> In his Passion of Christ, Gregory makes Christ, the Virgin Mary, and John (the so-called "Beloved Disciple") the three main characters, putting into their mouths lines once spoken by Dionysos, Agaue, and others in Euripides' *Bakkhai*. He also creates a chorus of women, in this case attendants of Mary, patterned after Euripides' chorus of Mad women.[10]

Like Gregory Nazianzus, other Christian writers were also influenced by the cult of Dionysus and the characteristics of the *Bacchae*.[11] Fulgentius, who was active in North Africa in the fifth or sixth century CE, wrote *Myths* (*Mitologiae*) in Latin in which he allegorically interpreted the *Bacchae* in both "physical and abstract terms."[12] They did not blindly use these essentials, but made them into genuine literary mimesis. When one investigates specific verses of the New Testament, therefore, the relationship between Dionysus and Christianity becomes clear, which will contribute to a better understanding of the Johannine Eucharist as well.

DIONYSUS AND EARLY CHRISTIAN LITERATURE

The figure of Dionysus appears not only in the Gospel of John, but also in other early Christian literature. Arthur Evans and Richard Seaford explicate the relationship between Dionysus and Christianity. They identify several Dionysiac characteristics in the New Testament. Particularly, Evans points out that the essence of Jesus appears in Euripides' *Bacchae* five hundred years before the New Testament writers composed their books.[13] Dionysus's persecution by Pentheus reminds one of Jesus' innocent suffering. Both Jesus and Dionysus are persecuted when they are born.

---

century, it still belonged to middle age. The full-scale of Renaissance began in the thirteenth century. See *Encyclopædia Britannica Online*, s.v. "Middle Age."

9. Tuilier, ed., *Passion du Christ*, 57–58.
10. Evans, *God of Ecstasy*, 151.
11. Evans, *God of Ecstasy*, 152.
12. Trzaskoma and others, eds., *Anthology of Classical Myth*, 268.
13. Evans, *God of Ecstasy*, 149.

Miraculous Escape

Scholars have observed literary similarities between Euripides' *Bacchae* and Acts of the Apostles.[14] Among them, with special focus on Acts 12, Otto Weinreich extensively argues the literary connection between the *Bacchae* and Acts.[15] Despite this mimesis between them, as John Weaver indicates, "commentators do not investigate or inter the possible interpretive significance of this parallel," which is "the prison–escape" in Acts as "a *topos* of Dionysian literature."[16] In fact, Acts 12:6–7 and *Bacchae* 443–448 are resonant with each other. In Acts, Peter, bound by double chains, is sleeping in the prison. The angel of the Lord taps Peter and arouses him, and "The chains fell from his wrists." In *Bacchae*, the maenads are chained in the dungeon by Pentheus, but suddenly they disappear. As Euripides reports, "The chains on their legs snapped apart by themselves. Untouched by any human hand."[17] In both cases, the followers of a new religion are wrongly arrested, then their chains are miraculously loosened by the power of their god. They continue practicing their religion.[18] In *Against Celsus*, Origen describes that Celsus, mocking Jesus, had related this story with *Bacchae*. Origen states that "This Jew of Celsus, ridiculing Jesus, as he imagines, is described as being acquainted with the *Bacchae* of Euripides, in which Dionysus says:– 'The divinity himself will liberate me whenever I wish'[*Bacchae* 498]."[19] Here, John Weaver comments that Celsus asks "why Jesus, if a god, could not escape his confinement on the cross."[20] This indicates that many Jews at that time compared Jesus with Dionysus, but thought that Dionysus was a god and Jesus was not. However, Origen wrote, "Now the Jews are not much acquainted with Greek literature; but suppose that there was a Jew so well versed in it (as to make such a quotation on his part appropriate), how (does it follow) that Jesus could not liberate Himself, because He did not do so?"[21] Origen had to defend that the story of miracles was already in the Bible against Celsus' statements. Here, the reason that Origen seriously refutes Celsus's argument ironically suggests the influence of Euripides' *Bacchae* on early Christian writing. Thus, Weaver mentions that "Origen deflects the

---

14. Regarding scholars' research, see footnote 7, 8 and 9 in Weaver, *Plots of Epiphany*, 151.
15. Weinreich, *Gebet und Wunder*, 317.
16. Weaver, *Plots of Epiphany*, 151.
17. Euripides, *Euripides V*, 172.
18. Evans, *God of Ecstasy*, 150.
19. Origen, "Against Celsus," 445.
20. Weaver, *Plots of Epiphany*, 60.
21. Origen, "Against Celsus," 445.

question by referring to the miraculous liberation of Peter in Acts 12 and Paul in Acts 16."[22]

Another example of the connection between a Christian miracle and Dionysus's miracle is found in Acts 16:25–26: "And toward midnight Paul and Silas prayed and praised God in a hymn. And the prisoners listened to them. And suddenly there was a great earthquake, so that the foundations of the prison were shaken. And immediately all the doors were opened and all the bonds were loosened." The author of Acts describes that the Jewish authorities wrongly persecute the members of a new religion by putting them into prison with chains, but the god of the new religion powerfully releases his followers from prison. Likewise, the local king, Pentheus unjustly persecutes Dionysus and his followers by putting Dionysus into prison, but the god of wine miraculously escapes. In *Bacchae* 576–641, Dionysus makes an earthquake, thunder, and lightning; then Dionysus appears in the joy of a chorus.[23] Dionysus says, "Let the earthquake come! Shatter the floor of the world!" (line 585).[24] Therefore, in this miraculous prison escape stories, "Jesus, in his own way, exhibited the same sort of divine power as Dionysus did when persecuted."[25]

The Resistance of Paul and Pentheus to the Will of God

A conspicuous Dianysiac feature is found in the story of Paul's conversion or call in Acts 9:1–19, 22:6–16, and 26:12–18.[26] Seaford states:

> The group hears the voice of the god but does not see him (*Bacchae* 578–95, Acts 9.7). To the lightning in *Bacchae* corresponds the description of the light appearing to Saul in terms of lightning (9.3, 22.6). The Dionysiac chorus falls to the ground and Pentheus collapses, and Saul falls to the ground (as does also, at 26.14, the group that accompanies him). The command to rise up, marking the transition, is given by Dionysos to the chorus and by the Lord to Saul. The chorus and Pentheus identify Dionysos with light; Saul saw the Lord, and it has been inferred the

---

22. Weaver, *Plots of Epiphany*, 60.
23. Seaford, *Dionysos*, 124.
24. Euripides, *Euripides V.*, 180.
25. Weaver, *Plots of Epiphany*, 60.
26. Stendahl, *Paul among Jews and Gentiles*, 7–23, especially, page 9. Stehdahl insists that Paul's story is "call" rather than "conversion."

'Saul's companions saw only a formless glare where he himself saw in it the figure of Jesus' (Haenchen).[27]

Here, Paul and Pentheus were the persecutors of the new religion and met the god whom they had persecuted. In *Bacchae* 794–795, the disguised Dionysus says, "Better slay victims unto him [Dionysus] than kick against the pricks, man raging against God."[28] And Acts 26:14 has a similar expression: "And all of us falling to the ground, I heard a voice speaking to me and saying in the Hebrew dialect, Saul, Saul, why do you persecute Me? It is hard for you to kick against the goads." This expression, "to kick against the goads," has been problematic for New Testament scholars because this striking phrase has not been discovered elsewhere in the Bible. This phrase appears only in some classical literature.[29] Particularly, the latter half of each Greek phrase is comparable in both Acts and the *Bacchae*.

Acts 26:14	*Bacchae* 794-795
πάντων τε καταπεσόντων ἡμῶν εἰς τὴν γῆν ἤκουσα φωνὴν λέγουσαν πρός με τῇ Ἑβραΐδι διαλέκτῳ· Σαοὺλ Σαούλ, τί με διώκεις; σκληρόν σοι πρὸς κέντρα λακτίζειν.	Θύοιμ ἄν αὐτῷ μᾶλλον ἤ θυμού μενος πρὸς κέντρα λακτίζοιμι θνητὸς ὤ θεῷ.

The πρὸς κέντρα λακτίζειν can be translated as "to kick against goads." This is a proverbial saying in Greek and Latin, which means to fight "against the will of the gods."[30] Obviously, even though the *Bacchae* and Acts use slightly different grammatical forms of the verb λακτίζω, the meaning is that rejecting the new god is like, as Evans explains, "kicking against the sharpened cattle prod."[31] Both Pentheus and Saul are cautioned "not to resist by the god whose new cult they are vainly persecuting."[32] Therefore, in Paul's conversion/call story, the author of Acts uses a literary imitation of the *Bacchae* in order to emphasize Paul's resistance to accept Jesus Christ.

---

27. Seaford, *Dionysos*, 125.
28. Euripides, *Euripides III*, 67.
29. Bruce, *Acts of the Apostles*, 501.
30. Buttrick, ed. *Acts of the Apostles*, 326.
31. Evans, *God of Ecstasy*, 151.
32. Seaford, *Dionysos*, 125.

THE DIONYSUS CULT AND THE GOSPEL OF JOHN

Jesus and Dionysus

John's portrait of Jesus is similar to that of Dionysus. Jesus defines himself as various symbols, such as light (1:4, 5, 9; 8:12), living water (4:14), living bread (6:48), a shepherd (10:11, 14), and a vine (15:1, 5). Dionysus appears as various symbols as well. He represents himself as a bull, goat, mule, vine, wine giver, and the king of the dead. Like Dionysus, Jesus is the miraculous figure in John. Jesus performs many miracles. He turns water into wine (2:1–12), heals disease (4:49–54; 5:8), feeds the five thousand (6:1–15), opens the eyes of a blind man (9:1–12), raises Lazarus from death (11:38–44), and defeats death (chapter 20 and 21).

Among the Olympian gods, Dionysus was the humanized deity. Indeed, like Hercules and Achilles, he was a hero. Although he was the son of Zeus, his mother was Semele and his divine origin was often challenged.[33] In the beginning of Euripides' *Bacchae*, Dionysus declares that "I am Dionysus, the son of Zeus, come back to Thebes, this land where I was born. My mother was Cadmus' daughter, Semele by name" (line 1–3).[34] In the same way, Jesus has a human character. While Jesus is Logos (John 1:1–5) and "Son of God" (John 1:18; 5:25; 10:36; 11:4, 27; 19:7; 20:31) in John's Gospel, Jesus is called the "Son of Joseph" Ἰησοῦν υἱὸν τοῦ Ἰωσὴφ (John 1:45; 6:42) as well. This description appears in John's Gospel only, saying, "Jesus of Nazareth, the son of Joseph" (1:45) and "Is not this Jesus, the son of Joseph, whose father and mother we know? How does He now say, 'I have come down out of heaven'?" (6:42).[35] In addition, in the prologue, John clearly declares that "the Word became flesh and dwelt among us" ὁ λόγος σὰρξ ἐγένετο καὶ ἐσκήνωσεν ἐν ἡμῖν (1:14). This verse points out that Jesus became a human being in flesh. In other Gospels, this high Christology and low Christology do not appear with the same emphasis.[36]

---

33. This is the main storyline of Euripides' *Bacchae*.

34. Euripides, *Euripides*, 155.

35. Jesus is called "Joseph's son" in Luke 4:22 where people similarly do not believe Jesus' divinity, saying that "And all spoke well of him, and wondered at the gracious words which proceeded out of his mouth; and they said, 'Is not this Joseph's son?'(οὐχὶ υἱός ἐστιν Ἰωσὴφ οὗτος;)."

36. Gregory Riley defines two types of Chritology: "The first, Low Christology, held that Jesus was at base a human being, born of human parents, who because of his wisdom, righteousness, and/ or obedience, was appointed by God to be the Messiah, or was in the providence of God predestined and appointed to such a position. Such a view was common among the so-called Jewish Christian sects in the East, and lay at the baseof Adoptionist Christology. The opposite view, High Christology, was that Jesus

Dionysus's birth story shows that Zeus and a human, Semele, are his parents, just as Jesus' parents are the Holy Spirit and the human, Mary, although John omits Jesus' birth story. Dionysus and Jesus had been persecuted since they were born. In the Gospel of John, Jesus was rejected (1:11), persecuted (15:20), and killed (19:28–30). Arthur Evans states that the significant influence of Dionysus on Christianity is the "concept of Dionysos as the suffering Son of God."[37] This figure is obvious in Euripides' *Bacchae*[38] where a violent Pentheus unjustly persecuted the Son of God (Zeus).[39] In John's Gospel, Jews persecute Jesus and finally kill him. In particular, John's passion narrative describes how much Jews unjustly oppressed and tormented Jesus, which leads to anti-Semitism later.

Jesus' travel from Galilee to Jerusalem or from city to city could be compared to Dionysus's travels through Thrace, Thebes, and so on. Just as Dionysus comes to his hometown, Thebes, but is rejected, Jesus comes to this world, but the world rejects him.[40] Dionysus's and Jesus' close relatives or family members refute them as divine beings. For instance, after many disciples desert Jesus (6:60–67), Jesus' brothers do not believe in him (John 7:6). Likewise, in the *Bacchae*, Dionysus's cousin, Pentheus, is most hostile toward him and his aunts negatively say that Dionysus is not the son of Zeus (line 28 and 44–51).[41]

Similarly, Jo-An Brant, who studies the dramatic elements in the Gospel of John, compares the prologue of the *Bacchae* and the Gospel. According to her, both literatures begin "by bringing sharply into focus the ambiguity of the hero's situation in a world of blind violence."[42] Her explanation is worthy of quotation:

---

was in reality in god, a divine being who descended to earth from heaven and took on some form of humanity and then reascended to where he had first belonged. This view was especially common among Gnostic groups, and lies at the base of the Christology of the Gospel of John." Accorcing to Riley, "Later orthodoxy made a valiant effort at melding these two views, developing in the fifthe century the doctrine of the Hypostatic Union, the teaching that Jesus was both God and Man in whom these two complete natures were present in one person." Riley, *I Was Thought to Be What I Am Not*, 10–11.

37. Evans, *God of Ecstasy*, 146.

38. Euripides, *Euripides V*, in the first half of the play, particularly, Dionysus is oppressed by Pentheus.

39. Evans, *God of Ecstasy*, 147.

40. In the Synoptics, Jesus was rejected by his people at his hometown, Nazareth (Mark 6:1–6; Matt 13:53–58; Luke 4:16–30), but in John, this story is missing.

41. Euripides, *Euripides V*, 156–57.

42. Brant, *Dialogue and Drama*, 20.

As in the prologue to Euripides' *Bacchae*, in which Dionysus gives an account of how he came to be in Thebes, the gospel's prologue explains how the divine came to be striding about Judea and the Galilee. This explanation then provides the conditions for the antagonism that greets Jesus. The bold claims of Jesus to possess an authority that goes beyond that of a prophet and an ancestry that is other than human will clash with what is known of Jesus' parentage and birthplace by those who inhabit the story. In *Bacchae*, Dionysus lays out the tension of claims about his status more baldly... His [Dionysus] incarnation is necessitated by the refusal of some to believe, among them his mother's sisters, who deny that he is the son of Zeus and accuse Semele of using Zeus to hide her seduction by a mortal. (27–29)[43]

Dionysus and Jesus made rulers jealous because of their many followers. Pentheus anxiously observes that many women of Thebes leave home dancing and brimming with wine in honor of Dionysus (line 215–25).[44] Pentheus is confident that Dionysus's miracle and attraction of women are impostures for threatening his country (line 245–50).[45] In a similar way, Jesus attracts many followers who have seen Jesus' miracles, which makes the chief priests and the Pharisees anxious. John describes their sense of political crisis in John 11:48–49: "So the chief priests and the Pharisees gathered the council, and said, "What are we to do? For this man performs many signs. If we let him go on thus, everyone will believe in him, and the Romans will come and destroy both our holy place and our nation." Because of their sense of crisis, they regard Jesus as demon possessed (John 8:48). According to Mark 3:21, even his family and friends think him mad, and according to John 7:5, his brothers do not believe him. Thus, Jesus' many opponents say, "He [Jesus] has a demon, and he is mad ($\mu\alpha\acute{\iota}\nu\varepsilon\tau\alpha\iota$) why listen to him?" (John 10:20). Dionysus is also a mad god. He not only makes his enemies mad, but also gives the blessing of madness to his followers. Apparently, Dionysus's ardent worshiper is a maenad whose name originates from $\mu\alpha\iota\nu\acute{\alpha}\varsigma$ which means "raving," "mad" or "frantic."[46]

Dionysus is often described in the *Bacchae* as a liberator who typically uses wine and dance to liberate humans from their sorrows. Moreover, when he is in chains, Dionysus often says that he will set himself free (line 493 and 649).[47] Dodds points out that Dionysus liberates human beings

43. Brant, *Dialogue and Drama*, 20.
44. Euripides, *Euripides V*, 163–64.
45. Euripides, *Euripides V*, 164–65.
46. Liddell, *Greek–English Lexicon*, 484.
47. Euripides, *Euripides III*, 42 and 56.

from "the bondage" of "reason and social custom."[48] The character of Jesus as a liberator extensively appears throughout the Gospels, especially in the Gospel of John.[49] In the controversial argument with the Jews, Jesus declares that he will make them free from sin (8:34–36). The verses of John 8:32–40 describe the bondage from which Jews need to be free:

> (32) and you will know the truth, and the truth will make you free." (33) They answered him, "We are descendants of Abraham, and have never been in bondage to any one. How is it that you say, 'You will be made free'?" (34) Jesus answered them, "Truly, truly, I say to you, everyone who commits sin is a slave to sin. (35) The slave does not continue in the house for ever; the son continues for ever. (36) So if the Son makes you free, you will be free indeed. (37) I know that you are descendants of Abraham; yet you seek to kill me, because my word finds no place in you. (38) I speak of what I have seen with my Father, and you do what you have heard from your father." (39) They answered him, "Abraham is our father." Jesus said to them, "If you were Abraham's children, you would do what Abraham did, (40) but now you seek to kill me, a man who has told you the truth which I heard from God; this is not what Abraham did.

Jesus affirms that the truth makes human beings (Jews) free (8:32). Obviously, the truth connotes Jesus himself (John 5:33, 14:6) because as a sacrificial lamb (1:29, 36), Jesus can erase the sin of the world. The Jews refute that they need to be free because they are descendants of Abraham (8:33). For these verses, Bultmann states that the Jews fail to recognize the eschatological aspect of freedom.[50] His point is reasonable that the freedom affirmed by Jesus is not a political one. However, Jesus' freedom is related to the knowledge of the truth that Jesus is the Son of God and the giver of eternal life. Bultmann also indicates that "The idea of freedom therefore is determined by the fact that the concept of bondage is defined as a ποιῶν τὴν ἁμαρτίαν."[51] Therefore, sin contains the eschatological aspect and present ignorance of the Jews who do not accept Jesus' word (8:37, ὁ λόγος οὐ χωρεῖ ἐν ὑμῖν) and even try to kill Jesus (8:40). Bultmann rightly describes the sinful situation of the Jews: "If the murderous will of the Jews is proof that they are

---

48. Dodds, ed., *Euripides Bacchae*, xx.
49. See Luke 4:18–19; 13:12.
50. Bultmann, *Gospel of John*, 437.
51. Bultmann, *Gospel of John*, 438.

88 THIS IS MY FLESH

not Abraham's children, and therefore also that they are not free, manifestly this murderous will is a particularly clear sign of their lack of freedom."[52]

An ancient painting shows Dionysus riding a mule in a victorious pose while "satyrs and followers hail him waving ivy branches (Kerényi, plate 54A)."[53] One of Dionysus's favorite animals is the mule because the mule represented "the invincible power of the sexual drive," which implies god's energy and frenzy associated with wine.[54] In John 12:12–17, with waving palm branches (12:13), the followers of Jesus greeted him as he rode on the back of a donkey just as the satyrs waving ivy branches acclaimed Dionysus who was also sitting on a mule.

Jesus' Wine Miracle and Dionysus

In John 2:1–11, the striking image of Dionysus appears when Jesus turns water into wine in a marriage in Cana of Galilee.[55] Jesus and his disciples are invited to the marriage. When wine becomes insufficient, prompted by his mother, Jesus turns six stone water-vessels of water into excellent wine which can satisfy the quite drunken guests. Riley assumes that Jesus turned "120 gallons of water into wine of excellent vintage."[56] This wine miracle indicates that the author of John describes Jesus in the image of Dionysus.

However, most scholars deny the Dionysiac influence on the wine miracle (2:1–11). Craig S. Keener and Brown briefly mention the Dionysus legends, but they prefer to the Old Testament model such as "echoes Moses' first sign in Exodus in Jesus' first sign in John."[57] While Edmund Little refutes the influence of Dionysus in Jesus' wine miracle, he criticizes the weakness of other scholars' arguments which, ironically, introduce the influence of Dionysus.[58] Although he accepts that Dionysian influence was well advanced in Palestine prior to Christianity, he favors the influence of Old

---

52. Bultmann, *Gospel of John*, 443.

53. Kerényi, *Dionysos*, 169. See Plate 54A; Evans, *God of Ecstasy*, 149.

54. Kerényi, *Dionysos*, 169–70. Refer to Plate 54A and 54B; In the *Bacchae*, Euripides compares the Bacchante with a colt, saying "Then, in ecstasy, like a colt by its grazing mother, the Bacchante runs with flying feet, she leaps!" (line 165–66) in Euripides, *Euripides V*, 161; The donkey is closely related to Jesus because the *Protevangelium of James* describes the pregnant Mary sitting on a donkey for the journey to Bethlehem and later Jesus also enters Jerusalem on a donkey, which stands for his humble character. Bauckham, "Imaginative Literature," 754, 794 and 1108.

55. Smith, "On the Wine God," 817; Wick, "Jesus gegen Dionysos?," 179–98.

56. Riley, *I Was Thought to Be What I Am Not*, 21.

57. Brown, *John I-VII*, 101–2; Keener, *Gospel of John*, 495.

58. See Little, *Echoes of the Old Testament*, 1–73.

Testament Jewish tradition because he thinks that "Wine symbolism played an important role in [Jewish] Temple cult and eschatological expectations."[59] Due to his favoritism for finding echoes of the Old Testament in the Christian faith, he often loses balance when he deals with Dionysiac materials. For instance, he states that "Linnemann suggests that the Cana story arose in a Christian community as part of a dialogue with Dionysian adherents. There was no question of syncretism. On the contrary, Christians were asserting that only in the crucified Jesus lay fullness of life."[60] Yet I argue that there does exist some syncretism in John 2:1–11, which is the influence of Dionysus, the famous wine god.[61] Actually, Little does not totally deny the Dionysian themes in John's Gospel. Thus, he adds "a Hellenistic stream" to the Jewish tradition:

> The Old Testament background to John's gospel must be acknowledged, but Dionysian themes should also be considered as part of a Hellenistic stream absorbed by Jewish thought. Jesus is the new Moses, the new Elijah and Elisha, the new Wisdom, the new Torah, the new Temple. His body and blood are new mana for the Jews, new and life-giving food for the pagans. With an eye on the pagan world, converted or unconverted, John is proclaiming Jesus as the new and greater Asclepius, a new and greater Dionysos, whose joy is more complete, and whose judgement is more just.[62]

I agree with Little that the Gospel of John describes Jesus as a greater hero than those of the Old Testament and Greco-Roman literature. Despite the varying levels of emphasis, the New Testament writers place on Jesus as the ultimate hero, they all knew that mimesis was a useful method to persuade an audience. The Hellenistic stream is stronger than Little allows it to be. In particular, in John 2:1–11, the Dionysian influence overwhelms the Jewish wine tradition. In addition, one may acknowledge that most of John's audience was made up of Gentiles, not Jews, though many texts deal with the various interactions between Jews and Jesus. Furthermore, most Jews in the first and second century CE. were Hellenized. Gentiles, especially Gentile Christians, were more familiar with Greek Literature than with the Old Testament. The wine miracle of Dionysus was more apparent to them than were the echoes of the Old Testament.

---

59. Little, *Echoes of the Old Testament*, 55.
60. Little, *Echoes of the Old Testament*, 55.
61. See Riley, *I Was Thought to Be What I Am Not*, 21.
62. Little, *Echoes of the Old Testament*, 58–59.

For this reason, Rudolf Bultmann points out that John 2:1–11 has "a typical motif of the Dionysus legend" and emphasizes "the epiphany of the God."[63] Contrary to Little's argument, Bultmann indicates that "The wine of the marriage at Cana does not come from the OT expectation of salvation but from the Dionysus cult in Syria."[64] After surveying various interpretation of Jesus' wine miracle at Cana, Martin Hengel further develops Bultmann's point. Then he concludes that Palestinian Judaism and early Christianity took directly and consciously the influence of Dionysus because of their "missionary adaptation."[65] His arguments are worthy of quotation:

> In this context the Palestinian 'Dionysus's is again impressed wholly with the stamp of the old Semitic vegetation-deities . . . The motif of the transformation of water into wine could have already penetrated in the popular Haggada of the Galilean rural population long before the first Christian narrative about a wine-miracle began circulating. *Since the OT–Jewish miracle tradition had included multiplication and transformation miracles in great numbers and since the wine symbolism played an important role even for the temple cult and the eschatological expectations, a transformation of water into wine would hardly have been seen as an alien element.* It was as suitable for the Messiah of Israel as it was for the pagan god (*italic* added).[66]

Hengel's statement shows that because of their familiarity with wine, Jews could easily accept the wine miracle, which implies that the Dionysus cult had already widely influenced the Jewish religion. Hengel states that "the wine and the vine play an important role in connection with the Jewish expectation of the Messiah," in Genesis 49:10–12.[67] In addition, he mentions that Jews in the first and second century kept this expectation; for "the wine-cup, pitcher, grape-leaf, and grape appear frequently on the coins of the uprisings of 66–73 and 132–5."[68] However, Hengel rightly points out that the wine–motif in the Old Testament is "the same one-sided interpretation for John" because "The Messianically interpreted blessing of Jacob in Gen. 49:10–12 describes the eschatological ruler in Dionysiac colours."[69] In this regard, the Jewish Christians may share the similar perspective of

---

63. Bultmann, *Gospel of John*, 119.
64. Bultmann, *Gospel of John*, 120. See footnote 1, too.
65. Hengel, "Interpretation of the Wine Miracle," 112.
66. Hengel, "Interpretation of the Wine Miracle," 112.
67. Hengel, "Interpretation of the Wine Miracle," 100.
68. Hengel, "Interpretation of the Wine Miracle," 100.
69. Hengel, "Interpretation of the Wine Miracle," 100.

wine-motif with the Jewish expectation of the Messiah.[70] For Gentile Christians, it is natural that changing water to wine is the clear sign of Dionysus. Thus, as Little unintentionally mentioned, they could naturally understand Jesus' power and quality as surpassing the power of Greek deities (also Jewish heroes).

On the one hand, Jesus' first miracle is significant for his ministry because "the first of his signs, Jesus did at Cana in Galilee, and manifested his glory (Ταύτην ἐποίησεν ἀρχὴν τῶν σημείων ὁ Ἰησοῦς ἐν Κανὰ τῆς Γαλιλαίας καὶ ἐφανέρωσεν τὴν δόξαν αὐτοῦ); and his disciples believed in him" (John 2:11). It is significant that Jesus' wine miracle shows "the concrete deed of the incarnate Logos."[71] In other words, the Logos which was in the beginning (John 1:1, Ἐν ἀρχῇ ἦν ὁ λόγος) reveals the first of his signs (2:11, ἀρχὴν τῶν σημείων) through the wine miracle which may come from Greek heritage. Thus, regarding John 2:1–11, Smith indicates that "by imitation of Dionysiac motifs," Christians were able to demostrate "religious ideas" that they wanted "both to appropriate and to contradict."[72] Riley further attests that "we must not be so ignorant as to fail to recognize its import: this is the signature miracle of Dionysus . . . So Jesus is here accomplishing what no ancient would have missed or misunderstood; he is a new Dionysus."[73] In doing so, at least the author of John presents that Jesus has an equal power to that of Dionysus.

On the other hand, this miracle story is "one of the most mysterious texts" in the New Testament.[74] It contains symbolism from the different traditions in short and delimited form.[75] Birger Olsson attests that "the symbolic meaning" dominates author's thinking when he shapes the wine miracles to show Jesus' glory and give his disciples firm faith in him.[76] One of the symbols of the wine miracle in 2:1–11 is "fullness" and "Joy" which the Messianic-Dionysus can bring. Indeed, Dionysus brings joy and happiness for those who drink wine. The wedding at Cana where Jesus makes abundant wine for the wedding guests is a perfect background for a symbol of the fullness of joy. After the guests are joyfully drunk, Jesus provides them

---

70. The pre-Christian expectation of the Messiah in Jewish tradition was a savior who can destroy the enemy and save the Jews from oppression. See. Charlesworth, "From Messianology to Christology," 5.

71. Hengel, "Interpretation of the Wine Miracle," 96.

72. Smith, "Wine God," 820.

73. Riley, *I Was Thought to Be What I Am Not*, 21.

74. Olsson, *Structure and Meaning*, 18.

75. See Hengel, "Interpretation of the Wine Miracle," 98 and Olsson, *Structure and Meaning*, 114.

76. Olsson, *Structure and Meaning*, 114.

with the premium wine, which means Jesus' ability to endow abundant joy and happiness. Here, all vocabularies such as wedding, feast, wine and wine miracle are drawing a strong image of a biding happiness.[77] Hengel indicates that the symbol of perfect joy is related to Jesus' vine saying several times.[78] For instance, Jesus says, "These things I have spoken to you, that my joy may be in you, and that your joy may be full" (5:11) and "Hitherto you have asked nothing in my name; ask, and you will receive, that your joy may be full" (16:24). Thus, the scene of John 2 is so similar to a Dionysus celebration that one could assume that John's community borrowed the idea from the Dionysus cult.[79] Thus, John chapter 2 is colored by the wine feature of Dionysus and portrays Jesus as Dionysus. This Dionysiac figure sporadically continues to appear throughout the Gospel of John, specifically, in John chapter 2, 4, 6, and 15. In particular, Riley emphasizes that "John chapter two. . . provides a key to the interpretation of chapter six."[80] In this respect, I also identify important clues in John 4:5–30 and John 6:16–59 that can show evidence of Dionysus.

The Dionysiac Motif in John 4:5–34 and 6:16–59

Here, I will agrue that like John 2:1–11, John 4 and John 6 include the Dionysiac elements. First, I will explain that John 4:11–34 parallels 6:20–35 in order, contents, and literal density; second, I will contend that John 4:5–34 parallels a Thrian story about Dionysus in an ancient myth, and 6:16–21 parallels the Dionysus' voyage on water in *Homeric Hymn*. By this, I will present that these two paralleds may be evidence of a memeric connection between John's Jesus and Dionysus. Therefore, I will begin to argue the similar connections that John 4:11–34 and 6:20–35 have to Dionysiac elements which contribute to the parallelism of both texts.

Jesus and the Samaritan Woman vs. Dionysus and the Shepherd

The literary structure and themes of John 4:5–34 and 6:16–59, especially 4:11–34 and 6:20–35, resonate with each other.

---

77. See footnote 73 in Hengel, "Interpretation of the Wine Miracle," 101.
78. Hengel, "Interpretation of the Wine Miracle," 101.
79. Smith, "Wine God," 817.
80. Riley, *I Was Thought to Be What I Am Not*, 21.

The Dionysus Cult and John's Eucharist 93

John 4:11–34	John 6:20–35
Sir, you have nothing to draw with (4:11)	You have no sign to do (6:30)
Our father Jacob drank water in this well (4:12)	Our fathers ate the manna in the desert, (6:31)
Every one who drinks of this water will thirst again (4:13)	Moses and people ate manna but they died in the desert (6:32)
The drink of Jesus shall give everyone eternal life (4:14).	the bread of God gives life to the world. (6:33)
The woman said to him, "Sir, give me this water" (4:15).	Then they said to him, "Lord, evermore give us this bread." (6:34)
Jesus said to her, "I who speak to you am he" (4:26).	And Jesus said to them, "I am the bread of life." (6:35)
"I have food to eat of which you do not know" (4:32). "My food is to do the will of him who sent me, and to accomplish his work" (4:34).	Do not labor for the food that perishes, but for that food which endures to everlasting life. (6:27)

Just as people ask Jesus in a skeptical manner what work he is performing in John 6:30, the Samaritan woman in 4:11 indicates in a negative manner that Jesus has nothing with which to draw water from the well. In 6:31, the multitude mentions that their fathers who had great faith ate the manna in the desert, and in the same way the woman says that "our father Jacob," who was great, drank water from the well and he died (4:12). Jesus points out that their ancestors ate the manna but they died (6:33), and analogously says that all people including Jacob drank water from the well but they thirsted again (4:14). The bread of God is Jesus himself who gives life (6:33) and likewise, the water that Jesus gives is "a spring of water welling up to eternal life" (4:14). The disciples request that Jesus always give them that bread (6:34) and in the same manner, the woman asks him to give her that water evermore (4:15). Jesus reveals that he is the bread of life to the multitude (6:35) and similarly, Jesus reveals that he is the messiah to the woman (4:26). Jesus gives food for everlasting life in 6:27 to those who seek perishable food, just as he gives food for everlasting life to people who do not understand the true meaning of the food in 4:32 and 4:34. While John 4:5–42 describes Jesus as "a spring of water welling up to eternal life," John 6:20–40 depicts Jesus as "the bread of life." As one sees in the above chart, both verses are parallel in many respects. Here, the point is that Jesus gives eternal life that can fill the spiritual thirst and hunger of human beings. The role of the woman is positively described, but the multitude in John 6 is seldom positively depicted. Unlike the woman in John 4, the multitude and some Jews did not believe that Jesus was bread from heaven (John 6:41–42). When one thinks that raw meat cannot be separated from blood, one can understand that Jesus' blood and flesh, which signifies living water or bread, satisfies thirst and hunger (John 6:35). This shows that the bread connotes his flesh which contains blood as well. Thus, despite some distinctiveness between two texts, the parallels are obvious. Then, why does the author of John delineate these parallels? I conjecture that in order to apply the cannibalistic terminologies of the Dionysus cult and identify Jesus with Dionysus in 6:51–59, the author contrives to prepare the literary structure for the reader.

For instance, the Samaritan woman recalls the shepherd who exchanged dialogues with Dionysus. Morton Smith indicates that the conversation between Jesus and the woman of Samaria in John 4:5–30 is influenced by the discussion between Dionysus and the shepherd in the myth as told by Achilles Tatius.[81] Although Achilles Tatius probably lived in the second century CE and wrote "The Story of Leucippe and Cleitophon" in eight books "shown by papyri to be circulating by the late 2nd cent. AD," his story is based on the ancient myth of Tyrians that was older than John's Gospel.[82] Regarding this story, Smith states that "the date of composition can hardly be later than the first half of the second century, and is probably earlier."[83] Achilles Tatius himself reports that his Dionysus story derives from a Tyrian story, "it almost seems an Attic tale" (II.2).[84] According to him:

> Dionysus once paid a visit to this herdsman, who set before him the produce of the earth and the result of the strength of his oxen: but their drink was the same as that of the oxen, since vines did not yet exist. Dionysus thanked the herdsman for his kindly cheer, and pledged him in a friendly cup; but his drink was wine. The herdsman, drinking of it, danced for joy, and said to the god: "Where did you get this purple water, my friend? Wherever did you find blood so sweet? For it is not that water which flows on the ground—that, as it descends into the midriff, affords but a faint pleasure, while this delights the sense of smell before ever it reaches the mouth; when you touch it, it is cold, but it leaps down into the belly and there, far down, lights

---

81. Smith, "Wine God," 819.

82. Hornblower and Spawforth, eds., *Oxford Classical Dictionary*, 7; E. H. Warmington conjectures that Achilles Tactius might write this story late in second century and "Achilles himself must be regarded as having compsed his novel earlier in that century." Warmington, "Introduction, ix-x.

83. Smith, "Wine God," 816.

84. Tatius, *Tatius*, 59.

up the fires of delight." "This," said Dionysus, "is harvest water, the blood of the grape" . . . and they keep that day as Dionysus' festival. (II.2–3)[85]

Here, after the Tyrian herdsman receives wine from Dionysus, he dances for joy. Then, he asks, "Where did you get this purple water, my friend? Wherever did you find blood so sweet?"(πόθεν, ὦ ξένε, σοὶ τὸ ὕδωρ τοῦτο τὸ πορφυποῦ; πόθεν οὕτως εὗρες αἷμα γλθκύ;).[86] In a similar way, the woman asks, "From where then do you have that living water?" (πόθεν οὖν ἔχεις τὸ ὕδωρ τὸ ζῶν; 4:11). Smith claims that the herdsman's question recurs in John 6:55, "My blood is the true drink."[87] Dionysus answers, "This is harvest water, the blood of the grape . . . it leaps down into the belly and there, far down, lights up the fires of delight."[88] Strikingly, Jesus answers, "The water that I shall give him shall be in him a well of water springing up into everlasting life" (τὸ ὕδωρ ὃ δώσω αὐτῷ γενήσεται ἐν αὐτῷ πηγὴ ὕδατος ἁλλομένου εἰς ζωὴν αἰώνιον. 4:14). Thus, Smith indicates that "The shepherd's words on the way wine enlivens the stomach are recalled by similar sayings of Jesus in Jn. 4:14 and 7:37ff. on the water of life."[89] As I investigated in chapter 2, in the Dionysus tradition, wine signifies the blood of Dionysus or of grapes. Grapes and wine are identified with Dionysus. I agree with Stephen Need that that blood and flesh serve as a metaphor for Jesus.[90] In not only John but also Paul and the Synoptics, wine and bread include metaphorical meanings of the suffering and resurrection of Jesus. Most scholars agree that those are represented in bread and wine. While Paul and the Synoptics indirectly explain the connection between wine and blood by using cup, John 6 directly explains it by using "blood" in the setting of the Dionysus cult.

Jesus' Walking on Water vs. Dionysus' Voyage on the Water

The entire flow of John 6 begins with the feeding of the five thousand (6:1–15). At first, many people followed Jesus because they witnessed a lot of Jesus' miracles (6:2). Jesus saw a multitude was coming to him and decided to give them bread (6:5–6). When the people saw Jesus' sign, they said, "This

85. Tatius, *Tatius*, 59–61.
86. Tatius, *Tatius*, 58–59.
87. Smith, "Wine God," 819.
88. Tatius, *Tatius*, 61.
89. Smith, "Wine God," 819.
90. Need, "Jesus the Bread," 200.

is indeed the prophet who is to come into the world!" Then Jesus withdrew again to the mountain because the people wanted him to be a king (6:14–15). Then, the walking on the sea discourse (6:16–21) serves to introduce the bread of life (6:27–34), the bread of life (6:35–48) that must be eaten.

Craig S. Keener approaches the story of Jesus' walking on water from a Jewish background, though he introduces various Greek figures who walked on water: "Orieon, a son of Poseidon; Xerxes, who thereby displayed a divine power; Pythagoras; and a Hyperborean magician."[91] Keener accepts that these Greek stories may parallel the Gospel and inform John 6:16–21, but he refutes their influence because these do not include "epiphany stories" as in John.[92] Thus, he suggests this story in John is rooted in a Jewish model which "recognized an epiphany of the one true deity" (Job 9:8 LXX, Ps 77:16–19 LXX, Ps 77:19 [76:20 LXX]).[93] However, the parallels between John 6:16–21 and the Old Testament references are not as clear as Keener suggests. His parallels are as follows:

> Psalm 77:16–19 When the waters saw thee, O God, when the waters saw thee, they were afraid, yea, the deep trembled. 17 The clouds poured out water; the skies gave forth thunder; thy arrows flashed on every side. 18 The crash of thy thunder was in the whirlwind; thy lightnings lighted up the world; the earth trembled and shook. 19 Thy way was through the sea, thy path through the great waters; yet thy footprints were unseen (ἐν τῇ θαλάσσῃ ἡ ὁδός σου καὶ αἱ τρίβοι σου ἐν ὕδασι πολλοῖς καὶ τὰ ἴχνη σου οὐ γνωσθήσονται.).

> Job 9:8 who alone stretched out the heavens, and trampled the waves of the sea (τανύσας τὸν οὐρανὸν μόνος καὶ περιπατῶν ὡς ἐπ' ἐδάφους ἐπὶ θαλάσσης.).

> John 6:16–21 When evening came, his disciples went down to the sea, 17 got into a boat, and started across the sea to Capernaum. It was now dark, and Jesus had not yet come to them. 18 The sea rose because a strong wind was blowing. 19 When they had rowed about three or four miles, they saw Jesus walking on the sea and drawing near to the boat. They were frightened (ἐληλακότες οὖν ὡς σταδίους εἴκοσι πέντε ἢ τριάκοντα θεωροῦσιν τὸν Ἰησοῦν περιπατοῦντα ἐπὶ τῆς θαλάσσης καὶ ἐγγὺς τοῦ πλοίου γινόμενον, καὶ ἐφοβήθησαν.). 20 but he said to them, "It is I; do not be afraid" (ὁ δὲ λέγει αὐτοῖς·ἐγώ εἰμι· μὴ φοβεῖσθε.).21 Then

---

91. Keener, *Gospel of John*, 672.
92. Keener, *Gospel of John*, 672.
93. Keener, *Gospel of John*, 673.

they were glad to take him into the boat, and immediately the boat was at the land to which they were going.

Although all three references include "θαλάσσης" and an ephipany of the deity, the purpose of the ephipany and key terms are different between John and the verses from the Old Testament. In particular, while the author of Job and Psalms emphasizes the greatness of God's work over the world, the author of John focuses on Jesus' power which removes fear through using ἐγώ εἰμι.[94] Job does not include any kind of "fear" or "frighten," though it does include περιπατῶν. Psalms 77 includes ἐφοβήθησαν καὶ ἐταράχθησαν (77:16), but no reference of περιπατῶν. Instead, Jesus' walking on water reminds one of Dionysus's voyage on the water. Even though the Homeric Hymn does not include θαλάσης and περιπατέω, it parallels Jesus' walking on water. Jesus says to the disciples, ἐγώ εἰμι μὴ φοβεῖσθε (It is I; do not be afraid) as Dionysus said, θάρσει. . . εἰμι δ' ἐγώ Διόνυσος ἐρίβρομος (take courage. . .I am loud-crying Dionysus.)[95] These verses parallel each other in some points. First, the followers of Jesus are frightened by the storm, and the sailors and a helmsman are frightened by the miraculous work of Dionysus. Second, both heroes reveal their identities with the phrase ἐγώ εἰμι to comfort their followers. As I noted earlier, the Old Testament model misses these important elements. Therefore, the Dionysiac image seems to appear in Jesus' walking on the water, which naturally connects the following Eucharist discourse (6:51–59) with the image of the Dionysus cult.

The Dionysiac Motif in John 15:1–11

The connection between Jesus and wine appears in John 15:1–11. Jesus characterizes himself as a vine (John 15:1). The Greek verse, Ἐγώ εἰμι ἡ ἄμπελος ἡ ἀληθινὴ ("I am the true vine") resounds Dionysus's remark in Homer's writing εἰμι δ' ἐγώ Διόνυσος ἐρίβρομος ("take courage . . . I am loud-crying Dionysus").[96] Observing that a vine signifies Dionysus, one may conclude that Jesus identified himself with Dionysus in John 15:1.[97] James George Frazer states that the "vine with its clusters" is the most noticeable feature of "the manifestation of Dionysus" and Dionysus is indeed a god of trees.[98] As I mentioned earlier in the discussion of Jesus' wine miracle, the perfect joy

94. See Meier, *Marginal Jew*, 914.
95. Homer, "VII to Dionysus," 433.
96. Homer, "VII to Dionysus," 433.
97. Seaford, *Dionysos*, 122.
98. Frazer, *New Golden Bough*, 351.

that Jesus gives to his followers is mentioned in 15:11; he says, "These things I have spoken to you, that my joy may be in you, and that your joy may be full." The characteristic of wine is naturally connected to joy. As the wine god, Dionysus removes all agony of his followers and liberates humans from all bondages so that he creates joyfulness. Therefore, in the *Orphic Hymns*, he is also called "Joyous Dionysos" (Διωνύσου πολυγνθοῦς).[99] What Jesus says "I am true vine" reverberates "I am true Dionysus."

In 15:1–16, the typical Dionysiac theme of "union with God" most frequently appears in the Bible. Here, the similar thematic phrase of ὁ μένων ἐν ἐμοὶ κἀγὼ ἐν αὐτῷ in 6:56 is positively repeated through using the vine tree metaphor:[100]

> 4 Abide in me, and I in you. As the branch cannot bear fruit by itself, unless it abides in the vine, neither can you, unless you abide in me. 5 I am the vine, you are the branches. He who abides in me, and I in him, he it is that bears much fruit, for apart from me you can do nothing. 6 If a man does not abide in me, he is cast forth as a branch and withers; and the branches are gathered, thrown into the fire and burned. 7 If you abide in me, and my words abide in you, ask whatever you will, and it shall be done for you. 8 By this my Father is glorified, that you bear much fruit, and so prove to be my disciples. 9 As the Father has loved me, so have I loved you; abide in my love. 10 If you keep my commandments, you will abide in my love, just as I have kept my Father's commandments and abide in his love . . . 16 You did not choose me, but I chose you and appointed you that you should go and bear fruit and that your fruit should abide; so that whatever you ask the Father in my name, he may give it to you. (John 15:4–16)

Just as Jesus keeps God's commandments and abides in God, his followers must observe the same pattern as Jesus. Just as God and Jesus are one, Jesus' disciples and Jesus must be one.[101] In John 15:4–11, Wilbert Howard and Arthur Gossip acknowledge that "The allegory of the vine and the branches is the most complete expression of the mystical union between Christ and

---

99. In the *Orphic Hymns* "To Semele" (line 3) in Athanassakis, trans., *Orphic Hymns*, 61.

100. Howard and Gossip, "St. John," 573.

101. Indeed, Jesus was God from the beginning (1:1) and he is God's begotten son, who is in the bosom of God (1:18). Thus, God and Jesus are inseparable; they are one.

the Christian in the Gospel."[102] They relate John 6:52-59 to 15:4-11 by symbolizing "constant union with Christ."[103]

THE INFLUENCE OF THE DIONYSUS CULT ON JOHN CHAPTER 6

I have discussed that the image of Dionysus is abundant in the Gospel of John. Notably, John 6:51-59 is the important evidence of the Dionysian influence on the Johannine Eucharist. However, like other mystery religions in the Greco-Roman period, the Dionysian ritual was veiled because of its secrecy. Many ancient writings describe its ritual in a fragmented way. Many of them focus more on Dionysus himself rather than his ritual. All evidence, however, witnesses that drinking wine and eating raw flesh with blood are the most unique elements of the Dionysian ritual. Unlike the eucharistic words of Jesus in the Synoptics, John's Jesus attests that "eating his flesh and drinking his blood" is the condition for having eternal life. As I mentioned in the dialogue between Dionysus and the shepherd, the wine itself signifies the blood of the grape [Dionysus]. Therefore, John's Jesus is speaking of the common elements of the ritual of the Dionysus cult: eating flesh and drinking blood.

Eating Flesh and Drinking Blood

The situation of Jesus' remarks is quite dramatic. When his disciples and the people searched for him, Jesus knew that they looked only for the loaves (John 6:25-26). The multitude knew that their ancestors ate the manna, bread from heaven (John 6:31). Jesus said to them, "I am the bread of life," while the Jews murmured at Jesus and disbelieved him (John 6:35-41). Jesus said, "I am the living bread which I shall give for the life of the world is my flesh," (John 6:51-52). "How can this man give us his flesh to eat?" (John 6:52). The Jews did not understand. Then, Jesus said again that his flesh and blood were food and drink (John 6:56) as Dionysus insisted that his blood was the true drink.[104] In brief, the questions and dialogue between Jesus and the multitude raised by 6:32-50 are emphatically reiterated in 6:51-59.[105]

102. Howard and Gossip, "St. John," 717.
103. Howard and Gossip, "St. John," 573.
104. Smith, "Wine God," 818.
105. Schnackenburg, *Gospel according to St. John*, 58; Brown says that in 6:51-58, the secondary eucharistic theme "comes to the fore and becomes the exclusive theme"

Greek literature indicates that Dionysus himself likes to eat raw flesh. Richmond Lattimore translates the *Bacchae*'s ὠμοφάγον χάριν (line 140) as "He [Dionysus] delights in the raw flesh"; Arthur Way does it as "for the taste of the feast raw-reeking"; John Sandys regards it as "for the enjoyment of a raw banqueting."[106] One of Orphic Hymns, "To Dionysus," also describes *omophagia* (ὠμοφαγία): "You [Dionysus] take raw flesh" (line 5).[107] Because of eating the raw flesh of Dionysus, Apostolos N. Athanassakis notes that through *omophagia* in the sacramental meals, the worshippers of Dionysus "became one with the god."[108] It is unclear how the Dionysus cult developed the notion of eating the god from eating the flesh. To emphasize the union with the god in the Dionysus ritual, however, the worshipers may connect the raw flesh and Dionysus himself as well as remember the renting death of baby Dionysus by the Titans. The common victim was a bull because Greeks described Dionysus as a bull in many places. Thus, in the Dionysus cult, Dionysus manifests in the form of an animal victim (usually a bull) and shows his torment and death in the sacrifice, then he becomes the sacrificial meal for his worshipers.

As I mentioned earlier, in the Paschal Lamb tradition, blood is not drunk despite its sacrificial use.[109] And Old Testament verses hardly mention that blood can imply wine.[110] In the Old Testament tradition, specifically to eat any kind of blood is strictly forbidden (Lev 3:17; 7:26) and one who eats meat with blood "shall be cut off from his people" (Lev 7:27) because blood is the root of life. Leviticus 17:14 clearly indicates, "For [as for the] life of all flesh, its blood is [identified] with its life. Therefore, I said to the sons of Israel, 'You are not to eat the blood of any flesh, for the life of all flesh is its blood; whoever eats it shall be cut off.'" In the Dionysus tradition, on the contrary, to eat raw flesh with dripping blood is a sacred ritual because the

---

in 6:35-50. Brown, *John I-VII*, 284.

106. Euripides, *Euripides V*, 160; Euripides, *Euripides III*, 14-15; Sandys, ed., *Bacchae of Euripides*, 118.

107. Athanassakis, trans., *Orphic Hymns*, 43. Regarding general introduction of the Orphic Hymns, see Athanassakis, trans., *Orphic Hymns*, vii-xiv.

108. Athanassakis, trans., *Orphic Hymns*, 122.

109. See Exod 12:7-23.

110. Edmund Little argues that in the Old Testament wine implies blood based on Genesis 49:11 in which "Judah, in Jacob's testimony, will wash his robes in the 'blood of grape'" and on Deuteronomy 32:14 in which "The Lord gives Israel the blood of the grape to drink." See Little, *Echoes of the Old Testament*, 25. However, both cases metaphorically describe the liquid of grape as the blood of grape. On the contrary, the Old Testament does not mean that wine implies blood. Generally, as Little mentions, wine is described in negative manners in the Old Testament. See Little, *Echoes of the Old Testament*, 26-31.

blood is giving a vital energy and life. Owing to a close connection to wine, Dionysus was called the wine god and wine often regarded as the blood of Dionysus. In the Dionysus cult, therefore, drinking wine is taking the blood of Dionysus, too. Strikingly, in the Synoptics, Jesus also claims that drinking wine signifies drinking his blood (Mark 14:24; Matt 24:28; Luke 22:20); in the Gospel of John, he directly insists drinking his blood for eternal life (6:54). Seaford argues that wine is imagined as the blood of Dionysus and Jesus.[111] He further explains the significance of grape for both:

> The association of the killing of the god with the crushing of the grapes (for wine-making) . . . as an allegorical interpretation of the mystic myth of the dismemberment and return to life of Dionysos, appears in Christian form in Clement's characterization of Jesus as 'the great grape-cluster, the word crushed for our sake' (*Paedagogus* II 19.3), as well as in Romanos' second *Hymn on the Nativity* (sixty century AD), in which Mary responds to her son's prediction of his crucifixion with the words 'O my grapevine (*botrus*), may they not squeeze you out.'[112]

Thus, from the Jewish or Hellenized Jewish background, many of his disciples said, "This is a hard saying; who can listen to it?" (John 6:60). After this statement, the multitude and many disciples rejected Jesus. Owing to their literal understanding of the flesh in 6:53 and 6:63, they fail to comprehend Jesus' sayings. The discussion between Jesus and the multitude (including disciples) shows that there are gradual tensions because of Jesus' identity. If Jesus had been presented as the Passover lamb or the new manna as in the Old Testament, the multitude and the disciples, although the multitude did not believe in Jesus, may not have said "This is a hard saying."

Jesus' Hard Saying in the Context of Dionysus

Jesus made them perplexed by representing himself as Dionysus because Dionysus was a problematic figure for the Jews. Sometimes before the Maccabean revolt in 168 BCE, "Yahweh was identified in Jerusalem with Zeus and Dionysus."[113] It is probably hard to think that the image of Jewish monotheistic God is mixed with Dinoysiac image. However, Morton Smith explains, "Some Jews identified the two deities, others at least chose Dionysus as the *interpretatio graeca* of Yahweh, and yet others contrasted

---

111. Seaford, *Dionysos*, 127.
112. Seaford, *Dionysos*, 127.
113. Smith, "Wine God," 822.

Yahweh—or his logos–as the true vine, with Dionysus, the false one."[114] Since Alexander the Great conquered Palestine, Jews had to adapt Hellenism either willingly or unwillingly. Their political leaders pushed them to follow the wave of Hellenism. Although the Maccabeans and Hasmonians tried to reject the Greek influence in their life, most Jews were already hellenized in their hearts. 2 Maccabees 6:7 reports that the Seleucid king Antiochus IV forced the Jews to honor Dionysus: "And in the day of the king's birth every month they were brought by bitter constraint to eat of the sacrifices; and when the feast of Bacchus was kept, the Jews were compelled to go in procession to Bacchus, carrying ivy" (KJA). Even ardent Jews who detested Greek customs unconsciously followed the way of Hellenism. The story in 2 Maccabees 10:1–10 shows that after Maccabeus and his company recover the temple and cleanse its altar, they celebrate the feast of the tabernacles with *thyrsoi* (θύρσοι).[115] Particularly, the description of 10:7 reminds one of procession of the maenads and satyrs carrying *thyrsoi*: "Therefore they bare branches (θύρσους) and fair boughs, and palms also, and sang psalms unto him [God] that had given them good success in cleansing his place" (KJA).[116] One may recognize that the term *thyrsos* (θύρσος) is specially used as the famous Bacchic wand "wreathed in ivy and vine–leaves with a pine–cone at the top."[117] Third Maccabees 2:27–30 describes the Dionysus cult:

> He [Philopator] proposed to inflict public disgrace upon the Jewish community, and he set up a stone on the tower in the courtyard with this inscription: "None of those who do not sacrifice shall enter their sanctuaries, and all Jews shall be subjected to a registration involving poll tax and to the status of slaves. Those who object to this are to be taken by force and put to death; those who are registered are also to be branded on their bodies by fire with the ivy-leaf symbol of Dionysus, and they shall also be reduced to their former limited status." In order that he might not appear to be an enemy to all, he inscribed below: "But if any of them prefer to join those who have been initiated into the mysteries, they shall have equal citizenship with the Alexandrians."

Although Philopator persecutes the Jewish community by forcing Jews to accept the initiation of the Dionysus cult, according to Weaver, "the

---

114. Smith, "Wine God," 824.

115. See Seaford, *Dionysos*, 121.

116. 2 Maccabees 10:7 reads, διὸ θύρσους καὶ κλάδους ὡραίους ἔτι δὲ καὶ φοίνικας ἔχοντες ὕμνους ἀνέφερον τῷ εὐοδώσαντι καθαρισθῆναι τὸν ἑαυτοῦ τόπον.

117. Liddell, *Greek-English Lexicon*, 372; Kerényi, *Dionysos*, 169.

plotline of 3 Maccabees bears a striking resemblance to the Dionysian resistance myths."[118] Judith also celebrates with *thyrsoi* (θύρσοι) after she kills her enemy, and the Jewish women dance for her victory (Jud 15:12).

In John 6:63–70, Jesus' hard saying which is related to the Dionysus cult causes many multitudes to leave Jesus. The identification of Jesus was an important factor that caused Jesus to be put to death, because the problematic figure of Jesus made people confused. For instance, as Jesus called God his own father and made himself equal with God the Father, people tried to kill Jesus (John 5:18). Brant argues this ambiguous identity of Greek heroes in the Greek tragic drama, and then compares it with that of Jesus in the Gospel of John.[119] She presents compelling comparison between John's Jesus and the Greek heroes:

> The Greek tragedians take the theatrical necessity of having characters identify themselves and each other and turn it into a feature of the plot whereby one character seeks to assert his or her own identity and others dispute it or puzzle over who that person really is. Who is a friend and who is an enemy? Who is a stranger and who is kin? Many plays end with realignment or recognition of friendships and relationships in the aftermath of *pathos* . . . [Likewise] Jesus' assertion of his identity alienates him from his society: he claims the power to name himself, and he rejects the ability of others to name him. His assertions render his identity ambiguous rather than known. Other characters take his self-assertions to be the sort of hubris that renders him God's rival, and like other tragic heroes who are lifted up too high to live among humankind, Jesus must die. Death and suffering are the great levelers of heroes and ordinary people by which *communitas* is reestablished.[120]

According to Morton Smith's argument, some Jews believed that Yahweh could be Dionysus, though some Jews rejected it.[121] In John's Gospel, many Jews could not accept Jesus as either Dionysus or God because Jesus was thought of as a mere man, the son of Joseph (6:42), who even could not be weighed with other Greek deities and prophets. Indeed, they were confident that Jesus was the son of Joseph in Galilee from where even the Jewish prophet could not rise in John 7:52, saying that "Are you from Galilee too? Search and you will see that no prophet is to rise from Galilee."

---

118. Weaver, *Plots of Epiphany*, 83.
119. Brant, *Dialogue and Drama*, 168–69.
120. Brant, *Dialogue and Drama*, 168–69.
121. Smith, "Wine God," 824.

Furthermore, Jews do not believe that Jesus is the Son of God, though they acknowledge that there are many sons of Zeus (God) in their world. According to dialogues between Jews and Pilate in John 19:7, Jews want Jesus to be crucified because Jesus claims himself as the Son of God: "The Jews answered him [Pilate], 'We have a law, and by that law he ought to die, because he has made himself the Son of God.'" As I argued earlier, in the Greek tradition, the sons of the god are famous heroes. Discussing Jesus as a hero, Brant states that "Whereas the Jesus of the Synoptic Gospels talks about the kingdom of heaven, the Johannine Jesus talks about himself."[122] In John 6:51–70, Jesus is talking about himself in the image of Dionysus and is presenting the eucharistic words in the setting of the Dionysus cult.

Plutarch describes that the Jews maintain a "connection with Dionysus when they keep the Sabbath by inviting each other to drink and to enjoy wine."[123] That Palestine was famous as "a grape growing country" supports why the Jews related Yahweh and Sabbath with wine.[124] According to Plutarch, the Jews hesitated to use honey which could spoil the wine in their religious services.[125] However, except for the twelve disciples, it was hard for the Jews to understand that Jesus was a new Dionysus as the revelation of Yahweh (6:68). Thus, John's Jesus tries to acquire the same authority of Dionysus through the imitation of the Dionysus cult. So Jesus identifies himself with Dionysus in John 6:51–59. Jesus reveals that he and the Father have a special relationship using the son and father relationship and equaling himself to God just as Dionysus has son and father relationship with Zeus (6:56–57). Through the lens of the Dionysus cult, therefore, Jesus' remarks become clear in John 6. Jesus' blood and flesh can be understood in light of the Dionysus cult. In other words, John's community emphasizes Jesus' power and divinity using the parallel of the Dionysus cult. While Dionysus is symbolized as a bull and wine, Jesus is symbolized as the bread of life and wine which represent Jesus' flesh and blood. For both traditions, wine represents the blood. John largely accepts the whole concept of the Dionysus cult, and he creatively modifies and changes it for his community. For instance, in the ritual of the Eucharist, John's community takes the bread instead of the flesh of the bull so that it can avoid the people's misunderstanding of the Eucharist as cannibalism. Although John 6:51–59 describes the Eucharist in cannibalistic language, it alludes to bread and wine in the ritual. In the Johannine Eucharist, the actual bread represents Jesus' flesh and wine Jesus'

---

122. Brant, *Dialogue and Drama*, 168 and 175–75.
123. Plutarch, "Table-Talk IV," 365.
124. Smith, "Wine God," 824.
125. Plutarch, "Table-Talk IV," 367.

blood. One knows that the bread signifies Jesus' body in the Synoptics and Paul's writings. This difference shows that John's Gospel has more affinity with the Dionysus cult than that of the Synoptics. Bultmann correctly states that "the use of σάρξ and αἷμα in Jn. 6:51b–58 instead of σῶμα and αἷμα to refer to the elements clearly agrees with the Syrian usage."[126] Philip K. Hitti argues that "immigrants from Syria introduced into Greece the alphabet, the art of mining and the worship of Dionysus."[127] Therefore, the cult of Dionysus was popular in Syria and it was a chief rival for Christianity in the first Century and after that.[128] If one interprets the flesh as a spiritual element or Logos (word), the following passage presents another problem, "It is the spirit that gives life, the flesh is of no avail" (John 6:63b) because the verse evidently differs spirit from flesh. One cannot object that Jesus' flesh and blood have spiritual elements, and humans' flesh does not have spirit in the perspective of the Gospel of John. Humans' flesh cannot inherit the Kingdom of God, but Jesus' flesh gives spirituality when one partakes in the Eucharist. These opposite descriptions of flesh in John 6 also create complicated problems for Jews and some disciples. Therefore, I have tried to avoid the literal interpretation of the flesh, but symbolic interpretation of the flesh. This approach deepens the meaning of the Johannine Eucharist in the perspective of the Dionysian sacrificial meal.[129]

Another aspect of Jesus' hard saying relates to the notion of the Jewish expectation of the messiah. In John 6:54, Jesus attests that he will raise up at the last day (τῇ ἐσχάτῃ ἡμέρᾳ) those who eat his flesh and drink his blood. The future figure of Jesus as a life-giver seems to betray the Jewish expectations for the messiah because the Jews and some disciples expect Jesus to be a current king (6:15). Just as Pilate wrote "the King of the Jews" on Jesus' cross (19:19), Jesus was indeed a king of the Jews, but a suffering king. Thus, the difference between the Jewish expectations of the messiah and the Johannine description of the messiah explain why Jesus' saying is hard to the Jews, but not to Jesus' twelve disciples.

---

126. Bultmann, *Gospel of John*, 235, see footnote 3.
127. Hitti, *History of Syria*, 109.
128. Hitti, *History of Syria*, 333.
129. Otherwise, whenever one tries to explain John chapter 6 in the various traditions, one can eventually discover inconsistency between verse 53 and 63. These two understandings of "flesh" in John 6 reveal that John's portrait of Jesus, on the one hand, is docetic, on the other hand, anti-docetic.

The Victorious Messiah and the Suffering Son of God in John 6:51–59

Many times, the Gospel of John describes Jesus as "Christ" or "Messiah."[130] Jesus himself eagerly accepts this title (10:25) and the author writes that the purpose of the Gospel of John is to manifest that "Jesus is the Christ, the Son of God, and that believing you may have life in his name" (20:31). Although Jews in John's Gospel are waiting for the messiah, they do not recognize Jesus as messiah. So they ask hm, "How long will you keep us in suspense? If you are the Christ, tell us plainly" (10:24). This question implies that the Jewish expectation for messiah is different from what Jesus reveals himself to them. Indeed, even though Jesus is the messiah, he is a suffering messiah.[131] Therefore, first, it is necessary to investigate what the pre-Christian expectations of the messiah among Jews are.

Jewish Expectation of the Messiah

In the Gospels, Jews reject belief in Jesus as Christ or Messiah because of their pre-expectation for the messiah. Christians often find that there are tensions between the image of Messiah in the Old Testament and the New Testament. In short, Jesus was not a Messiah for whom Jews had waited. Instead, Jesus appears as a suffering Messiah, though the title Christ or Messiah is important to define Jesus' identity. This image of the suffering messiah is obvious in John's Jesus. In this point, J. H. Charlesworth points out the invalid assumptions that Jewish messianology is closely related to Christian Christology.[132] He mentions that there is no proof to support the claim that "Jews expected the coming of a Messiah," as many Christians have believed.[133] The term "Messiah" does not appear in the Old Testament.[134] Instead, "Messiah" comes from the Hebrew participle *mashiach* meaning "anointed one" who can be a king, a prophet, or a priest.[135] In particular, "the king of Israel" was often described as the anointed one.[136]

---

130. John 1:17, 41; 4:25, 29; 7:31; 9:22; 11:27; 17:3; 20:31.

131. It is questionable that a suffering servant in Isaiah 53:1–12 stands for the Jewish messiah.

132. Charlesworth, "From Messianology to Christology," 6.

133. Charlesworth, "From Messianology to Christology," 5.

134. Charlesworth, "From Messianology to Christology," 11.

135. Cullmann, *Christology*, 113.

136. Cullmann, *Christology*, 113.

In Christian tradition, Deuteronomy 18:15 has inspired the Messiah's coming; The Messiah will become like Moses. It says, "The Lord your God will raise up for you a prophet like me from among you." The Psalmist relates that David and his descendants will rule forever (Ps. 18:50) and the Messiah will come out from the horn of David (Ps. 132:17). The famous messianic verses are Isaiah 9:6–7, which also explain that the Messiah will govern the world on the throne of David. In Isaiah 45:1–5, the unexpected passage about the Messiah is the introduction of Cyrus as God's anointed one, the Messiah. Here, the Hebrew adjective term is exact לִמְשִׁיחוֹ (45:1). Cyrus was a foreigner, however, the writer of Isaiah saw that Cyrus released Israel from the exile and made Israel rebuild the second temple. Thus, the figure of the Messiah is a powerful king who can liberate Israel from the enemies. While the relationship between David and the Messiah projects the future figure of the Messiah, Cyrus does not appear as the future Messiah. J. J. M. Roberts states, "Despite the positive expectations associated with Cyrus, he, like Jeremiah's Nebuchadnezzr, was a contemporary ruler, not an expected figure of the future."[137] Both David and Cyrus reinforce this political and military image of the Messiah, and for the Jewish people, the descendant of David has continued to maintain this image.

Although the pseudepigrapha's most important thoughts include that "God is about to bring an end to all normal history, bring in the promised day, and inaugurate the end of time,"[138] the role of the Messiah is not emphasized in the pseudepigrapha. Among fifty-one, only five writings in the pseudepigrapha have the term "Messiah," "the Anointed one," or "the Christ."[139] The Psalms of Solomon contains the famous passage that says that the role of the Messiah is "to smash the arrogance of sinners like a potter's jar; to shatter all their substance with an iron rod; to destroy the unlawful nation with the word of his mouth" (17: 21–33).[140] Here, the Messiah is not totally described as a bloody warrior; however the writer expects the Messiah to deliver from the profane enemies.[141] Unlike the Old Testament tradition, the notion of the Messiah is generally absent in the literature of Early Judaism.[142]

137. Roberts, "Old Testament's Contribution to Messianic Expectations," 40.
138. Charlesworth, "Concept of the Messiah," 193.
139. Charlesworth, "Concept of the Messiah," 197.
140. Charlesworth, "Concept of the Messiah," 197.
141. Charlesworth, "Concept of the Messiah," 199.
142. Charlesworth indicates, "The noun, term, or title 'the Messiah' appears rarely in the literature of Early Judaism or from roughly 250 BCE to 200 CE. But it is also true that in the whole history of Israel and Pre-Rabbinic Judaism 'the Messiah' appears with unusual frequency and urgency only during this period, especially from the first

In the Targums, the Messiah also appears as a military figure. In the Mishnah, the greatest Rabbi of the time, Akiba named Simon Bar Kokhba, who led a revolt 132–135 CE. as the Messiah.[143] Here, the focus is the contemporary figure of Messiah, as well. According to Jacob Neusner, a renowned Jewish Scholar, "the Messiah as an eschatological figure makes no appearance in the system of the Mishnah."[144] When I carefully investigate 4 Ezra and 2 Baruch, I agree with Charlesworth's descriptions, "Jews did not profess a coherent and normative messianology."[145]

L. H. Schiffman indicates that most documents in the Dead Sea Scrolls do not emphasize the Messiah. For instance, the Zadokite Fragments (Damascus Document) contain the term *māšîah*, but it is referring to the prophets, which is "virtually unequivocal meaning of 'Messiah.'"[146] Among the Megillat HaSerakhim (Rule Scroll), Rule of the Community and Rule of the Congregation show that both David and Davidic descendants do not play an important role as the Messianic figure.[147] Instead, two messiahs, priestly and royal, appear as the messiahs of Aaron and Israel in Rule of the Community 9:11.[148] Moreover, the War Scroll, containing the clear portrait of an eschatological battle, and Pesher Habakkuk do not have any specific messianic figures.[149] Although the Thanksgiving Scroll includes the birth of the Messiah, the focus of the document is "the destruction of the wicked."[150]

Trypho, who lived at Corinth around the early second century, represented how the Hellenic Jews understood the Messiah.[151] He believed that the Messiah must have been glorious. He said that "These and such like Scriptures, sir, compel us to wait for Him who, as Son of man, receives from the Ancient of days the everlasting kingdom. But this so-called Christ of yours was dishonorable and inglorious, so much so that the last curse contained in the law of God fell on him, for he was crucified."[152] If there is a slight expectation for the Messiah in the Dead Sea Scrolls and pseudepigrapha, and the glorious figure of the Messiah in the Old Testament, why does

---

century BCE to 135 CE." Charlesworth, "From Messianology to Christology," 12.

143. Charlesworth, "From Messianology to Christology," 15.
144. Neusner, *Messiah in Context*, 18–19.
145. Charlesworth, "From Messianology to Christology," 35.
146. Schiffman, "Messianic Figures and Ideas," 117.
147. Schiffman, "Messianic Figures and Ideas," 120–21.
148. Riley, *River of God*, 212.
149. Schiffman, "Messianic Figures and Ideas," 123.
150. Schiffman, "Messianic Figures and Ideas," 123.
151. Coxe, ed., *Justin Martyr and Irenaeus*, 194.
152. Coxe, ed., *Justin Martyr and Irenaeus*, 210.

the New Testament describe Jesus as suffering, humble and even the future figure of the Messiah?

Justin Martyr wrote an apologetic letter to a Roman emperor, explaining that Jesus Christ, who was crucified, died, rose again, and ascended into heaven, was nothing different from the sons of Zeus.[153] Justin compared Jesus to one of Zeus' sons such as Asclepius, Hermes, Dionysus, Dioscure, Perseus of Danae, and Bellerophon.[154] The story of the sons of Zeus was "paradigms for the early church in its understanding of Jesus."[155] While the notion of the suffering Messiah does not appear in the Old Testament and the Jewish literature, in Greek tradition, the suffering sons of Zeus were a common observation.[156] Exceptionally, Dionysus stands for the suffering son of the god because of Euripides' *Bacchae* and Orphic characteristics of Dionysus. Justin said, "If somebody objects that he [Jesus] was crucified, this is in common with the sons of Zeus."[157]

Hesiod gives a clue to explain the future figure of the Messiah in *Works and Days* (line 106–201).[158] According to him, the origin of the world began from the Golden Age, and then moved to the Silver Age, the Bronze Age, and to the present Age of Iron. Although his characteristic of the structure is "degeneration," "the heroes are not a degeneration at all."[159] They are a "divine race of hero-men who are called demigods, the generation before our own" (lines 159–160).[160] Therefore Jesus was described as the imitation of one of the Greek heroes in early Christianity. For instance, Tertullian states that Jesus had two fathers, as Hercules did in the birth stories.[161] Because gods and humans "sprang from one source," they could mate (line 108).[162] God mated Mary, and their offspring was Jesus. Similarly, Zeus intercoursed many female mortals, and their offspring were many Greek heroes. Among them, Dionysus's birth story is distinctive for this hero tradition.

The *Odyssey* shows that Achilles went to battle when his best friend Patroclus died, although he knew that he would die there. This is strikingly

---

153. Richardson, ed., *Christian Fathers*, 255.

154. Richardson, ed., *Christian Fathers*, 255.

155. Riley, *One Jesus Many Christs*, 19.

156. Jesus as the suffering servant in Isaiah 53 and the lamb of the Passover in the Old Testament is the understanding of the Post-Easter thoughts.

157. Richardson, ed., *Christian Fathers*, 256.

158. Hesiod, "Works and Days," 10–17.

159. Riley, *One Jesus Many Christs*, 34.

160. Hesiod, "Works and Days," 14–15.

161. Tertullian, *Against Marcion*.

162. Hesiod, "Works and Days," 11.

similar to Jesus' journey to Jerusalem, in spite of knowing of his impending death there. Prometheus endures an eternal suffering by "an eagle to daily eat his liver, which regrew each night" for the sake of humans which reminds that Jesus suffers a great deal, even crucifixion for humans.[163] Riley states that our human generation is the "age of injustice," which needs final divine judgment.[164] The righteous hero will come and judge. "Yet Hesiod in his artistry has given the melded tales both example and hope: the previous race had been that of the righteous heroes, and the one to come a return to the Golden Age."[165] Therefore, the eschatological feature of the Messiah has directly come from the model of the Greek heroes. The writers of the New Testament borrowed this concept of the hero to articulate their Messiah, Jesus Christ. Jesus must have been the best hero of the Greek heroes for them. In John 6:54, the author strikingly avers that eating his flesh and blood is essential for resurrection of the last day: "he who eats my flesh and drinks my blood has eternal life, and I will raise him up at the last day." This view of resurrection implies the future figure of the Messiah. Bultmann also points out that "This of course, is quite different from the Johannine view" because other of John's verses (3:18–21; 5:24; 11:25–27. etc.) insist the present resurrection and life rather than eschatological salvation.[166] Therefore, in John's Gospel, the future and present figure of the Messiah appear. In particular, in 6:51–59, along with the image of the suffering son of God and the future figure of the messiah, the author borrows the image of Dionysus and describes the Johannine Eucharist in light of the hero's sacred meal.

The Suffering Son of God in John 6:51–59

I have discussed the sacrificial death of Jesus of John 6:51–59 in this book in chapter 3. I have argued that to provide his flesh and blood, like a sacrificial animal, Jesus must first endure suffering and die for "the substance of food" of the world (6:51c).[167] The ingestion of Jesus' flesh and blood emphasizes Jesus' torment and death as the necessary steps for the Johannine Eucharist. The Synoptics and Paul's writings focus on the remembrance of Jesus' suffering and death as such they state "This is my body" and "This is my blood." As I have discussed, John's eucharistic words include "flesh" instead of "body," and encourage eating Jesus' flesh and drinking his blood

163. Riley, *River of God*, 186.
164. Riley, *One Jesus Many Christs*, 34.
165. Riley, *One Jesus Many Christs*, 34–35.
166. Bultmann, *Gospel of John*, 236.
167. Webster, *Ingesting Jesus*, 83.

The Dionysus Cult and John's Eucharist   111

instead of taking his body and blood. John emphasizes the special aspect of the Eucharist that his readers can experience Jesus' suffering and even death when they participate in the Eucharist. Indeed, John vividly develops Jesus' passion narrative in chapters 18 and 19, especially in 18:22, 19:1–3, 19:15–18, and 19:28–30:

> 18:22 When he had said this, one of the officers standing by struck Jesus with his hand, saying, "Is that how you answer the high priest?" . . . 19:1 Then Pilate took Jesus and scourged him. 2 And the soldiers plaited a crown of thorns, and put it on his head, and arrayed him in a purple robe; 3 they came up to him, saying, "Hail, King of the Jews!" and struck him with their hands . . . 15 They cried out, "Away with him, away with him, crucify him!" Pilate said to them, "Shall I crucify your King?" The chief priests answered, "We have no king but Caesar." 16 Then he handed him over to them to be crucified. 17 So they took Jesus, and he went out, bearing his own cross, to the place called the place of a skull, which is called in Hebrew Golgotha. 18 There they crucified him, and with him two others, one on either side, and Jesus between them . . . 28 After this Jesus, knowing that all was now finished, said (to fulfil the scripture), "I thirst." 29 A bowl full of vinegar stood there; so they put a sponge full of the vinegar on hyssop and held it to his mouth. 30 When Jesus had received the vinegar, he said, "It is finished"; and he bowed his head and gave up his spirit.

Regarding the above descriptions of Jesus suffering and death, Brant indicates an important observation compared to the Synoptics that "pay little attention to Jesus' body" in the process of his suffering and death.[168] She claims that John concentrates on the "corpus on the cross" as "the signs of suffering that [set] Jesus apart from others."[169] For example:

> He [Jesus] bears his won cross like a "real man." The description of the soldiers casting lots for his clothing is followed immediately by the picture of the women standing near the cross where Jesus hangs naked (19:23–25). Jesus describes the experience of his body when he says, "I am thirsty," and the narrator describes how he drinks sour wine from a hyssop branch, utters his final words, bows his head, and gives up his spirit (19:28–30). The eye continues to linger upon the body when the soldiers come to break his legs and look and the body to see that he is dead

---

168. Brant, *Dialogue and Drama*, 242.
169. Brant, *Dialogue and Drama*, 243.

and when they pierce his cadaver, out of which spews blood and water (19:32–34).[170]

From the perspective of Jewish expectations for the Messiah, the early Christians, especially the Jewish Christians, must not have understood Jesus' suffering, taking insult and miserable death. However, when they put them in relation to Greek heroes, Jesus' suffering was not a difficult matter to understand; instead they could rationalize his suffering and death comparing his life with that of other Greek heroes. For John's Gospel, the best model must have been Dionysus because of the legend of his famous suffering by Hera, the Titans, and Pentheus. Dispite being the joyful wine god, Dionysus was indeed the suffering son of the god at the same time. Thus, the author interprets the Johannine Eucharist in light of the Dionysus cult. This Dionysiac approach to the Johannine Eucharist needs to include "eating flesh and drinking blood"; for the purpose of John's writing makes his readers believe that "Jesus is the Christ, the [suffering] Son of God" for life (John 20:31).

Dionysiac Reading of John 6:51–59

From this Dionysiac perspective, one may revisit John 6:51–59, which is the main part of the discourse on the Bread of Life in John 6.[171]

---

170. Brant, *Dialogue and Drama*, 243.

171. Beutler, "Structure of John 6," 122. Beutler states that the Bread of Life discourse framed verses 6:22–59 with "the double narrative of vv. 1–15, 16–21" and "the two sections about the decision of faith in vv. 60–65, 66–71."

The Dionysus Cult and John's Eucharist   113

51 ἐγώ εἰμι ὁ ἄρτος ὁ ζῶν ὁ ἐκ τοῦ οὐρανοῦ καταβάς· ἐάν τις φάγῃ ἐκ τούτου τοῦ ἄρτου ζήσει εἰς τὸν αἰῶνα, καὶ ὁ ἄρτος δὲ ὃν ἐγὼ δώσω ἡ σάρξ μού ἐστιν ὑπὲρ τῆς τοῦ κόσμου ζωῆς. 52 Ἐμάχοντο οὖν πρὸς ἀλλήλους οἱ Ἰουδαῖοι λέγοντες· πῶς δύναται οὗτος ἡμῖν δοῦναι τὴν σάρκα [αὐτοῦ] φαγεῖν; 53 εἶπεν οὖν αὐτοῖς ὁ Ἰησοῦς· ἀμὴν ἀμὴν λέγω ὑμῖν, ἐὰν μὴ φάγητε τὴν σάρκα τοῦ υἱοῦ τοῦ ἀνθρώπου καὶ πίητε αὐτοῦ τὸ αἷμα, οὐκ ἔχετε ζωὴν ἐν ἑαυτοῖς. 54 ὁ τρώγων μου τὴν σάρκα καὶ πίνων μου τὸ αἷμα ἔχει ζωὴν αἰώνιον, κἀγὼ ἀναστήσω αὐτὸν τῇ ἐσχάτῃ ἡμέρᾳ. 55 ἡ γὰρ σάρξ μου ἀληθής ἐστιν βρῶσις, καὶ τὸ αἷμά μου ἀληθής ἐστιν πόσις. 56 τρώγων μου τὴν σάρκα καὶ πίνων μου τὸ αἷμα ἐν ἐμοὶ μένει κἀγὼ ἐν αὐτῷ. 57 καθὼς ἀπέστειλέν με ὁ ζῶν πατὴρ κἀγὼ ζῶ διὰ τὸν πατέρα, καὶ ὁ τρώγων με κἀκεῖνος ζήσει δι᾽ ἐμέ. 58 οὗτός ἐστιν ὁ ἄρτος ὁ ἐξ οὐρανοῦ καταβάς, οὐ καθὼς ἔφαγον οἱ πατέρες καὶ ἀπέθανον· ὁ τρώγων τοῦτον τὸν ἄρτον ζήσει εἰς τὸν αἰῶνα. 59 Ταῦτα εἶπεν ἐν συναγωγῇ διδάσκων ἐν Καφαρναούμ.	51 "I am the living bread which came down from heaven; if any one eats of this bread, he will live for ever; and the bread which I shall give for the life of the world is my flesh." 52 The Jews then disputed among themselves, saying, "How can this man give us his flesh to eat?" 53 So Jesus said to them, "Truly, truly, I say to you, unless you eat the flesh of the Son of man and drink his blood, you have no life in you; 54 he who eats my flesh and drinks my blood has eternal life, and I will raise him up at the last day. 55 For my flesh is food indeed, and my blood is drink indeed. 56 He who eats my flesh and drinks my blood abides in me, and I in him. 57 As the living Father sent me, and I live because of the Father, so he who eats me will live because of me. 58 This is the bread which came down from heaven, not such as the fathers ate and died; he who eats this bread will live for ever." 59 This he said in the synagogue, as he taught at Capernaum.

Verse 51 ἐγώ εἰμι ὁ ἄρτος ὁ ζῶν ὁ ἐκ τοῦ οὐρανοῦ καταβάς· ἐάν τις φάγῃ ἐκ τούτου τοῦ ἄρτου ζήσει εἰς τὸν αἰῶνα, καὶ ὁ ἄρτος δὲ ὃν ἐγὼ δώσω ἡ σάρξ μού ἐστιν ὑπὲρ τῆς τοῦ κόσμου ζωῆς. In the first part of verse 6:51, Jesus seems to identify himself as manna from heaven, but he declares that ἐγώ εἰμι ὁ ἄρτος ὁ ζῶν. Marcus Dods points out that Jesus reveals himself "to be not 'the bread of life,' but 'ὁ ἄρτος ὁ ζῶν' 'the living bread.'"[172] This living bread connotes the living flesh in 51c. While the manna itself is not living and can not give life, Jesus himself is the living bread and can impart life.[173] Actually, while the manna that the forefathers ate never imparted eternal life, Jesus insists that he is the Bread of Life in 6:48 (ἐγώ εἰμι ὁ ἄρτος τῆς ὁ ζωῆς), which essentially differentiates the manna and Jesus himself. The only thing in common is that both the manna and Jesus came down from heaven (6:31 and 6:51).[174] The phrase ὁ ἐκ τοῦ οὐρανοῦ καταβάς alludes to Jesus'

---

172. Dods, "Gospel of St. John," 757.
173. Dods, "Gospel of St. John," 757.
174. "The aroist here may be compared with the present 'comes down' in vs. 50; we saw the same variation concerning 'gives' and 'has given' in vss. 37, 39." Brown,

incarnation, in which Jesus came to the world in human flesh.[175] Although Jesus made a great quantity of bread using two barley loaves and fed the multitude, that bread was only food that spoils (βρῶσιν τὴν ἀπολλυμένην).[176] Likewise, God gave manna and fed the Israelite people in the desert, but the manna never gave eternal life. Up to this point, the author of John uses two images of the bread (temporal and eternal; the manna and the Bread of Life) in order to present Jesus as "the living bread" in flesh.[177] Thus, by presenting himself as "the living bread," Jesus relates that the bread (ἄρτος) is his flesh (σάρξ), rather than his body. For this reason, accepting the significant difference between John's Eucharist and the Synoptics's, Brown attempts to solve this problem by stating:

> However, there is really no Hebrew or Aramaic word for "body," as we understand the term; and many scholars maintain that at the Last Supper what Jesus actually said was the Aramaic equivalent of "This is my flesh" ... It may be, then, that in this respect John is the closest of the Gospels to the original eucharistic language of Jesus. That John vi 51 resembles a eucharistic formula was noticed in early times, for both the OL and Syr. Witnesses read for this verse: "This bread which I shall give is my *body* for the life of the world."[178]

Brown's argument importantly pays attention to Jesus' original saying that is "This is my flesh" rather than "This is my body" owing to the lack of an equivalent word for "body" in Hebrew and Aramaic. This point suggests that "This is my body" originates from "This is my flesh," which means that John's Eucharist may contain a more original form of the Christian Eucharist, at least in the formula, "This is my flesh." Despite some textual witnesses' support for "my body" in 6:51, the majority of witnesses still strongly support for "my flesh."[179] In the other New Testament books, although σάρξ often means "the body itself" (Eph 5:29; Col 2:1; 5; 1 Cor 5:5; and 2 Cor 7:1), in John 6:51–59, it signifies the "atoning sacrifice" of Jesus.[180] For this

---

John I–VII, 282.

175. Brown indicates that καταβάς includes the incarnation. Brown, *John I–VII*, 282.

176. Dods, "Gospel of St. John," 757; in addition, the multiplied bread does not come from heaven.

177. "The evangelist may also be influencecd by a desire to distinguish the symbolic eating of the heavenly bread (φαγεῖν ἐκ, 51b) from real sacramental eating" (Schnackenburg, *Gospel according to St. John*, 62).

178. Brown, *John I–VII*, 285.

179. The *Novum Testamentum Graece* (both 25th and 27th edition) does not accept the textual variants of OL and Syr.

180. Dods, "Gospel of St. John," 757.

purpose, Jesus' flesh contains "the material that covers the bones of a human or animal body."[181] Therefore, the living bread is naturally akin to "raw flesh" in the Dionysiac term *omophagia* (ὠμοφαγία). In 51b, Jesus says that anyone who eats (φάγῃ) the flesh that Jesus will give in the future will live forever; his flesh will be given for "the life of the world" (ὑπὲρ τῆς τοῦ κόσμου ζωῆς). The term φάγῃ and its variant forms appear about 154 times throughout the New Testament.[182] This high frequence of use for this term cannot be specialized in John, but it indicates the universal eating of Jesus' flesh "for the life of the world." Here, Jesus is the living bread in the present, but his flesh is the bread in the future at the same time. Regarding the future aspect of Jesus' flesh, Dods indicates that "The giving of His flesh, a still future giving which is spoken of as a definite act, is, then, most naturally referred [referring] to the death on the cross... ὑπὲρ τῆς τοῦ κόσμου ζωῆς, for the sake of the life of the world ... It is only hinted that somehow the death of Christ is needed for the world's life."[183] Brown also mentions that "the connection between the Eucharist and the death of Jesus may be hinted at in John."[184] However, Jesus' statement only perplexes the crowd in the next verse.

Verse 52: Ἐμάχοντο οὖν πρὸς ἀλλήλους οἱ Ἰουδαῖοι λέγοντες· πῶς δύναται οὗτος ἡμῖν δοῦναι τὴν σάρκα [αὐτοῦ] φαγεῖν; Verse 52 begins with the striking expression, "The Jews then disputed among themselves," for μάχομαι means "to fight" (Act 7:26), "to be quarrelsome" (2 Tim 2:24), and "dispute" (John 6:52 and Jas 4:2). This expression reminds one of the multitude's "murmuring" of 6:41 and of Israel people's "arguing" with Moses (Exod 17:2; Num 20:3).[185] Relating this verse to "the event in the wilderness," Rudolf Schnackenburg states that the Jews rebel against God "in unbelief" by "murmuring and arguing among themselves about" Jesus.[186] Thus, for Schnackenburg, the Jews' disputes are not caused by "the fact the consumption of the blood involved in eating (living) 'flesh' was forbidden to the Jews and abhorrent to them (cf. Gen 9:4; Lev 3:17; Dt 12:23)," but

181. Bauer, *Greek-English Lexicon*, 914–16.

182. Matt 6:25, 31; 9:11; 11:18–19; 12:1, 4; 14:16, 20–21; 15:2, 20, 27, 32, 37–38; 24:49; 25:35, 42; 26:17, 21, 26; Mark 1:6; 2:16, 26; 3:20; 5:43; 6:31, 36–37, 42, 44; 7:2ff, 28; 8:1–2, 8; 11:14; 14:12, 14, 18, 22; Luke 4:2; 5:30, 33; 6:1, 4; 7:33–34, 36; 8:55; 9:13, 17; 10:7–8; 12:19, 22, 29, 45; 13:26; 14:1, 15; 15:16, 23; 17:8, 27–28; 22:8, 11, 15–16; 24:43; John 4:31ff; 6:5, 23, 26, 31, 49ff, 58; 18:28; Acts 9:9; 10:13–14; 11:7; 23:12, 21; 27:35; Rom 14:2–3, 6, 20–21, 23; 1 Cor 8:7–8, 10, 13; 9:4, 7, 13; 10:3, 7, 18, 25, 27–28, 31; 11:20ff, 26ff, 33–34; 15:32; 2 Thess 3:8, 10, 12; Heb 10:27; 13:10; Jas 5:3; Rev 2:7, 14, 20; 10:10; 17:16; 19:18.

183. Dods, "Gospel of St. John," 757.

184. Brown, *John I-VII*, 282, refers to Schnackenburg, *Gospel according to St. John*, 68.

185. Schnackenburg, *Gospel according to St. John*, 60.

186. Schnackenburg, *Gospel according to St. John*, 60.

by "their unbelief."[187] However, "πῶς δύναται . . . φαγεῖν;" clearly indicates that their disputes originate from cannibalism (eating Jesus' flesh). In fact, according to J. Albert Harrill, "Cannibalism was one of the prime images of factionalism in ancient Mediterranean culture and is the key image of John 6";[188] and "Jesus' cannibalistic language also provokes a fight" among the Jews (6:52).[189] In addition, the Jews quarrel with each other due to Jesus' remark that recalls again the ambiguous characteristics of Jesus who is presenting himself as Dionysus. The Jews had observed the Dionysiac image of Jesus in 2:1–11, though they were reluctant to accept it. According to Dods, in 6:52, the Jews had controversial views in their judgment of Jesus because "Some impatiently denounced Him [Jesus] as insane: others suggesting that there was truth in His words."[190]

All their disputes focus on the question, πῶς δύναται . . . φαγεῖν; They assume a physical eating of Jesus' flesh.[191] Thus their reaction seems to be reasonable and even natural, for humans do not eat other humans. However, their understanding of Jesus' remark is wrong in that Jesus uses the image of the Dionysiac *omophagia*, emphasizing his sacrificial death in a cannibalistic term that "functions to divide insiders and outsiders" in 6:52–66.[192] Although *omophagia* includes the actual eating of the raw flesh, the author of John vividly implies the idea of *omophagia* only to reinvent the Johannine Eucharist, not the Dionysiac ritual. Due to this Dionysiac influence on the Johannine Eucharist, Christians were accused of cannibalism in the first and second century; for "flesh and blood" imagery is apparent "in reference to continuing Eucharistic meals."[193] While the Synoptics and Paul use "body and blood," John implies "flesh and blood" in the Eucharist, which naturally reinforces the image of cannibalism. Later John Chrystostom, who died in 407 CE, vivaciously described how Jesus gave his flesh to eat: "He [Jesus] hath given to those who desire Him not only to see Him, but even to touch, and eat Him, and fix their teeth in His flesh, and to embrace Him, and satisfy all their love" (*Hom.* XLVI.3).[194] Although Chrystostom emphasizes the spiritual eating of the Son of man, his language signifies the

---

187. Schnackenburg, *Gospel according to St. John*, 60.
188. Harrill, "Cannibalistic Language," 149.
189. Harrill, "Cannibalistic Language," 157.
190. Dods, "Gospel of St. John," 757.
191. Dods, "Gospel of St. John," 757.
192. Harrill, "Cannibalistic Language," 158.
193. McGowan, "Eating People," 413.
194. Chrysostom, *Chrysostom*, 166.

world of cannibalism (*Hom.* XLVII.2).[195] In particular, the vocabulary and idea of the Johannine Eucharist indicate Dionysiac cannibalism. One of the important reasons that Christians were persecuted by pagans was the rumor of cannibalism. Explaining the social aspect of cannibalism rather than the ritual aspect, McGrowan asserts, "If the accusation against Christians had not existed, someone would have had to invent it."[196] Whether the rumor was true or not, pagans saw the Christian Eucharist as cannibalism owing to cannibalistic image in the Gospels, especially in John 6. This negative image of cannibalism actually came from ancient literature before the Gospel writers and Paul described it. For example, Homer negatively describes cannibalism as a barbarically cruel habit. In *Odyssey* 9:289–290, Polyphemus, the Cyclope devours Odyseus's comrades like this:

> So I spoke, but from his pitless heart he made no answer, but sprang up and laid his hands upon my comrades. Two of them together he seized and dashed to the earth like puppies, and their brains flowed forth upon the ground and wetted the earth. Then he cut them limb from limb and made ready his supper, and ate them like a mountain-nurtured lion, leaving nothing— ate the entrails, and the flesh, and the bones and marrow.[197]

Because the early Christian writers were aware of this barbaric cannibalism in the Greco-Roman world, they used it for attacking their pagan rivals. According to Harrill, "Cannibalism thus belongs to ancient polemics against rival forms of government and community self-definition."[198] The *Acts of Andrew*, written around the second century, describes pagan cannibalism vividly for this apologetic purpose:

> They [cannibals] would seize all who came to their city, dig out their eyes, make them drink a drug prepared by sorcery and magic. When forced by them to drink the drug, the victims' hearts became muddled and their minds deranged ... they would eat hay like cattle or sheep ... the executioners came into the prison to carry people away to eat. (chapter 1–3)[199]

Thus, MacDonald indicates that the author of *Acts of Andrew* implied the story of Greek cannibalism in order to "fend off pagan criticism

---

195. Chrysostom, *Chrysostom*, 170.
196. McGowan, "Eating People," 434.
197. Homer, *Odyssey Books 1–12*, 337.
198. Harrill, "Cannibalistic Language," 140.
199. MacDonald, *Acts of Andrew and Matthias*, 71–77.

of Christians as cannibals."²⁰⁰ McGrowan also states that "the Apologists pointed out, Kronos and Zeus are both credited with devouring children" because "both cannibalism and incest are prominent in myths concerning the origins of the Gods."²⁰¹ While arguing the dense and sequential parallels between Mark 14:13–16 and the *Odyssey* (10.100–5 and 109–16), MacDonald shows how Mark modifies negative cannibalism into the Christian interpretation of cannibalism, "eating Jesus' body and blood."²⁰² He points out the parallel of two texts:²⁰³

Odyssey 10.100–105 and 109–116	Mark 14:13–16
Odysseus sent two comrades (plus a herald) to seek out hospitality.	Jesus sent two disciples to seek out a guest room.
They went out and met a woman drawing water to take back to the city.	They went out and met a man carrying water back to the city.
The messengers asked questions and were shown a "high-roofed house."	The messengers asked questions and were shown an "upper room."
An orge "made ready his meal."	The disciples readied the Passover.

MacDonald further explains that "In both accounts the following of the water carriers ends in a cannibalistic feast: the eating of Odysseus's companions and the symbolic eating of Jesus' body and blood."²⁰⁴ This positive cannibalism is highlighted in John 6.

As I have illustrated, Dionysus is described as both raw flesh eater and raw flesh giver. Although the emphasis between the two images is different according to literature, unlike other ancient literature, the story of Dionysus contains two aspects of cannibalism: negative and positive. The description of Dionysus as a raw flesh giver shows that he was torn apart and devoured by the Titans, which is linked to "continuing cultic practice."²⁰⁵ Therefore, the Dionysiac ritual of *omophagia* and *sparagmos* is another name for the ritual of cannibalism in a positive sense. The participants are tearing and eating raw flesh, which signifies eating Dionysus. In this regard, Harrill describes that in John 6:52–66, "The Johannine author revaluated the cultural taboo of cannibalism in positive terms."²⁰⁶ While John 6:51–56 reveals this

200. MacDonald, *Homeric Epics and the Gospel of Mark*, 66.
201. McGowan, "Eating People," 428.
202. MacDonald, *Homeric Epics and the Gospel of Mark*, 120–23.
203. MacDonald, *Homeric Epics and the Gospel of Mark*, 123.
204. MacDonald, *Acts of Andrew*, 123.
205. McGowan, "Eating People," 428; see Burkert, *Homo Necans*, 112 and 123.
206. Harrill, "Cannibalistic Language," 136.

The Dionysus Cult and John's Eucharist   119

Dionysiac cannibalism in Jesus' eucharistic words, the Jews's question, πῶς δύναται... φαγεῖν; in 6:52 implies that the Jews do not understand Jesus as a giver of his flesh and blood. Thus, while cannibalism is striking evidence that Christianity and the Dionysus cult closely share construction of their core ritual, John demonstrates the best model for it.

Verse 53: εἶπεν οὖν αὐτοῖς ὁ Ἰησοῦς· ἀμὴν ἀμὴν λέγω ὑμῖν, ἐὰν μὴ φάγητε τὴν σάρκα τοῦ υἱοῦ τοῦ ἀνθρώπου καὶ πίητε αὐτοῦ τὸ αἷμα, οὐκ ἔχετε ζωὴν ἐν ἑαυτοῖς. Jesus' claim about the flesh is insistent because he asserts that if one does not take flesh *and* blood, one has no life. Jesus is talking about present life by taking his flesh and blood, which emphasizes the present possession of life through participating in the Johannine Eucharist. Thus, while the role of "Son of Man" in 6:53 may be literally present, "Final eschatology is also implied in the reference to eating the flesh of the Son of Man (53) who is an eschatological figure."[207] Definately the figure of the Son of Man is eschatological in 6:27. Schnackenburg informs us that "The three Son of man sayings (6:27, 53, 62) can be given a common interpretation" where the Son of man will give an eternal food, and will return from whence he came. This future figure of the Son of Man is another version of that of Son of God, who is described in the New Testament as the eschatological figure of the Messiah and suffering Messiah at the same time.[208] This eschatological figure is emphasized in 6:54.

The manna, the bread from heaven in the Old Testament, is not accompanied by drinking wine or water. The idea that eating flesh and drinking blood guarantees life does not originate in the Old Testament, but in the Dionysus cult in the Greco-Roman religion. According to Dods' interpretation, Jesus avers that his actual flesh and blood, which represents his real human life, are given for humans because "σάρξ καὶ αἷμα form together one conception and are equivalent to the με of ver. 57."[209] For this verse, Brown states that "the Hebrew idiom 'flesh and blood' means the whole man."[210] If Brown's explanation is right, then John would seem to be advocating cannibalism. σάρξ and αἷμα are emphasized by φάγητε and πίητε for "the 'eating and drinking' can only mean the complete acceptance of Him and union with Him as thus manifested."[211] Like the term φάγητε, πίητε is

---

207. Brown, *John I–VII*, 292.

208. A minor difference between the Son of Man and the Son of God is each figure's inclination to eschatological figure or the suffering figure. The latter more focuses on the suffering messiah.

209. Dods, "Gospel of St. John," 758.

210. Brown, *John I–VII*, 282.

211. Dods, "Gospel of St. John," 758; see also Schnackenburg, *Gospel according to St. John*, 62.

frequently used in the New Testament.²¹² However, both terms do not come with σάρξ and αἷμα in which they indicate to eat flesh and to drink blood except for John 6:51-58. Regarding John's shocking expressions, Schnackenburg points out: "For Christian hearers there could be no doubt of the reference to the eucharistic meal. But why the sharp wording with a negative conditional sentence, making participation in the Eucharist an essential condition for the possession of life? Probably the evangelist is attacking a gnostic or docetic group within his community which rejected the reception of the Eucharist."²¹³

Schnackenburg does not consider the Dionysiac influence on this verse, but he tries to explain why John uses the term "flesh" in the Eucharist. He supposes that the Johannine Eucharist functions "as a weapon against any docetic dilution of Christology."²¹⁴ His view supports the idea that the Johannine Eucharist (6:51-59) uses "the cannibalistic language"²¹⁵ for an "antidocetic purpose."²¹⁶ Obviously, the ritual of Dionysus is anti-gnostic or anti-docetic because it includes the cannibalistic terms "tearing and eating raw flesh" in its core system.

Verse 54: ὁ τρώγων μου τὴν σάρκα καὶ πίνων μου τὸ αἷμα ἔχει ζωὴν αἰώνιον, κἀγὼ ἀναστήσω αὐτὸν τῇ ἐσχάτῃ ἡμέρᾳ. John uses a unique word, τρώγων, which appears in Matt 24:38, and John 6:54, 56-68, and 13:18 only.²¹⁷ It does not even appear in LXX. The literal meaning of τρώγων is "gnaw," "munch," "nibble," or "eat," which has been used from "the time of Homer for the eating of animals, especially herbivorous animals" and "from the time of Herodotus . . . [for] the eating of men."²¹⁸ Matthew 24:38 also includes the

212. About 54 times of πίητε and its variant forms are found in the New Testament: Matt 6:25, 31; 11:18-19; 20:22-23; 24:38, 49; 26:27, 29, 42; 27:34; Mark 10:38-39; 14:23, 25; 16:18; Luke 1:15; 5:30, 33, 39; 7:33-34; 10:7; 12:19, 29, 45; 13:26; 17:8, 27-28; 22:18, 30; John 4:7, 9-10, 12ff; 6:53-54, 56; 7:37; 18:11; Acts 9:9; 23:12, 21; Rom 14:21; 1 Cor 9:4; 10:4, 7, 21, 31; 11:22, 25ff; 15:32; Heb 6:7; Rev 14:10; 16:6; 18:3.

213. Schnackenburg, *Gospel according to St. John*, 61.

214. Schnackenburg, *Gospel according to St. John*, 68.

215. Harrill, "Cannibalistic Language," 134.

216. Schnelle, *Antidocetic Christology*, 207.

217. Matt 24:38, "For as in those days before the flood they were eating and drinking, marrying and giving in marriage, until the day when Noah entered the ark" (ὡς γὰρ ἦσαν ἐν ταῖς ἡμέραις [ἐκείναις] ταῖς πρὸ τοῦ κατακλυσμοῦ τρώγοντες καὶ πίνοντες, γαμοῦντες καὶ γαμίζοντες, ἄχρι ἧς ἡμέρας εἰσῆλθεν Νῶε εἰς τὴν κιβωτόν); John 13:18, "I am not speaking of you all; I know whom I have chosen; it is that the scripture may be fulfilled, 'He who ate my bread has lifted his heel against me'" (Οὐ περὶ πάντων ὑμῶν λέγω· ἐγὼ οἶδα τίνας ἐξελεξάμην· ἀλλ' ἵνα ἡ γραφὴ πληρωθῇ· ὁ τρώγων μου τὸν ἄρτον ἐπῆρεν ἐπ' ἐμὲ τὴν πτέρναν αὐτοῦ.).

218. Barrett, *St John*, 247; See Bauer, *Greek-English Lexicon*, 1019; Dods, "Gospel of St. John," 758.

The Dionysus Cult and John's Eucharist   121

same phrase "eating and drinking" (τρώγοντες καὶ πίνοντες) in the setting of a marriage meal. In John 13:18, in which Jesus predicts Judas's betrayal by quoting Ps 41:9, the form of τρώγων is the same as in John 6:54–58. John modifies ὁ ἐσθίων of Ps 40:10 (LXX) into ὁ τρώγων.[219] Baur indicates that in John 13:18 ὁ τρώγων μου τὸν ἄρτον is "a symbol of close comradeship," but this phrase also shows a close connection with the eucharistic discouse in 6:51–59.[220] The term τρώγων provides the similar eucharistic setting for John 6:51–59 and 13:1–38. Each reference of τρώγων in the New Teastament appears in the meal setting and it indicates that this verb is importantly used for the Johannine cannibalistic Eucharist, which is closely associated with the Dionysus cult.[221] Indeed, although Paul uses ἐσθίειν in 1 Cor 11:26–27, John never uses this term, but includes φαγεῖν, "the usual supplement of the defective."[222] Both τρώγων and φαγεῖν occur four times in John 6:51–59. Particularly, while appearing six time in the Bible, τρώγων exists five times in the Gospel of John (6:54–58; 13:18), especially four times in 6:54–58. John's special vocabulary hints that John was influenced by a cannibalistic sacrificial meal and its ritual, which 1 Cor 11 and Mark do not share because Mark and 1 Cor 11 place greater emphasis on λαβὼν and ἔκλασεν.[223]

Verse 55: ἡ γὰρ σάρξ μου ἀληθής ἐστιν βρῶσις, καὶ τὸ αἷμά μου ἀληθής ἐστιν πόσις. John also uses ἀληθής βρῶσις and ἀληθής πόσις to explain Jesus' flesh and blood, which have no parallel in the Synoptics or Paul's writings. Investigating the common usage of these words in the New Testament and other Christian literature, Walter Bauer defines βρῶσις as (1) "eating," (2) "consuming," or (3) "food"; and πόσις as (1) "drinking" or (2) "a drink."[224] Observingly, Liddell and Scott define βρῶσις as (1) "meat," (2) "eating," or (3) "corrosion"; for the primary definition of "meat" is naturally related to "flesh."[225] Thus, Jesus' flesh and blood are genuine food (meat) and drink that endure to eternal life, but do not perish (6:27). His flesh and blood confirm a close relationship with the participants. Eating Jesus' flesh is true eating and drinking Jesus' blood is true drinking in order to obtain true life and to become one with Jesus, a notion which is not found in the Synoptics or Paul. Indeed, Jesus' desire to provide his flesh and blood as

219. Psalm 41:9, "Even my bosom friend in whom I trusted, who ate of my bread, has lifted his heel against me."

220. Bauer, *Greek-English Lexicon*, 1019.

221. Riley, *I Was Thought to Be What I Am Not*, 22.

222. Barrett, *St John*, 247.

223. Bauer explains that Jesus uses τρώγων against docetism that tries to spiritualize the Load's Supper. See Bauer, *Greek-English Lexicon*, 1019.

224. Bauer, *Greek-English Lexicon*, 184–85 and 855.

225. Liddell, *Greek-English Lexicon*, 158.

true food (βρῶσις) and drink (πόσις), and thereby save human beings from sin through his sacred suffering and sacrificial death only appears in the Johannine Eucharist. The immortal Greek gods eat special food, "ambrosia" (ἀμβρῶσια) and drink "nectar" (νέκταρ) in Homer's writings because their food must be immortal.[226] Riley indicates that "this food of gods was able to strengthen and preserve humans: it is applied to the dead body of Sarpedon to preserve him for burial (*Il.* 16.670, 680), and given to Achilles to instill in him divine strength" (*Il.* 19.347, 353).[227] Likewise, humans can possess eternal life by eating Jesus' flesh and blood, which are usually represented as bread and wine in the Eucharist.[228] In this regard, the phrase "bread from heaven" (ὁ ἄρτος ὁ ἐξ οὐρανοῦ) in John 6:58 highlights the bread as a special divine food. Justin Martyr also mentions that the Eucharist is food that consists of Jesus' flesh and blood:

> This food we call Eucharist... for forgiveness of sins and for rebirth... handed down to us. For we do not receive these things as common bread or common drink; but as Jesus Christ our Saviour being incarnate by God's word took flesh and blood for our salvation, so also we have been taught that the food consecrated by the word of prayer which comes from him, from which our flesh and blood are nourished by transformation, is the flesh and blood of that incarnate Jesus. (*Apology* 1.66)[229]

Although later, Justin introduces the Synoptic and Pauline traditions of the Eucharist, he notes that the consecrated bread and wine are Jesus' flesh and blood, which also nourish the participants' flesh and blood. Through his profound knowledge of Greek literature and myths, he relates the Eucharist to a Greek regimen such as: what humans eat determines human character. In this respect, a human can be a god if he or she eats the food of the god. In addition, by following a divine regimen, at the least, humans can more easily have communion with the god. This regimen is different from Jewish dietary law in Leviticus in which God emphasizes his holiness through dietary law because a holy God requires his people to be holy. In this context, although humans eat holy food, they can never be like God, and food is not the means through which people commune with God. In the Jewish dietary system, humans and God are separate in their original nature. In

---

226. Riley, *I Was Thought to Be What I Am Not*, 17.

227. Riley, *I Was Thought to Be What I Am Not*, 18.

228. In Homer, *ambrosia* is "the food of the gods and of their steeds" or "ointment" for embaiming and perfume; nectar is "the drink of the gods" or "applied as a preservative against decay." See Autenrieth, *Homeric Dictionary*, 19 and 196.

229. Richardson, ed., *Christian Fathers*, 286.

John 6:53, 54 and 55, Jesus even recommends drinking "blood," which is abominable for the Jewish God. Although Schnackenburg does not include the Dionysiac feature of the Johannine Eucharist in his discussion, he does comment that the most important "sacramental function of the meal," is "to make available the flesh and blood of Jesus as a food which gives life," which is also crucial in the Dionysus cult.[230]

Verse 56: ὁ τρώγων μου τὴν σάρκα καὶ πίνων μου τὸ αἷμα ἐν ἐμοὶ μένει κἀγὼ ἐν αὐτῷ. The author repeats the Dionysiac cannibalistic phrase "He who eats my flesh and drinks my blood." The cannibalistic language also connects "the sense of taste (γεύεσθαι), imaged mostly in depictions of eating and drinking" to the union with God for eternal life.[231] Strikingly, in the cannibalistic terms, the sense of taste or the ingesting metaphor emphasizes immortal life in 6:51–58:[232]

> If any one eats of this bread, he will live for ever . . . Truly, truly, I say to you, unless you eat the flesh of the Son of man and drink his blood, you have no life in you . . . he who eats my flesh and drinks my blood has eternal life, and I will raise him up at the last day . . . He who eats my flesh and drinks my blood abides in me, and I in him . . . he who eats this bread will live for ever.

Later, in John 8:52, the close relationship between taste and eternal life appears in the polemic dialogue with the Jews, describing "Now we know that you have a demon. Abraham died, as did the prophets; and you say, 'If any one keeps my word, he will never taste death' (ἐάν τις τὸν λόγον μου τηρήσῃ, οὐ μὴ γεύσηται θανάτου εἰς τὸν αἰῶνα.)."[233] The Jews modify Jesus' actual words, "he will never *see* death" into "he will never *taste* death" after Jesus says, "Truly, truly, I say to you, if any one keeps my word, he will never see death" (8:51). For this, Dorothy Lee explains that "the two are parallel: sight and taste, vision and gestation, both express, in their own ways access to the

---

230. Schnackenburg, *Gospel according to St. John*, 69.

231. Lee, "Gospel of John and the Five Senses."

232. I have investigated Webster's argument about the "ingesting motif" in chapter 3 above. See Webster, *Ingesting Jesus*. Particularly, she concludes that "the ingesting motif is an effective vehicle for conveying the soteriology of the gospel and ites this expression of soteriology to the Eucharistic tradition" (153).

233. γεύομαι appears in various meanings in the New Testament: "taste," "partake of," "enjoy" in Luke 14:24; John 2:9; Acts 20:11; and Col 2:21; "eat" in Acts 10:10; "come to know," "experience" in Mark 9:1; John 8:52; Heb 2:9; 1 Pet 2:3; "obtain" in Heb 6:4. See Bauer, *Greek-English Lexicon*, 195. In particular, Mark 9:1 describes that "Truly, I say to you, there are some standing here who will not taste death (οὐ μὴ γεύσωνται θανάτου) before they see that the kingdom of God has come with power," which is similar to John 8:52.

deathless life that the Johannine Jesus bestows."[234] Lee's point is reasonable until one sees John's skillful literary art indicating that the Jews who once claimed "How can this man give us his flesh to eat?" (6:52), now sarcastically say how Jesus makes one never taste death. Here, by refusing that Jesus and his words can impart life, the Jews show the same attitude as they did when they did not understand Jesus' eucharistic words of 6:51. While Jesus continues to insist that his flesh is the source of life, the Jews are too stubborn to accept this idea and their unwillingness here later contributes to their willingness to kill Jesus. The author of John shows to the reader that both 6:52 and 8:52 are "eyewitness accounts of events," which depict the Jews' enacted disbelief of Jesus' eucharistic words.[235]

Haenchen argues that verse 6:56 does not mean to partake "the elements of the eucharist," but means the union with Jesus in faith.[236] However, as I have discussed, the entire setting of John 6 comes to focus on the Eucharist, though John does not mention the actual elements of bread and wine as in the Synoptics and Paul's writings. The genuine character of food and drink relates to μένει because Jesus "becomes as truly assimilated to the life of the individual as the nourishing elements in food enter into the substance of the body."[237] Barrett rightly observes the significance of μένει: "μένει is John's most important word. The Father abides in the Son (14.10), the Spirit abides upon Jesus (1.32f.); believers abide in Christ and he in them (6.56; 15.4). There are variations of the same thought: the word of Christ abides in Christians and they in it (5.38; 8.31; 15.7); Christ abides in the love of God and the disciples must abide in the love of Christ (15.9f.)."[238] Brown also indicates that the statement of ἐν ἐμοὶ μένει resembles the description of the true vine in John 15:3–7, which is a "eucharistic symbol."[239] For a human being, a strong communion with Jesus is only possible when one eats Jesus' flesh and drinks his blood (6:56). Therefore, Riley relates John 6:54 and 56 to the Dionysus cult:

> One of the central features of the mysteries of Dionysiac religion was the ritual and symbolic consumption of the flesh and blood of the god: the raw flesh of a young animal was touched to the lips as a reenactment of the eating of the young deity by the

---

234. Lee, "Gospel of John and the Five Senses," 122–23.

235. I borrow this expression, "eyewitness accounts of events" from Gould, "Myth, Memory, and the Chorus: 'Tragic Rationality,'" 108.

236. Haenchen, *John 1*, 296.

237. Dods, "Gospel of St. John," 758.

238. Barrett, *St John*, 247.

239. Brown, *John I–VII*, 283.

Titans. Thus he was celebrated, as one who had survived death and granted immortality, as Lord of Souls. This symbolic act brought union with Dionsys, Dionysus within the celebrant, who granted eternal life. So in the Gospel of Johh, Jesus says of himself (6:54–56): "54 Those who eat my flesh and drink my blood have eternal life . . . 56 Those who eat my flesh and drink my blood abide in me, and I in them."[240]

Verse 57: καθὼς ἀπέστειλέν με ὁ ζῶν πατὴρ κἀγὼ ζῶ διὰ τὸν πατέρα, καὶ ὁ τρώγων με κἀκεῖνος ζήσει δι' ἐμέ. The expression of "the living Father" (ὁ ζῶν πατὴρ), which is unique in the New Testament, is established by "the living bread" (ὁ ἄρτος ὁ ζῶν) in 6:51.[241] The usage of fa,gh| and trw,gwn functions to highlight both phrases, the living Father and the living bread. Dods explains this relationship by stating, "The living Father has sent Christ forth as the bearer of life . . . The Father is the absolute source of life; the Son is the bearer of that life to the world . . . Every one that eateth [eats] Christ will by that connection participate in the life of God."[242] Because Jesus is with God and is the Son of God, his flesh and blood are divine elements, and people can live if they eat them; for Jesus says that "he who eats me will live because of me" (6:57). Brown indicates that "vs. 57 is a most forceful expression of the tremendous claim that Jesus gives *man a share in God's own life*, an expression far more real than the abstract formulation of II Pet I 4."[243] Brown's problem is that he disregards the Greek tradition of the union with the god and the divine characteristics of the Greek hero. Thus, instead of seeing the Dionysiac union with the god, in this verse, he relates "sharing God's life" to the covenant theme in the Synoptics and Jeremiah 24:7 and 31:33.[244]

Verse 58: οὗτός ἐστιν ὁ ἄρτος ὁ ἐξ οὐρανοῦ καταβάς, οὐ καθὼς ἔφαγον οἱ πατέρες καὶ ἀπέθανον· ὁ τρώγων τοῦτον τὸν ἄρτον ζήσει εἰς τὸν αἰῶνα. The antecedent of οὗτός clearly indicates "the flesh of Jesus."[245] The similar expression, "The bread . . . is my flesh" (ὁ ἄρτος . . . ἡ σάρξ μού ἐστιν) in 6:51c reiterates in "my flesh is the bread" (οὗτός ἐστιν ὁ ἄρτος). These expressions are compared to that of the Synoptics and Paul, "This is my body" (τοῦτό ἐστιν τὸ σῶμα μου) in which one can find "no suggestion of

---

240. Riley, *I Was Thought to Be What I Am Not*, 22.

241. Brown, *John I–VII*, 283; Haenchen, *John 1*, 296.

242. Dods, "Gospel of St. John," 758; see also Brown, *John I–VII*, 283.

243. Brown, *John I–VII*, 292; 2 Pet 1:4, "by which he has granted to us his precious and very great promises, that through these you may escape from the corruption that is in the world because of passion, and become partakers of the divine nature."

244. See Brown, *John I–VII*, 293.

245. Brown, *John I–VII*, 284.

cannibalism."²⁴⁶ Schnackenburg claims that "The essence of the eucharistic doctrine and of the whole bread discourse can now be presented" in 6:58.²⁴⁷ Although Jesus is the bread from heaven, like manna, he is also bread which is "something of a different and superior nature to the manna."²⁴⁸ Actually, the bread "such as the fathers ate and died" (58) is totally different from the bread that is Jesus' flesh. This difference is emphasized in the parallelism of two opposite vocabularies: ἔφαγον . . . ἀπέθανον ὁ τρώγων . . . ζήσει. According to Udo Schnelle's explanation, "The antithesis to the ancestors in the desert connects this verse back to v. 49, and the promise of eternal life refers to v. 51b."²⁴⁹ By using two words from 6:49, "your fathers," and 6:51, "live forever," the author clearly contrasts the manna and Jesus' bread (flesh) in order coherently to create the Johannine Eucharist in "a very skilful piece of work."²⁵⁰ By doing so, contrary to some scholars' arguments such as those of Brown, Schnackenburg, and Vollert, the bread from heaven (ὁ ἄρτος ὁ ἐξ οὐρανοῦ) does not imitate the Jewish traditional model such as the manna, the paschal lamb, and Moses' typology. Instead, it refers to the cannibalistic tradition that is common in the Dionysus cult.

Verse 59: Ταῦτα εἶπεν ἐν συναγωγῇ διδάσκων ἐν Καφαρναούμ. John ends with the story of Jesus teaching the Eucharist in the synagogue at Capernaum. John 6:24 already mentions the town of Capernaum, but 6:59 first indicates that the teaching of Jesus was held at this synagogue.²⁵¹ There is some controversy as to whether verse 59 is included in the pericope of the eucharistic words or not. But this verse clearly explains the geographical setting of Jesus' eucharistic discourse. In the Synoptics, Jesus delivers the eucharistic words at night in the upper room; however, John's Jesus speaks his discourses in the daytime in a larger space than that of the Synoptics. The author of John demonstrates that Jesus openly delivers his new teaching in the synagogue, which is the center of Jewish education and worship. Despite his emphasis on the Jewish influence on this discourse, Schnackenburg points out that by teaching in the synagogue, Jesus confronted "the Judaism of his time" in order to reveal his identity as the Son of God.²⁵² Thus, the author of John lets the reader anticipate that Jesus' new teaching will be public and widespread among Jewish Christians as well as Greeks.

---

246. Riley, *I Was Thought to Be What I Am Not*, 19.
247. Schnackenburg, *Gospel according to St. John*, 64.
248. Dods, "Gospel of St. John," 758.
249. Schnelle, *Antidocetic Christology*, 206.
250. Schnackenburg, *Gospel according to St. John*, 65.
251. Schnackenburg, *Gospel according to St. John*, 65.
252. Schnackenburg, *Gospel according to St. John*, 65.

SUMMARY

The cult of Dionysus has challenged the Christian faith because of its parallel ritual and the similarities between the figures of Jesus and Dionysus. Early Church fathers acknowledged these similarities, so they accused Dionysus and his cult of being a diabolic imitation of Christianity. As an antecedent religion, the Dionysiac cult was more popular than Christianity when the Gospel of John was written.[253] Because the notions of the suffering son of God and the resurrection are apparent in the cult of Dionysus, Christianity might have adapted them either consciously or unconsciously. Imitating the *Bacchae*, for example, Gregory of Nazianzus wrote *The Passion of Christ* and Fulgentius wrote *Myths* for apologetic purpose. The New Testament writers might be also aware of the Dionysus cult. The characteristics of Dionysus appear in Jesus' birth story and his unjust suffering at the hand of his enemies. In the *Bacchae* and Acts, as Origen reported through Celsus' words, the followers of the new religion miraculously escape from their enemy's prison. In addition, just as Dionysus escapes from prison with the occurrence of earthquake, thunder, and lightning, Paul and Silas escape from prison as the result of a sudden earthquake (Acts 16:25–26). Saul's conversion/call story (Acts 9:1–19; 22:6–16; and 26:12–18) follows some paterns of Pentheus's resistance to accept Dionysus: both fall to the ground when they meet a divine being accompanied by light, and they are warned not to resist the new religion through a proverbial saying "against the will of the gods." Strikingly, this phrase of Acts 26:14 is not found in other New Testament writings; it is only found in the *Bacchae* 794–795.

This Dionysiac feature mostly appears in John's Jesus who turns water into wine as does Dionysus, and identifies himself as grape vine (John 15:1–11). In the Gospel of John, along with a high Christology (1:1–18), a low Christology also appears, which describes Jesus as the son of Joseph. Like Dionysus, Jesus is challenged because of his origin and his birth. Dionysus and John's Jesus are the miracle workers and also the most human of gods at the same time. John's eucharistic words (6:51–59) and passion narratives (chs. 18–19) show the notion of the innocent suffering of god's son that also appears in the *Bacchae*, but does not appear in the pre-Christian expectations of the Messiah. As John 20:31 describes, the purpose of John's writing is to address that Jesus is the Christ, the suffering Son of God, which indicates that John borrows the image of suffering Dionysus for the sake of the suffering Jesus. In the stories, both heroes are rejected by their closest

---

253. The daily cult of Greco-Roman religion in "street corner shrines and home altars" continued, "even after the Christianization of the Empire." Riley, *I Was Thought to Be What I Am Not*, 12.

family members and relatives. One of the reasons that Jesus and Dionysus face death is the jealousy of their enemies (rulers, Hera, Pentheus, etc.) due to their potential power to attract many people. Thus, the enemies of Jesus and Dionysus often call them mad. However, Dionysus uses the blessing of madness to liberate humans from their bondage and agony, in addition to using wine and dance. Likewise, John's Gospel describes Jesus in the image of a liberator who releases the captives, and sets at liberty those who are oppressed (John 8:32–34).

Jesus' wine miracle in John 2:1–11 is one of the most remarkable Dionysiac images in the Bible. The motif that Jesus turns water into wine does not come from the Jewish tradition, but originates from a typical Dionysiac legend. Hengel's arguments show that Palestinian Judaism and Christianity adapted the wine miracle of the Dionysiac cult under the massive Hellenistic stream. Through this Dionysiac wine miracle and its symbolism, Jesus reveals his glory and makes his disciples believe in him. In particular, this story includes the Dionysiac symbol of perfect joy, which also relates to Jesus' vine sayings. The literary structure and themes in John 4:5–30 and 6:16–59 exhibit the influence of Dionysus as well. The dialogue between Jesus and the Samaritan woman recalls the dialogue between Jesus and the multitude, as well as the dialogue between Dionysus and the shepherd in Morton Smith's argument.[254] Thus, 4:5–30 functions to interpret John 6 in the Dionysiac image. Jesus' walking on the water discourse (6:16–21) reinforces this Dionysiac motif so that it serves to introduce the bread of life discourse (6:35–48) and the eucharistic words (6:51–59). In this aspect, unlike the Synoptics and Paul's eucharistic descriptions, the eucharistic words in John 6:51–59 reflect the Dionysiac influence because it replaces the term "body" with "flesh" and indicates Jesus' flesh and blood is real food for everlasting life. The Dionysiac sacrificial ritual and its purpose, which absorbs the god's power by the eating of raw flesh and blood, explains the meaning of eating Jesus' flesh and drinking his blood in 6:51–59. Indeed, here Jesus' remarks reinforce the Dionysiac rituals of *omophagia* and *sparagmos* in cannibalism. As MacDonald investigated, cannibalism is negatively depicted in ancient literature, especially Homer's *Iliad* 10 and *Acts of Andrew*. In many cases, cannibals are the enemies of the main characters, but in the case of cannibalism in the Dionysus cult, Dionysus is both the raw flesh eater and a victim of cannibalism at the same time, and the two features are not clearly separated in him. In this point, the author of John 6:51–59 revaluates cannibalism in positive terms by imparting life through Jesus' flesh and blood. Thus, Jesus' hard saying is a consequence of (1) cannibalistic elements, (2) ambigious

---

254. Smith, "Wine God," 819.

features of Dionysus and Jesus, (3) the opposite meaning of flesh in 6:53 and 6:63, and (4) the deep chasm between Jewish expectation of the Messiah and the Dionysiac suffering son of the god. In other words, because of the cannibalistic language of John and the syncretistic characteristics of Dionysus for the Jewish people, Jesus' words complicate this issue. As a result, Dionysus was intentionally or unintentionally identified with Yahweh among Jewish people and the culture of Dionysus signified the world of cannibalism. Furthermore, contrary to the divine character of Dionysus, Jesus is the mere son of Joseph from Galilee from whence no prophet is supposed to rise. Thus, that a mere human Jesus is comparing himself with God by using the cannibalistic image of Dionysus causes a problem for the multitude so that they do not accept Jesus' words nor his divinity, and they leave him. Indeed, John portrays Jesus as a better Dionysus by refuting the literal interpretation of the flesh, and instead suggesting the symbolic interpretation of it.

5

Conclusion

I HAVE DISCUSSED THE Johannine Eucharist by focusing on Greco-Roman sacred meals and the Dionysiac cult. After investigating scholars' arguments on the Johannine Eucharist, I have presented the redactional problems of the eucharistic texts of the Synoptics, 1 Cor 11:23–25, and John 6:51–59 in order to trace the history of the eucharistic ideas. To argue my thesis, throughout my book I have applied two methodologies: the history of ideas and literary criticism.

On the one hand, as I discussed in chapter 2, redaction criticism and the history of ideas show that the Johannine Eucharist is somewhat dependent on the Synoptics and 1 Cor 11:23–25 because references to the Eucharist in the New Testament are related to the sacrificial death of Jesus and the sacrificial meal tradition. On the other hand, they also show that the Johannine Eucharist is unique because it replaces "body" with "flesh" and "cup" with "blood," which leads to the discussion of the influence of the Dionysus cult. In John's eucharistic texts specifically, literary criticism reveals how the author of John's Gospel develops the Greco-Roman idea of sacred meals through literary means.

In chapter 3, I have argued that John's feeding stories, which reflect equal banquets among participants, and the Last Supper scene, support the notion that Greco-Roman meal customs are integrated in the Johannine Eucharist by the presence of reclining, giving thanks, praying, and drinking wine. The Greek sacred meal traditions mainly occur in the *thysia* sacrifice, with its emphasis on the powerful union between the god and the worshippers as well as the fellowship among the participants. Eating the animal's body and blood represents ingesting divine power, which does not appear in the Jewish sacrifice.

An investigation of sacred meals and hero traditions in Greco-Roman religion reveals that the Dionysus cult played an important role in many aspects of Greco-Roman religion. Throughout the Greco-Roman world and the early Christian world, diverse features are collected in the characteristics of Dionysus: he was a hero, the ruler of death and resurrection, the suffering son of a god, the wine giver, the god of trees, the mad god, the giver of raw flesh, the eater of raw flesh, a sacrificial bull, a liberator, and the initiator of dance and drama.[1] In particular, as a Greek hero, he possesses both human and divine features. Similarly, John describes Jesus as both logos (1:1) and the Son of Joseph (6:42), which focuses on Jesus' dual origins: human and divine. In the Homeric tradition, Dionysus stands on the edge of heroes and gods. Compared to Achilles, Hector, Odysseus, and other heroes, Dionysus is more divine, while compared to Olympian gods, Dionysus is more human. This explains why Dionysus is the last to join the group of twelve Olympian gods. Because of his two birth stories, dual natures, many forms of mythical masks, and various literary traditions, it is often difficult to conceive the whole picture of Dionysus. Nevertheless, one likely finds a deep influence of the Dionysus cult on the Eucharist of John 6 due to the cannibalistic description of "eating flesh and drinking blood."

In chapter 4, I have discussed how the Dionysus cult provides ample evidence of the sacred meal, which emphasizes the union with the god. The climax of the union with the god happens in the Dionysiac rituals of *omophagia* and *sparagmos*. Unlike other Gospels, John reiterates this union with God. Just as God dwells in Jesus and he dwells in God, Jesus says that he will abide in his followers and they must remain in Jesus in order to bear fruit (John 15:7). Using the Dionysiac cannibalistic image, John's eucharistic words (6:51–59, especially 6:56) highlight the Johannine interpretation of the communion with God. Jesus requires his disciples to abide in him as he does in God. The relationship between God and Jesus is the ultimate model for his disciples. In addition, the grapevine discourse (15:1–11), which implies the union with God, is also closely related to the cult of Dionysus.

Even though Dionysus was a god of foreign origin, he was popular in the Greco-Roman world. In a sense, the different versions of his birth

---

1. "Plutarch comments sardonically that while some supporters welcomed Antony with Bacchic processions hailing him as 'Dionysus,' most of the crowd understood him to be the 'Eater of Raw Flesh' that the hail named him (Plutarch, *Vit. Ant.* 24.4)" in Harrill, "Cannibalistic Language," 140.

story and the various meanings of his name strengthened this popularity. Although the Orphic tradition of Dionysus mentions the persecution and torment of baby Dionysus, Euripides' *Bacchae* describes Dionysus as the unique image of the suffering son of the god, which is also closely related to his nature as a Greek hero. As I argued in chapter 4, that the Dionysiac notion of the suffering son of the god influenced the concept of Jesus' innocent suffering and death as the suffering son of God is indirectly reflected in the Church fathers' accusation that the sons of Zeus were a diabolic imitation of Jesus. This Dionysiac interpretation continues throughout the Gospel of John. For instance, although there are numerous characteristics of Dionysus in Jesus' image in John, the author selects only positive aspects of Dionysus. In contrast, the destructive characteristic of Dionysus in Jesus is described by the opponent of the Johannine Jesus. For instance, the Jews and Jewish authorities call Jesus "mad" and "demon possessed." Just as Dionysus bestowed wine on his worshipers and changed them, so did Jesus show his power and glory through the wine miracle (2:1–11) and the eucharistic words (6:51–59). Just as Dionysus' blood represents wine, Jesus' blood also signifies wine, though the bread and cup disappear in John 6:51–59. In John 2 and 6, the author of John tries to present to the reader that Jesus has equal power to Dionysus. Likewise, flesh represents Dionysus' powerful epiphany, whereas the bread represents Jesus' flesh. In order to avoid accusations of cannibalism, the Christian Eucharist has taken the bread and wine (or cup) to represent Jesus' body and blood, instead of real flesh and blood, though John still contains the Dionysiac influence that appears in the statement "to eat flesh and to drink blood." Thus, if one misses the Dionysus tradition in John 6, one also misses the vivid color of the biblical interpretation in John 6, such that John's Eucharist becomes monochromatic, as are the descriptions of the Eucharist in Paul and the Synoptics. In the Johannine eucharistic words and some Johannine texts, the author presents Jesus as a new, better model of Dionysus to his audience. Therefore, John's Eucharist is more richly understood under the influence of the Dionysus cult so that one can interpret the enigmatic verses in John 6:51–59 in the broader context of the history of religion. In this respect, the Dionysus cult undergirds John's eucharistic discourse in 6:51–59, not eroding John's tradition but reinforcing its theology. Unlike other negative descriptions of cannibalism in ancient literature, Dionysus is described as both an eater of raw flesh and a giver of raw flesh. Through positively reevaluating the negative term of cannibalism, the Johannine author takes the tradition of a raw giver of the Dionysus cult for the Eucharist. Thus, Jesus' hard saying (6:60) is a consequence of this cannibalistic language and ambiguous features of Dionysus. In the Greco-Roman religion, therefore, while the Dionysus cult most shows the cannibalistic and manic ritual of sacred meals, in the New Testament, the Johannine Eucharist demonstrates the best model of the Dionysus cult.

There are several benefits to reading John 6:51–59 from the perspective of the Greco-Roman Sacred meal and the influence of Dionysus on the Christian Eucharist. First, it brings out the emphasis on Jesus' suffering and his death because of the vivid description of Jesus as bloody food. To eat Jesus' flesh and to drink his blood presupposes Jesus' submission to death. Paul and the Synoptics also allude to Jesus' suffering and death in the eucharistic words. However, they seem to delineate them in a disinterested attitude, at a distance from the passion of Jesus. At first, they show the bread and cup to their audience, then, they write that the elements are Jesus' body and blood. In addition, their descriptions are wrapped in the neutralized terms for the passion of Jesus (body, cup, covenant, etc). However, John's description is different from them; for it uses vivid cannibalistic language. John's Jesus does not discuss the bread and cup. Instead, he reveals himself to his audience as the living flesh for the life of the word (6:51). While the Synoptics and Paul describe Jesus' suffering and death through the bread and cup, John does so through Jesus' flesh and blood. In addition, John specifically focuses on Jesus' torment and death using the image of a sacrificial lamb for the sin of the world (1:29).

Second, this reading explains why John consistently emphasizes communion with God throughout the Gospel. This typical motif appears in the statement of 6:56, "He who eats my flesh and drinks my blood abides in me, and I in him" (ὁ τρώγων μου τὴν σάρκα καὶ πίνων μου τὸ αἷμα ἐν ἐμοὶ μένει κἀγὼ ἐν αὐτῷ), which is a crucial element for the union of humans and Jesus Christ. It is not surprising that this motif continues in the grapevine discussion in 15:4–16 where a Dionysiac image emerges. In the Jewish tradition, however, humans do not unite with God by eating flesh and drinking blood. Thus, the Johannine Eucharist will lead Christians to a close relationship with God when they participate in the Eucharist. Furthermore, this reading promotes the unity of Christian community through the Eucharist.

Third, this reading illuminates the deeper meaning of Jesus' flesh by explaining why John omits "body" and replaces it with "flesh" in the eucharistic words (6:51–59). Along with the famous eucharistic phrase "This is my body," "This is my flesh" could be used in the Christian Eucharist in order to emphasize the passion of Christ. Compared to the Jewish expection of the victorious Messiah, it better explains the violent death of Jesus as the suffering Son of God.

Fourth, this reading contributes to understanding the diversity of Christology in the Gospel of John. There are "a dozon or more Christologies" in the Gospel of John.[2] Among them, "Jesus on the model of Dionysus, the Son of God as Son of Zeus" presents "the inclusive Christology."[3] As Nietzsche already implied, Western Christianity oppressed the Dionysiac features (such as madness and emotion), and focused on reason and beauty, characteristics of the god Apollo. Howerver, by seeing Jesus in the Dionysiac tradition, one may better understand the cannibalistic language and mood in the Johannine Eucharist and Jesus' tragic death and resurrection in the broad Greco-Roman concept, which lead the reader to the inclusive religious dimentions.

Fifth, this reading pays attention to the Greco-Roman religion and Greek literature as useful resources for the study of the New Testament. Although the Gospel of John quotes many verses from the Old Testament to explain the fulfillment of scripture, John 6:51–59 seems not to have the Old Testament as its background, but the Dionysus cult of cannibalistic language. The function of the *thysia* sacrifice also contributes to the interpretation of the Johannine Eucharist in the intrinsic value of the Greco-Roman religion and literature. Except for Bultmann, many commentators have tried to interpret John 6:51–59 in the eucharistic discourse from the Jewish perspective. They have not investigated the Dionysiac influence on the Johannine Eucharist, but some of their literary analysis and theological insights are useful for tracing the idea of Dionysiac ritual in the Johannine eucharistic discourse (6:51–59). Thus, my argument does not claim the direct influence of the ancient sources for the Gospel of John that I discussed in chapters 2 and 3; instead, I have explored the literary mimetic flags and the "unit of idea" of each source that appears in John 6:51–59. Therefore, apart from all favoritism for the Jewish paschal interpretation, John 6:51–59 manifests the heritage of the Dionysus cult, though it is modified by John's Greco-Roman tradition as well as by the Jewish background.

Despite uncovering the above advantages of the Dionysus cult and Greco-Roman sacred meal traditions for understanding the Johannine Eucharist, this book has not completely examined the Dionysiac traditions and the sacred meals in the Greco-Roman world due to my limitation to access all Greek literature and religions. In particular, the triumphal return of Dionysus from India would be an important subject to study the future figure of the Messiah in the Johannine Christology; the Orphic influence on the Dionysus cult would be another step to trace the unit of the idea for Christian notions of death and resurrection, though I have briefly sketched these in this study. Although I have not much dealt with the ritual aspects of the Johannine Eucharist in this book, my study includes rich implications for ritual studies.

2. Riley, *I Was Thought to Be What I Am Not*, 22.
3. Riley, *I Was Thought to Be What I Am Not*, 22.

Bibliography

Aeschylus. *The Seven Against Thebes*. Translated by Christopher M. Dawson. Englewood Cliffs, NJ: Prentice-Hall, 1970.

Aland, Kurt. *Synopsis Quattuor Evangeliorum: Locis Parallelis Evangeliorum Apocryphorum et Patrum Adhibaitis*. Stuttgart: Deutsche Bibelgesellschaft, 2005.

Athanassakis, Apostolos N. *The Orphic Hymns: Text, Translation, and Notes*. Texts and Translations 12. Missoula, MT: Scholars, 1977.

Aulén, Gustaf. *Eucharist and Sacrifice*. Translated by Eric H. Wahlstrom. Philadelphia: Muhlenberg, 1958.

Autenrieth, Georg. *A Homeric Dictionary*. Translated by Robert P. Keep. Rev. ed. Norman: University of Oklahoma Press, 1958.

Barrett, C. K. *The Gospel according to St John: An Introduction with Commentary and Notes on the Greek Text*. London: SPCK, 1958.

Barth, Markus. *Rediscovering the Lord's Supper*. Atlanta: John Knox, 1988.

Bauckham, Richard. "Imaginative Literature." In *The Early Christian World*, edited by Philip F. Esler, 791–812. London: Routledge, 2000.

Bauer, Walter. *A Greek-English Lexicon of the New Testament and Other Early Christian Literature*. Translated by William F. Arndt and F. Wilbur Gingrich. 3rd ed. edited by Frederick W. Danker. Chicago: University of Chicago Press, 2000.

Beardslee, William A. *Literary Criticism of the New Testament*. Guides to Biblical Scholarship: New Testament Series. Philadelphia: Fortress, 1969.

Belayche, Nicole. "Sacrifice and Theory of Sacrifice during the 'Pagan Reaction': Julian the Emperor." In *Sacrifice in Religious Experience*, edited by Albert I. Baumgarten, 101–26. Studies in the History of Religions 93. Leiden: Brill, 2002.

Bethune-Baker, J. F. B. *An Introduction to the Early History of Christian Doctrine: To the Time of the Council of Chalcedon*. 7th ed. London: Methuen, 1942.

Beutler, Johannes. "The Structure of John 6." In *Critical Readings of John 6*, edited by R. Alan Culpepper, 115–27. Biblical Interpretation Series 22. Leiden: Brill, 1997.

Bevir, Mark. *The Logic of the History of Ideas*. Cambridge: Cambridge University Press, 1999.

Bonner, Campbell. "A Dionysiac Miracle at Corinth." *American Journal of Archaeology* 33 (1929) 368–75.

Bornkamm, Günther. "Die eucharistische Rede im Johannes-Evangelium." *ZNW* (1956) 161–69.

———. *Paul*. Translated by D. M. G. Stalker. New York: Harper, 1971.
Brandon, S. G. F. "Doctrine of Transubstantiation." In *A Dictionary of Comparative Religion*, edited by S. G. F. Brandon, 622. New York: Scribner, 1970.
———. "Eucharist." In *A Dictionary of Comparative Religion*, edited by S. G. F. Brandon, 269. New York: Scribner, 1970.
Brant, Jo-Ann A. *Dialogue and Drama: Elements of Greek Tragedy in the Fourth Gospel*. Peabody, MA: Hendrickson, 2004.
Brown, Raymond E. *The Gospel according to John I–XII*. AB 29. Garden City, NY: Doubleday, 1966.
Bruce, F. F. *The Acts of the Apostles: The Greek Text with Introduction and Commentary*. 3rd rev. and enl. ed. Grand Rapids: Eerdmans, 1951.
Bultmann, Rudolf. *The Gospel of John: A Commentary*. Translated by G. R. Beasley-Murray, edited by R. W. N. Hoare and J. K. Riches. 1971. Reprint, Johannine Monograph Series. Eugene, OR: Wipf & Stock, 2014.
Burkert, Walter. *Greek Religion*. Translated by John Raffan. Cambridge: Harvard University Press, 1985.
———. *Homo Necans: The Anthropology of Ancient Greek Sacrificial Ritual and Myth*. Translated by Peter Bing. Berkeley: University of California Press, 1983.
Buttrick, George Arthur, ed. *The Acts of the Apostles, The Epistle to the Romans*. IB 9. Nashville: Abingdon, 1954.
Carpenter, Thomas H., and Robert J. Gula. *Mythology: Greek and Roman*. New York: Longman, 1977.
Chadwick, John. *Linear B and Related Scripts*. Reading the Past 1. London: British Museum, 1987.
Charlesworth, James H. "The Concept of the Messiah in the Pseudepigrapha." In *Aufsteig und Niedergang der römischen Welt*, II.19.1: 188–218. Berlin: de Gruyter, 1979.
———. "From Messianology to Christology: Problems and Prospects." In *The Messiah: Developments in Earliest Judaism and Christianity*, edited by James H. Charlesworth, 3–35. Minneapolis: Fortress, 1992.
Chatman, Seymour Benjamin. *A Theory of Meter*. Janua linguarum. Series minor 36. The Hague: Mouton, 1965.
Chilton, Bruce. *The Temple of Jesus: His Sacrificial Program within a Cultural History of Sacrifice*. University Park: Pennsylvania State University, 1992.
Chrysostom, John. *Chrysostom: Homilies on the Gospel of Saint John and the Epistle to the Hebrews*. Vol. 14. 14 vols. 2nd ed. Nicene and Post-Nicene Fathers, edited by Philip Schaff. Peabody, MA: Hendrickson, 1994.
Clement. "Exhortation to the Greeks." In *Clement of Alexandria*, 3–263. Cambridge: Harvard University Press, 1919; reprint, 1982.
Coldstream, J. N. "Hero Cults in the Age of Homer." *Journal of the Hellenic Society* 96 (1976) 8–17.
Coxe, A. Cleveland, ed. *The Apostolic Fathers with Justin Martyr and Irenaeus*. Vol. 1. The Ante-Nicene Fathers: Translations of the Writings of the Fathers down to A.D. 325. Grand Rapids: Eerdmans, 1950.
Creed, John Martin. *The Gospel according to Luke: The Greek Text with Introduction, Notes, Indices*. London: Macmillan, 1930.
Crossan, John Dominic. "It is Written: A Structuralist Analysis of John 6." *Semeia* 26 (1983) 3–21.

Cullmann, Oscar. *The Christology of the New Testament*. Translated by Shirley C. Guthrie and Charles A. M. Hall. Philadelphia: Westminster, 1963.

———. *Early Christian Worship*. Translated by A. Stewart Todd and James B. Torrance. 1953. Reprint, Philadelphia: Westminster, 1978.

Davies, W. D., and Dale C. Allison. *A Critical and Exegetical Commentary on the Gospel according to Saint Matthew*, vol. 3. 3 vols. International Critical Commentary. Edinburgh: T. & T. Clark, 1988.

Dix, Gregory. *The Shape of the Liturgy*. London: Dacre, 1945.

Dodd, Charles H. *The Interpretation of the Fourth Gospel*. Cambridge: Cambridge University Press, 1953.

Dodds, E. R., ed. *Euripides Bacchae*. London: Oxford University Press, 1960.

———. *The Greeks and the Irrational*. Boston: Beacon, 1957.

Dods, Marcus. "The Gospel of St. John." In *The Expositor's Greek Testament: Gospels, St. John*, edited by W. Robertson Nicoll, 1:653–872. Grand Rapids: Eerdmans, 1956.

Dunn, James D. G. "John 6: A Eucharistic Discourse?" *NTS* 17 (1971) 328–38.

Ekroth, Gunnel. "Heroes and Hero-Cults." In *A Companion to Greek Religion*, edited by Daniel Ogden, 100–114. Blackwell Companions to the Ancient World. Malden, MA: Blackwell, 2007.

Eliade, Mircea. *Rites and Symbols of Initiation: the Mysteries of Birth and Rebirth*. Translated by Willard R. Trask. New York: Harper & Row, 1965.

Eliot, T. S. *Points of View*. Edited by John Hayward. London: Faber, 1951.

———. *The Sacred Wood: Essays on Poetry and Criticism*. 2nd ed. London: Methuen, 1928.

Euripides. *Bakkhai*. Edited by Reginald Gibbons and Charles Segal. New York: Oxford University Press, 2000.

———. *Euripides III*. Translated by Arthur S. Way. Vol. III. IV vols. Edited by T. E. Page and W. H. D. Rouse. London: William Heinemann, 1912. Reprint, 1919.

———. *Euripides V*. The Complete Greek Tragedies, edited by David Grene and Richmond Alexander Lattimore. Chicago: The University of Chicago Press, 1959.

Evans, Arthur. *The God of Ecstasy: Sex-Roles and the Madness of Dionysos*. New York: St. Martin's, 1988.

Faraone, Christopher A. "Introduction." In *Masks of Dionysus*, edited by Thomas H. Carpenter and Christopher A. Faraone, 1–12. Ithaca, NY: Cornell University Press, 1993.

Foakes-Jackson, F. J. *Josephus and the Jews: The Religion and History of the Jews as Explained by Flavius Josephus*. New York: Richard R. Smith, 1930.

Frazer, James George. *The New Golden Bough*. New York: Criterion, 1959.

Frye, Northrop. *Anatomy of Criticism: Four Essays*. Princeton: Princeton University Press, 1971.

Genette, Gérard. *Figures III*. Paris: Seuil, 1972.

Gill, David. *Greek Cult Tables*. Harvard Dissertations in Classics. New York: Garland, 1991.

———. "*Trapezomata*: A Neglected Aspect of Greek Sacrifice." *Harvard Theological Review* 67 (1974) 117–37.

Gould, John. "Myth, Memory, and the Chorus: 'Tragic Rationality.'" In *From Myth to Reason?: Studies in the Development of Greek Thought*, edited by Richard Buxton, 107–16. Oxford: Oxford University Press, 1999.

Grassi, Joseph A. "Eating Jesus' Flesh and Drinking His Blood: The Centrality and Meaning of John 6:51–58." *Biblical Theology Bulletin* 17 (1987) 24–30.

Griffiths, Gwyn. "The Great Egyptian Cults of Oecumenical Spiritual Significance." In *Classical Mediterranean Spirituality*, edited by A. H. Armstrong, 39–65. New York: Crossroads, 1986.

Haenchen, Ernst. *John 1: A Commentary on the Gospel of John Chapters 1–6*. Translated by Robert W. Funk, edited by Robert Walter Funk and Ulrich Busse. Hemeneia. Philadelphia: Fortress, 1984.

Hard, Robin. *The Routledge Handbook of Greek Mythology: Based on H. J. Rose's "Handbook of Greek Mythology."* London: Routledge, 2004.

Harrill, J. Albert. "Cannibalistic Language in the Fourth Gospel and Greco-Roman Polemics of Factionalism (John 6:52–66)." *JBL* 127 (2008) 133–58.

Hengel, Martin. "The Interpretation of the Wine Miracle at Cana: John 2:1–11." In *The Glory of Christ in the New Testament: Studies in Christology in Memory of George Bradford Caird*, edited by L. D. Hurst et al., 84–112. Oxford: Clarendon, 1987.

Henrichs, Albert. "'He Has a God in Him': Human and Divine in the Modern Perception of Dionysus." In *Masks of Dionysus*, edited by Thomas H. Carpenter and Christopher A. Faraone, 13–43. Ithaca, NY: Cornell University Press, 1993.

Herodotus. *Herodotus*. Translated by A. D. Godley. Vol. 1. Cambridge: Harvard University Press, 1926. Reprint, 1966.

Hesiod. "Theogony." In *Hesiod; Homeric Hymns; Epic Cycle; Homerica*, edited by Jeffrey Henderson, 78–154. LCL. Cambridge: Harvard University Press, 1936. Reprint, 2000.

———. "Works and Days." In *Hesiod; Homeric Hymns; Epic Cycle; Homerica*, edited by Jeffrey Henderson, 2–65. LCL. Cambridge: Harvard University Press, 1936. Reprint, 2000.

Hitti, Philip Khuri. *History of Syria: Including Lebanon and Palestine*. London: Macmillan, 1951.

Homer. *Homer: Iliad Books 1–12*. Translated by A. T. Murray. Vol. 1. 2nd ed. LCL. Cambridge: Harvard University Press, 1924. Reprint, 2003.

———. *Homer: Odyssey Books 1–12*. Translated by A. T. Murray. Vol. 2. 2nd ed. LCL. Cambridge: Harvard University Press, 1919. Reprint, 2002.

———. "The Homeric Hymn I to Dionysus." In *Hesiod; Homeric Hymns; Epic Cycle; Homerica*, 286–89. LCL. Cambridge: Harvard University Press, 1936. Reprint, 2000.

———. "The Homeric Hymn VII to Dionysus " In *Hesiod; Homeric Hymns; Epic Cycle; Homerica*, 428–32. LCL. Cambridge: Harvard University Press, 1936. Reprint, 2000.

Honea, Sion M. "Homer's *Daitos Eises*, The Greek Sacrificial Meal." *Journal of Ritual Studies* 7 (1993) 53–68.

Hornblower, Simon, and Antony Spawforth, eds. *The Oxford Classical Dictionary*. Oxford: Oxford University Press, 1996.

Howard, Wilbert F., and Arthur John Gossip. "The Gospel according to St. John." In *The Interpreter's Bible: Luke, John*, edited by George Arthur Buttrick, 7:436–811. New York: Abingdon, 1952.

Hubert, Henri, and Marcel Mauss. *Sacrifice: Its Nature and Function*. Translated by W. D. Halls. Chicago: University of Chicago Press, 1964.

Jeremias, Joachim. *The Eucharistic Words of Jesus*. Translated by Arnold Ehrhardt. 2nd ed. New York: Macmillan, 1955.

———. *The Eucharistic Words of Jesus*. Translated by Norman Perrin. 3rd ed. Philadelphia: Fortress, 1977.

———. "This is My Body . . . " *Expository Times* 83 (1972) 196–203.

John, John St. "The Sacred Meal: The Roots of Christian Ritual." *Dialogue & Alliance* 6/3 (1992) 52–69.

Josephus. *Josephus: The Jewish War*. Translated by H. St J. Thackeray. Vol. 3. LCL. Cambridge: Harvard University, 1930.

Justin. "Dialogue with Trypho." In *Apostolic Fathers, Justin Martyr, Irenaeus*, edited by Alexander Roberts, James Sir Donaldson, and A. Cleveland Coxe, 194–270. Peabody, MA: Hendrickson, 1995.

———. "The First Apology of Justin, the Martyr." In *Early Christian Fathers*, edited by Cyril C. Richardson, 225–37. New York: Touchstone, 1996.

Keener, Craig S. *The Gospel of John: A Commentary*. Vol. 1. 2 vols. Peabody, MA: Hendrickson, 2003.

Kennedy, George A. *A New History of Classical Rhetoric*. Princeton: Princeton University Press, 1994.

Kerényi, C. *Dionysos: Archetypal Image of Indestructible Life*. Translated by Ralph Manheim. Vol. 2. Bollingen Series 65. New Jersey: Princeton University Press, 1976.

LaCocque, André. "Sin and Guilt." In *Encyclopedia of Religion*, edited by Lindsay Jones, 12:8402–7. Detroit: Macmillan Reference USA, 2005.

Lada-Richards, Ismene. *Initiating Dionysus: Ritual and Theatre in Aristophanes' Frogs*. Oxford: Oxford University Press, 1999.

Lang, Bernhard. "This Is My Body: Sacrificial Presentation and the Origins of Christian Ritual." In *Sacrifice in Religious Experience*, edited by Albert I. Baumgarten, 189–206. Studies in the History of Religions 93. Boston: Brill, 2002.

Larson, Jennifer. *Ancient Greek Cults: A Guide*. New York: Routledge, 2007.

Lee, Dorothy. "The Gospel of John and the Five Senses." *JBL* 129 (2010) 115–27.

Liddell, Henry George. *An Intermediate Greek-English Lexicon: Founded upon the Seventh Edition of Liddell and Scott's Greek-English Lexicon*, edited by Robert Scott. Oxford: Clarendon, 1983.

Lietzmann, Hans, and Robert D. Richardson. *Mass and Lord's Supper: A Study in the History of the Liturgy*. Translated by Dorothea H. R. Reeve. Leiden: Brill, 1979.

Lightfoot, R. H. *History and Interpretation in the Gospels*. New York: Harper, 1935.

"Literary Criticism." In *Encyclopædia Britannica Online* (2010). http://search.eb.com/eb/article-9110461.

Little, Edmund. *Echoes of the Old Testament in the Wine of Cana in Galilee (John 2:1–11) and the Multiplication of the Loaves and Fish (John 6:1–15)*. Cahiers de la Revue Biblique. Paris: Gabalda, 1998.

Lovejoy, Arthur O. *The Great Chain of Being: A Study of the History of an Idea*. Cambridge: Harvard University Press, 1936.

MacDonald, Dennis Ronald. *The Acts of Andrew and the Acts of Andrew and Matthias in the City of the Cannibals*. Texts and Translations Christian Apocrypha Series. Atlanta: Scholars, 1990.

———. *Does the New Testament Imitate Homer?: Four Cases from the Acts of the Apostles*. New Haven: Yale University Press, 2003.

———. *The Homeric Epics and the Gospel of Mark*. New Haven: Yale University Press, 2000.

Martiz, Petrus, and Gilbert Van Belle. "The Imagery of Eating and Drinking in John 6:35." In *Imagery in the Gospel of John*, edited by Jörg Frey, Jan G. van der Watt and Ruben Zimmermann, 333–52. Wissenschaftliche Untersuchungen zum Neuen Testament 200. Tübingen: Mohr/Siebeck, 2006.

Mayerson, Philip. *Classical Mythology in Literature, Art, and Music*. New York: Wiley, 1971.

McConnell, John F. "The Eucharist and the Mystery Religions." *CBQ* 10 (1948) 29–41.

McGowan, Andrew. "Eating People: Accusations of Cannibalism Against Christians in the Second Century." *Journal of Early Christian Studies* 2 (1994) 413–42.

McKnight, Scot. *A Light Among the Gentiles: Jewish Missionary Activity in the Second Temple Period*. Minneapolis: Fortress, 1990.

Meier, John P. *A Marginal Jew: Rethinking the Historical Jesus*. Vol. 2. New York: Doubleday, 1991.

Meyer, Marvin W., ed. *The Ancient Mysteries: A Sourcebook of Sacred Texts*. Philadelphia: University of Pennsylvania Press, 1987.

"Middle Age." In *Encyclopædia Britannica Online* (2010). http://search.eb.com/eb.com/eb/article-9110461.

Moore, Clifford Herschel. *The Religious Thought of the Greeks, from Homer to the Triumph of Christianity*. Cambridge: Harvard University Press, 1925.

Moore, Francis John. "Eating the Flesh and Drinking the Blood: A Reconsideration." *ATR* 48 (1966) 70–75.

Need, Stephen W. "Jesus the Bread of God: the Eucharist as Metaphor in John 6." *Theology* 105 (2002) 194–200.

Neusner, Jacob. *Messiah in Context*. Philadelphia: Fortress, 1984.

Nietzsche, Friedrich W. *The Birth of Tragedy*. Translated by Douglas Smith. Oxford: Oxford University Press, 2000.

Nilsson, Martin P. *The Dionysiac Mysteries of the Hellenistic and Roman Age*. Ancient Religion and Mythology. 1957. Reprint, New York: Arno, 1975.

Nock, Arthur Darby. "The Cult of Heroes." *HTR* 37 (1944) 141–73.

Nonnos. *Nonnos Dionysiaca I*. Translated by W. H. D. Rouse; Mythological Introduction and Notes by H. J. Rose; and Notes on Text Criticism by L. R. Lind. Vol. 1. LCL. Cambridge: Harvard University Press, 1940.

Noy, David. "The Sixth Hour Is the Mealtime for Scholars: Jewish Meals in the Roman World." In *Meals in a Social Context: Aspects of the Communal Meal in the Hellenistic and Roman World*, edited by Inge Nielsen and Nanne Sigismund Nielsen, 134–44. Aarhus Studies in Mediterranean Antiquity 1. Aarhus: Aarhus University Press, 1998.

Olsson, Birger. *Structure and Meaning in the Fourth Gospel: A Text-Linguistic Analysis of John 2:1–11 and 4:1–42*. Coniectanea biblica. New Testament Series 6. Lund: Gleerup, 1974.

Origen. "Against Celsus." In *Ante-Nicene Fathers: The Writings of the Fathers Down to A. D. 325*, edited by Alexander Roberts and James Donaldson, vol. 4. New York: Christian Literature, 1890.

Otto, Walter F. *Dionysus: Myth and Cult*. Translated by Robert B. Palmer. Bloomington: Indiana University Press, 1965.

Overman, J. Andrew. *Matthew's Gospel and Formative Judaism: The Social World of the Matthean Community*. Minneapolis: Fortress, 1990.
Parker, Robert. *Miasma: Pollution and Purification in Early Greek Religion*. Oxford: Clarendon, 1983.
Parsons, Jotham. "Defining the History of ideas." *JHI* 68 (2007) 683–99.
Pausanias. "Elis II." In *Pausanias Description of Greece 3*, edited by T. E. Page. Cambridge: Harvard University Press, 1933.
Perrin, Norman, and Dennis C. Duling. *The New Testament, an Introduction: Proclamation and Parenesis, Myth and History*. 2nd ed. San Diego: Harcourt Brace Jovanovich, 1982.
Perry, John M. "The Evolution of the Johannine Eucharist." *NTS* 39 (1993) 22–35.
Pindar. *The Odes of Pindar: Including the Principal Fragments*. Translated by John Sandys, edited by John Edwin Sandys. Cambridge: Harvard University Press, 1937.
Plato. "Cratylus." In *The Collected Dialogues of Plato: Including the Letters*, edited by Edith Hamilton and Huntington Cairns, 421–74. Bollingen Series 71. New York: Pantheon, 1961.
———. *Critias*. In *The Collected Dialogues of Plato Including the Letters*, edited by Edith Hamilton and Huntington Cairns, 1212–24. Bollingen Series 71. New York: Pantheon, 1961.
———. *Phaedrus*. In *The Collected Dialogues of Plato Including the Letters*, edited by Edith Hamilton and Huntington Cairns, 475–525. Bollingen Series 71. New York: Pantheon, 1961.
———. *Republic*. In *The Collected Dialogues of Plato Including the Letters*, edited by Edith Hamilton and Huntington Cairns, 575–844. Bollingen Series 71. New York: Pantheon, 1961.
———. *Symposium*. In *The Collected Dialogues of Plato Including the Letters*, edited by Edith Hamilton and Huntington Cairns, 526–74. Bollingen Series 71. New York: Pantheon, 1961.
Plutarch. "The Eating of Flesh I." In *Plutarch's Moralia* XII, edited by E. H. Warmington, 537–79. LCL Cambridge: Harvard University Press, 1957.
———. "Isis and Osiris." In *Plutarch Moralia* V, edited by T. E. Page, 3–193. LCL. Cambridge: Harvard University Press, 1936. Reprint, 1999.
———. *Plutarch's Moralia*. Vol. XV. XVI vols., edited by T. E. Page. LCL. Cambridge: Harvard University Press, 1939. Reprint, 1967.
———. "Reply to Colotes." In *Plutarch's Moralia* XIV, edited by T. E. Page, 153–317. LCL. Cambridge: Harvard University Press, 1939. Reprint, 1967.
———. "Table-Talk IV." In *Plutarch's Moralia* VIII, edited by T. E. Page, 283–515. LCL. Cambridge: Harvard University Press, 1936.
———. "Whether the Affections. . ." In *Plutarch's Moralia* VI, edited by T. E. Page, 378–94. LCL Cambridge: Harvard University Press, 1939. Reprint, 1962.
Posener, Georges. *Dictionary of Egyptian Civilization*. Translated by Alix Macfarlane. New York: Tudor, 1962.
Preston, James J. "Purification: An Overview." In *Encyclopedia of Religion*, edited by Lindsay Jones, 11:7503–511. Detroit: Macmillan Reference USA, 2005.
Richards, I. A. *Principles of Literary Criticism*. New York: Harcourt, 1928.
Richardson, Cyril C., ed. *Early Christian Fathers*. New York: Touchstone, 1996.
Riesner, Rainer. "A Pre-Christian Jewish Mission?" In *The Mission of the Early Church to Jews and Gentiles*, edited by Jostein Ådna and Hans Kvalbein, 211–50.

Bibliography

Wissenschaftliche Untersuchungen zum Neuen Testament 127. Tübingen: Mohr/Siebeck, 2000.

Riley, Gregory J. *I Was Thought to Be What I Am Not: Docetic Jesus and the Johannine Tradition.* Claremont: IAC, 1994.

———. *One Jesus Many Christs: How Jesus Inspired not One True Christianity but Many.* 1997. Reprint, Minneapolis: Fortress, 2000.

———. *The River of God: A New History of Christian Origins.* San Francisco: HarperSanFrancisco, 2003.

Roberts, J. J. M. "The Old Testament's Contribution to Messianic Expectations." In *The Messiah: Developments in Earliest Judaism and Christianity*, edited by James H. Charlesworth, 39–51. Minneapolis: Fortress, 1992.

Ruggieri, Giuseppe, and Miklós Tomka, ed. *The Church in Fragments: Towards What Kind of Unity?* Maryknoll, NY: Orbis, 1997.

Sandys, John Edwin, ed. *The Bacchae of Euripides with Critical and Explanatory Notes.* Cambridge: Cambridge University Press, 1880.

Schürmann, Heinz. *Der Einsetzungsbericht, Lk 22, 19-20: II. Teil einer quellenkritischen Untersuchung des Lukanischen Abendmahlsberichtes, Lk 22, 7–38.* Neutestamentliche Abhandlungen 20. Münster: Aschendorff, 1955.

Schiffman, L. H. "Messianic Figures and Ideas in the Qumran Scrolls." In *The Messiah: Developments in Earliest Judaism and Christianity*, edited by James H. Charlesworth, 116–29. Minneapolis: Fortress, 1992.

Schnackenburg, Rudolf. *The Gospel according to St. John.* Translated by Cecily Hastings, et al. Vol. 2. New York: Seabury, 1980.

Schnelle, Udo. *Antidocetic Christology in the Gospel of John: An Investigation of the Place of the Fourth Gospel in the Johannine School.* Translated by Linda M. Maloney. Minneapolis: Fortress, 1992.

Schweizer, Eduard. *The Good News according to Matthew.* Translated by David E. Green. Atlanta: John Knox, 1975.

Seaford, Richard. *Dionysos.* Gods and Heroes of the Ancient World. London: Routledge, 2006.

Shapiro, Alan. "Introduction." In *Bakkhai*, edited by Reginald Gibbons and Charles Segal. New York: Oxford University Press, 2000.

Smith, Dennis E. *From Symposium to Eucharist: The Banquet in the Early Christian World.* Minneapolis: Fortress, 2003.

———. "Meal Customs (Greco-Roman)." In *ABD*, edited by David Noel Freedman, 4:650–53. New York: Doubleday, 1992.

———. "Meal Customs (Sacred Meals)." In *ABD*, edited by David Noel Freedman, 4:653–55. New York: Doubleday, 1992.

Smith, Dennis E., and Hal Taussig. *Many Tables: the Eucharist in the New Testament and Liturgy Today.* London: SCM, 1990.

Smith, Morton. "On the Wine God in Palestine (Gen. 18, Jn. 2, and Achilles Tatius)." In *Salo Wittmayer Baron: Jubilee Volume on the Occasion of His Eightieth Birthday*, edited by Saul Lieberman and Artghur Hyman, 2:815–29. New York: Columbia University Press, 1974.

Spencer, Aída Besançon. "Literary Criticism." In *New Testament Criticism & Interpretation*, edited by David Alan Black and David S. Dockery, 225–51. Grand Rapids: Zondervan, 1991.

Stendahl, Krister. *Paul among Jews and Gentiles and Other Essays.* London: SCM, 1977.

Tatius, Achilles. *Achilles Tatius*. Translated by S. Gaselee. Revised and reprinted ed. LCL. Cambridge: Harvard University Press, 1917. Reprint, 1969.
Temple, Patrick J. "The Eucharist in St. John 6." *CBQ* 9 (1947) 442–52.
Thomas, Ruth Edith. "The Sacred Meal in the Older Roman Religion." Ph.D Dissertation, University of Chicago, 1935.
Toynbee, Jocelyn. M. C. "Life, Death, and Afterlife on Roman-Age Mosaics." In *Jenseitsvorstellungen in Antike und Christentum: Gedenkschrift für Alfred Stuiber*, 210–14. Jahrbuch für Antike und Christentum. Ergänzungsband 9. Münster: Aschendorff, 1982.
Trzaskoma, Stephen M. et al., eds. *Anthology of Classical Myth: Primary Sources in Translation*. Indianapolis: Hackett, 2004.
Tuilier, André, ed. *La Passion du Christ: Tragédie*. Paris: Cerf, 1969.
Visser, Margaret. "Worship Your Enemy: Aspects of the Cult of Heroes in Ancient Greece." *Harvard Theological Review* 75 (1982) 403–28.
Vollert, Cyril. "The Eucharist: Insights from Scripture." *TS* 21 (1960) 404–43.
Warmington, E. H. "Introduction." In *Achilles Tatius*, ix–xvi. Cambridge: Harvard University Press, 1917. Reprint, 1969.
Weaver, John B. *Plots of Epiphany: Prison-Escape in Acts of the Apostles*. Beihefte zur Zietschrift für die neutestamentliche Wissenschaft und die Kunde der älteren Kirche. Berlin: de Gruyter, 2004.
Webster, Jane S. *Ingesting Jesus: Eating and Drinking in the Gospel of John*. Atlanta: Society of Biblical Literature, 2003.
Weinreich, Otto. *Gebet und Wunder*. Religionsgeschichtliche Studien. Stuttgart: Kohlhammer, 1968.
Wick, Peter. "Jesus gegen Dionysos? Ein Beitrag zur Kontextualisierung des Johannesevangeliums." *Biblica* 85 (2004) 179–98.
Wilson, Daniel J. *Arthur O. Lovejoy: An Annotated Bibliography*. New York: Garland., 1982.
———. "Lovejoy's The Great Chain of Being after Fifty Years." *JHI* 48 (1987) 187–206.
Xenophon. *Xenophon: Symposium*. Translated by A. J. Browen. Warminster, UK: Aris & Phillips, 1988.
Yerkes, Royden Keith. *Sacrifice in Greek and Roman Religions and Early Judaism*. London: A. & C. Black, 1953.

Subject Index

Abraham, 87–88, 123
Achilles, 84, 94, 109, 122, 131
Alexander the Great, 65, 102
animal sacrifice, 27, 29–30, 34, 48, 63, 67
Asclepius, 33, 89, 109

Bacchae, 34, 37, 40, 45–47, 49, 79–86, 100, 109, 127, 132
Bellerophon, 33, 109
body, ix–x, 1–2, 5, 8, 12–13, 16–17, 23–24, 30, 36–38, 45–46, 49, 67, 70, 89, 105, 109–11, 114–16, 118, 122, 124–25, 128, 130–33
bread and wine, 2–3, 5, 8–9, 12, 14, 23, 30, 49, 65, 74, 95, 104, 122, 124, 132
bread of life, 4–6, 14, 16, 54, 59, 66, 68, 77, 99, 104, 113–14, 128
Bromius, 34
Bultmann, Rudolf, 14, 53, 61, 69–72, 74, 76, 87, 90, 105, 110, 134

Cana, 6, 88–91
cannibalism, x, 5–6, 49, 104, 116–19, 126, 128–29, 132
Catholics, 5
Christian Eucharist, 1–3, 6–7, 20, 23–24, 28, 31, 43, 48, 50–51, 65–66, 117, 132–33
Christian ritual, 18, 28
Christianity, 2, 7, 22, 42, 43, 48, 65, 78, 79, 80, 85, 88, 90, 105, 109, 119, 127, 128, 134

Christology, ix, 9, 54, 74–75, 77, 84–85, 91, 106, 120, 127, 134
Church Fathers, 2, 43, 48, 50, 79, 127
communion, 3, 28–30, 44, 50, 63–64, 76, 122, 124, 131

daitos eises, 27–28, 48
Demeter, 38, 50, 65
demon, 30, 79, 86, 123, 132
Dionysus cult, ix–x, 1, 7, 18, 20–23, 30–31, 34, 39, 41–42, 44, 47–51, 53, 69, 75, 78–79, 90, 92, 94, 99–105, 112, 119, 121, 123–24, 126–28, 130–34
deipnon, 25–26, 52, 56
demigod, 31, 109
Dioscure, 33, 109
divine fathers, 32
drinking blood, 6, 8, 19, 29, 48, 50, 69–70, 74, 99, 112, 131
drinking of blood, 5, 70

eating flesh, 6, 8, 19, 69–71, 74, 99, 112, 119, 131, 133
eating of the flesh, 5, 49
ecstasy, 31, 40–41, 45, 50, 88
epiphany, 40, 49, 90, 96, 132
eternal life, 8, 36, 42, 49, 56, 67, 68–69, 77, 87, 93, 99, 101, 110, 113–14, 121–23, 125–26
everlasting life, 93, 95, 128
Evius, 34

Subject Index

flesh and blood, 5–9, 28, 30, 49, 50, 66–69, 71, 73, 77, 99, 104–5, 110, 116, 119, 121–25, 128, 132–33
food, 17, 25, 27–28, 30, 34, 48, 55–56, 67–68, 89, 93, 99, 110, 113–14, 119, 121–24, 133
foot washing, 55, 58, 76
gentile, 43, 65, 89, 91

Gospel of John, 9, 48, 52–56, 59, 64, 66, 69, 75–76, 79–80, 84–85, 87, 89, 92, 99, 101, 103, 105–6, 121, 127, 132–34
Gospels, 1, 17, 19, 34, 56, 84, 87, 104, 106, 114, 117
Greco-Roman banquet, 20, 52, 76
Greco-Roman Meal Custom, ix, 24–25, 48, 55–56, 58, 75, 130
Greco-Roman Religion, ix–xi, 1, 18, 22–23, 42, 65, 119, 127, 131–32, 134

Hera, 36, 49, 112, 128
Hermes, 28, 33, 109
hero cult, ix, 20, 23–24, 31–34, 48–49, 51
heaven, 5, 17, 33, 43, 55–56, 66, 68–69, 73, 75, 79, 84–85, 94, 96, 99, 104, 109, 113–14, 119, 122, 126
Hercules, 84, 109
history of ideas, ix, 18–20, 130
homoeopathic effects, 46, 50

imagery of flesh, 68, 71, 77
incarnation, 46, 72–73, 86, 114
initiation, 45, 47, 102

Jerusalem, 2, 4, 63–65, 77, 85, 88, 101, 110
Jerusalem temple, 63, 65, 77
John the Baptist, 6, 60.
Johannine Eucharist, ix, x, 1, 2, 4, 6, 14, 17–23, 51, 54, 74–77, 80, 99, 104–5, 110, 112, 116–17, 119–20, 122–23, 126, 130, 132–34
Johannine literature, 2, 19, 52, 55
Judaism, 43, 93, 107, 126, 128
Justin Martyr, 79, 109, 122

lamb, 3, 6, 7, 23, 26, 59–64, 70, 76–77, 87, 100–101, 109, 126, 133
Lamb of God, 6, 59–63, 76
Last Supper, 2–5, 8–10, 13–14, 17, 33, 53, 55–58, 76, 114, 130
libation, 25, 33, 52
life, xii, 1, 4–9, 14, 16–17, 32, 36, 38–39, 42–43, 45–46, 49–50, 54, 56, 59, 66–71, 73–74, 77, 80, 87, 89, 93, 95–96, 99, 100–102, 104–6, 110, 112–15, 119–26, 128, 133
life of the world, 16–17, 68, 73, 68, 73, 99, 113–15
literary criticism, ix, 18–20, 130
living bread, 16, 23, 31, 68–69, 84, 99, 113–15, 125
living Father, 113, 125
Logos, 8, 84, 91, 102, 105, 131

MacDonald, Dennis R., xi, 10, 75, 117–18, 128
mad god, 86, 131
madness, 39, 134
maenad, 35, 39, 81, 86, 102
manna, 73–74, 93, 99, 101, 113–14, 119, 126
Mary, 80, 85, 88, 101, 109
Mediterranean world, 1, 65
Messiah, 84, 90–91, 93, 105–10, 112, 119, 127, 129, 133–34
messianology, 108
miasma, 63, 76
mimesis, 75, 80–81, 89
mimesis criticism, 75
mission, 43, 65
Moses, 29, 43, 66–67, 89, 93, 107, 115, 126
my body, 5, 12–13, 16–17, 23, 49, 67, 110, 114, 125, 133
mystery religion, 7, 22, 43, 99

New Testament, ix–xi, 1, 3, 8, 10, 17–18, 25–26, 29, 40, 49, 51, 55, 57, 59–60, 65–66, 70, 75–77, 80, 83, 89, 91, 106, 109, 110, 114–15, 119–21, 123, 125, 127, 130, 133–34

Odyssey, 109, 118
Old Testament, 5–6, 26, 40, 60–62, 70, 76, 79, 88–90, 96–97, 100–101, 106–9, 119, 134
omophagia, 20, 23, 46–48, 50, 100, 115–16, 118, 128, 131
orgies, 44, 48
Origen, 76, 81, 127
Orpheus, 50
Orphic Hymns, 36, 47, 49, 98, 100
Osiris, 38, 42–43, 47, 50, 78

Paschal Lamb, 7, 60–61, 64, 76, 100, 126
Passion of Christ, 79–80, 127, 133
Passover lamb, 6, 60, 101
Passover meal, ix, 2–4, 24, 29, 48
Paul, ix, 2–5, 7–10, 12–13, 16–17, 19–20, 22–23, 26, 28, 30–31, 33–34, 65, 69, 82–83, 95, 105, 110, 116–17, 121–22, 124–25, 127–28, 132–33
Perseus of Danae, 33, 109
Pentheus, 37, 47, 80–86, 112, 127–28
Pharisees, 58, 86
pious fraud, 41
Protestants, 2, 5

rabbinic Judaism, 65
raw flesh, 20–21, 23, 30, 46, 48, 50, 99–100, 115–16, 118, 120, 124, 128, 131–32
raw flesh eater, 21, 118, 128
raw flesh giver, 21, 118
reclining, 20, 24, 26, 48, 52, 55–58, 76, 130
resurrection, 2, 36, 42, 46, 49–50, 53, 74, 78, 80, 95, 110, 127, 131, 134
revel, 44
Riley, Gregory J., 8–9, 19, 30–32, 49, 84–85, 88–89, 91–92, 110, 122
Roman emperor, 32, 109
Roman Empire, x, 18, 65, 79

sacred meal, ix–x, 1, 7–8, 18–30, 33–34, 48, 51–53, 59, 64, 130–31, 133–34
sacrificial death, 67, 69, 71–75, 110, 116, 122, 130

sacrificial lamb, 59–62, 64, 76–77, 87, 133
sacrificial meals, ix, 26, 29, 49
Samaritan woman, 23, 92–94, 128
sarx (σάρξ), 68–69, 73–75, 77, 105, 1141, 119, 125
Saul, 82–83, 127
scapegoat, 61–62, 69, 76
Semele, 7, 35–37, 43, 49, 84–86, 98
Simon Bar Kokhba, 108
Socrates, 25, 39
Son of God, 37, 49, 71, 84–85, 87, 104, 106, 119, 126, 133–34
son of Joseph, 68, 84, 103, 127, 129, 131
Son of man, 5, 9, 56, 68, 71–73, 103, 113, 116, 119, 123
sons of Zeus, 33, 49, 104, 109, 132
sparagmos, 20, 46–48, 118, 128, 131
suffering son of God, 36–38, 49, 85, 106, 110, 127, 132–33
synagogue, 14, 113, 126
Synoptics, ix, 2–5, 7–17, 20, 22–23, 26, 33–34, 60, 75, 85, 95, 99, 101, 105, 110, 111, 114, 116, 121, 124–26, 128, 130, 132–33

temple, 27, 41, 60, 62–65, 77, 89–90, 102, 107
thysia, 27–30, 33, 48, 61–66, 70, 76–77, 130, 134
thysia sacrifice, 30, 33, 48, 61, 63–64, 66, 70, 76–77, 130, 134
Titan, 7, 30, 36, 42, 49–50, 100, 112, 118, 125
transubstantiation, 5, 29
Trapezomata, 28, 33, 34, 48
Trypho, 43, 108

unit-ideas, 19
vital energy, 101

wine god, 21, 40, 42, 49, 91, 98, 101, 112
wine miracles, 20, 91

Zeus, 7, 33, 35–36, 47, 49, 65, 79, 84–86, 101, 104, 109, 118, 132, 134

Ancient Document Index

OLD TESTAMENT

Genesis

9:4	70, 115
49:10–12	90

Exodus

12:46	60
17:2	115
24:8	29

Leviticus

3:17	70, 115
7:27	70
16:7–10	61–62
17:10–14	70

Numbers

9:12	60
20:3	115

Deuteronomy

12:23	70, 115
18:15	107

1 Samuel

14:33	70

Psalms

18:50	107
34:20	60
41:9	121
40:10 (LXX)	121
132:1	107

Proverb

31:6	40

Isaiah

9:6–7	107
45:1–5	107
45:1	107
53:5–6	23
53:7	61

Jeremiah

15:16	5
24:7	125
31:33	125

Ezekiel

3:3	5

Amos

6:4	26

APOCRYPHA

Tobit

2:1	26

Judith

7:9	26
12:15–16	26
15:12	103

2 Maccabees

6:7	102
10:1–10	102
10:7	102

3 Maccabees

2:27–30	102

NEW TESTAMENT

Matthew

9:13	66
12:7	66
13:52	75
15:35	25
24:38	120
26:26	13, 24
26:28	29

Mark

2:15	52
3:21	86
6:39	52
6:40	25, 57
8:6	52
9:49	66
12:33	66
14	13
14:3	52
14:13–16	118
14:13–15	4
14:13	4
14:18	52
14:22–25	9, 11, 15, 23
14:22	12–13, 24
14:23	12, 52
14:24	17, 29, 101
14:26	52
26:26–29	9, 11

Luke

4:18–19	87
7:36	52
10:34	40
11:37	25, 52
13:1	66
13:12	87
14:7–24	52
14:7	52
14:10	25
16:22	25
17:7	25
22:14	26
22:15–20	9, 11, 23
22:15–19a	12
22:9	24
22:19	13
22:20	26, 29
22:24–28	58

John

1:1–18	127
1:1–5	84
1:1	91, 131
1:4	84
1:5	84
1:7	61
1:9	61, 84
1:11	85
1:14	8, 71, 84
1:18	84
1:23	60
1:29	20, 61–62, 76, 87, 133
1:29b	62
1:32	124
1:36	76, 87
1:45	84
1:51	72

Ancient Document Index   151

2:1–14	23
2:1–12	84
2:1–11	x, 21, 55, 88–92, 116, 128, 132
2	92
2:2	61
2:4	55
2:11	91
3:5	61
3:18–21	110
4	92
4:5–42	93
4:5–34	21, 23, 92.
4:5–30	92, 94, 128
4:10–15	66
4:11–34	92–93
4:11	93
4:12	93
4:14	84
4:32–34	55
4:32	67
4:49–54	84
5:8	84
5:11	92
5:18	103
5:21	71
5:24	108
5:25	84
5:38	124
6	1, 3–9, 14, 21, 23, 53, 66–67, 72–75, 77, 92, 95, 104, 112, 116–18, 124, 128, 132
6:1–71	55, 59
6:1–15	9, 55, 57, 66, 77, 84
6:1–14	56
6:2	67
6:3–4	67
6:4	8
6:5	66–67
6:6	67
6:9	67
6:10–11	57
6:10	25
6:11	26, 57, 67,
6:12–15	12
6:14–15	96
6:15	71, 105
6:16–59	92
6:16–24	9
6:16–21	66, 92, 96, 128
6:16–19	21
6:20–40	93
6:20–35	92–93
6:20–35	92–93
6:22–59	54, 66
6:22–50	77
6:24	126
6:25–51a	9
6:25–26	99
6:25	69
6:26	55
6:27–34	66, 96
6:27	56, 119
6:27a	56
6:29	72–73
6:30	93
6:31–40	56
6:31	99, 113
6:32–50	99
6:35–48	96, 128
6:35–41	99
6:35–40	68
6:35	54, 56, 59, 66, 73, 94
6:36	73
6:38	74
6:39	42
6:40	73
6:41–42	94
6:41	115
6:42	68, 84, 103, 131
6:44–46	68
6:44	42
6:47	42, 73
6:48–51a	68
6:48	5, 84
6:49	126
6:50	74
6:51–52	99
6:51–70	74, 104
6:51–59	x, 4, 6, 9, 15, 20–21, 23, 31, 50, 53, 56, 66–67, 69–70, 72–74, 77, 94, 97, 99, 104, 106, 110, 112, 120–21, 127–28, 130–34.
6:51–58	120, 123
6:51–56	118
6:51–53	69

John (continued)

Reference	Pages
6:51	16, 23, 69, 113–14, 133
6:51a	16
6:51b–58	74
6:51b–57	14
6:51b	126
6.51c–58	14, 72
6:51c	16, 68, 72, 110
6:52–66	116, 118
6:52–59	99
6:52–58	68
6:52	69, 71, 99, 115–16, 119, 124
6:53–57	29
6:53–54	9, 14, 67
6:53	7, 8–9, 66, 68, 71, 73, 101, 119, 123.
6:54–58	121
6:54	17, 69, 105, 119–20, 123–24
6:55	95, 121, 123
6:56–68	120
6:56	5, 70, 99, 123–24, 131, 133
6:57	6, 71, 119
6:58	16, 42, 66, 126
6:59	14, 126
6:60–71	9, 53, 66, 72
6:60–67	85
6:60–65	54
6:60–63	72
6:60	69, 71, 101, 132
6:61	72
6:62	119
6:63–70	103
6:63	71–72, 74, 77, 101
6:63b	105
6:64	71
6:66–71	54
6:66	71
6:68	104
7:5	86
7:6	85
7:8	55
7:36	58
7:37–39	55
7:44–46	58
7:52	103
8:12	84
8:30–40	53, 72
8:30	53
8:31	124
8:32–40	87
8:32–34	128
8:32	87
8:33	87
8:34–36	87
8:48	86
8:51–52	55
8:51	123
8:52	123–24
9:1–12	84
9:2–6	12
10:20	86
10:24	106
10:25	106
10:36	84
11:4	84
11:25–27	110
11:27	84
11:38–44	84
11:48–49	86
12:1–8	55
12:12–17	88
12:13	88
12:20–33	53
12:24	55
12:31–32	12
13–17	4, 56
13:1—17:26	9, 14, 53
13:1—17:24	9
13	3–4, 8, 14, 53, 58, 121
13:1–38	121
13:1–30	55–56
13:1–18	8
13:1–17	58
13:3–5	52
13:6–9	58
13:11	71
13:12–16	58
13:12	26
13:18	14, 120–21
13:23	25
13:26	14
14:2–4	56
14:10	124
15:1–12	23
15:1–11	21, 131
15:1–7	55

15:1	84
15:3–7	124
15:4–16	133
15:4	124
15:5	6, 84
15:7	124, 131
18–19	127
18	111
18:1	4
18:21–35	12
18:22	111
19:1–3	111
19:7	84, 104
19:14	60
19:15–18	111
19:19	105
19:23–25	111
19:28–37	55
19:28–30	111
19:32–34	112
19:34	70
19:42	60
20:31	84, 106, 112, 127
21:1–25	55
21:15–17	56

Acts

2:13	31
7:26	115
9:1–19	82, 127
9:7	82
12:6–7	81
12	81–82
16:25–26	82, 127
16	82
22:6–16	82, 127
26:12–18	82, 127
26:14	83, 127

Romans

12:1	66

1 Corinthians

5:5	114
10:16–21	30
10:16	30
10:17	30
11	8, 14, 17, 121
11:19–22	28
11:23–25	6–7, 9, 11–13, 15, 23, 130
11:23–24	26
11:23b–25	26
11:24–25	12
11:24	13, 24, 29–30
11:24b	16
11:25	26, 29
11:26–27	121
11:26	30

2 Corinthians

7:1	114

Ephesians

5:29	114

Colossians

2:1	114

2 Timothy

2:24	115

Hebrews

5:1	66
8:3	66
9:9	66
9:23	28, 66
9:26	28
10:1	66
10:5	66
10:8	66
10:11–12	66
10:12	28
11:4	66
13:15–16	66

James

4:2	115

1 Peter

1:18–19	61
2:5	66

1 John

5:6–6	70

DEAD SEA SCROLLS

Rule of the Community

9:11	108

GRECO-ROMAN WRITINGS

Aeschylus

Severn Against Thebes	43–44

Euripides

Bacchae

28	85
44–51	85
100	47
138	46
443–448	81
493	86
498	81
576–641	82
578–595	82
585	82
649	86
705–707	40
734–740	46
794–795	83, 127
1017	47
1125–1137	46
1159	47

Cretans

472	46

Hesiod

Theogony

940–942	35

Works and Days

106–201	109
108	109
159–160	109

Homer

The Homeric Hymn VII to Dionysus

line 1	36

The Homeric Hymns to Dionysus

line 8–9	35
line 17–18	35

Iliad

1.458–474	27
2.420–431	27
6.130ff	35
7.327–330	27
10.575–579	25
10	128
16.670	122
16.680	122
19.347	122
19.353	122
22.461	35

Odyssey

9.289–290	117
10.109–116	118
10.100–105	118
14.418–438	28
14.434–436	28

Josephus

The Jewish War

6.93–94.	64
6.271–82.	65

Pindar

Olympian

1.90–93	33

Plato

Critias

120a–b	25

Republic

372b	24
421b	24
618–619	24
662	24

Symposium

176a	25

Plutarch

The Eating of Flesh

996B–C	42

Isis and Osiris

364E	42
364F	47

Reply

1119F	44

Xenophon

Symposium

II.1	25

EARLY CHRISTIAN WRITINGS

Nonnos

Dionysiaca

	47

Justin Martyr

Apology 1.66	122

Psalms of Solomon

17:21–33	107

www.ingramcontent.com/pod-product-compliance
Lightning Source LLC
Chambersburg PA
CBHW050821160426
43192CB00010B/1841